but, he spit in my coffee ...

A reads-like-fiction memoir about adopting a child with Reactive Attachment Disorder (RAD)

Keri Williams

This book is memoir based on a true story and reflects the author's present recollections of experiences over time. Some names and characteristics have been changed, some events have been compressed, and some dialogue has been recreated. Some parts have been fictionalized to varying degrees.

Copyright © 2019/2022
Keri Williams
All rights reserved.

A memoir based on a true story.

DEDICATION

This book is dedicated to mothers of troubled children who, like me, have been blamed and shamed into silence. This story is not only mine; it is our story, and it must be told.

PROLOGUE

I surge out of my chair, my face flushing, and I can't keep the tremble out of my voice. "He's threatening to stab his little brother and strangle me. How can you *still* think he's safe to come home?"

"Devon is not a threat to anyone," Wanda says, with an exasperated sigh. Devon, my 11-year-old son, is in the psych ward because he claims he's seeing hallucinations of a man ordering him to stab his little brother and to strangle me. Wanda is his therapist.

The sour smell of the hospital hangs thick in the air and gums to the inside of my mouth as I look around the table at the social worker, the nurse, and Wanda. Devon is using these "hallucinations" to threaten me. Can't any of them see that?

"You need to be supportive of what is in Devon's best interest," Wanda says.

I sink back into my chair and months of family therapy lurch through my mind. I know Wanda thinks Devon's behaviors are my fault and that I'll try to use this latest hospitalization to keep him from moving back home.

Panic curls its fingers around my throat.

Wanda is right.

I'll do whatever it takes to keep him from coming home.

Part I
Denial

1

8 years earlier

"As far as foster kids go, they're pretty much perfect," says Tina, a state of Florida adoption worker. "Makayla is two and Devon is three. Devon's such a bright, funny, handsome young man. And Makayla loves to wear dresses and have her hair done."

As her words fan my long-held dreams to adopt, I gaze out of my office window at the palm trees shading the parking lot and Devon and Makayla form like mirages in my imagination.

Tina lowers her voice, like a friend taking me into her confidence. "Since they're so young and haven't been abused, there are several other prospective families interested in them. But we want to find the right family. I know y'all recently decided not to adopt, but we're hoping you might reconsider?"

I eagerly agree, wondering how this unsolicited call could be anything but fate.

"We think you're a good match for a couple of reasons. You have other children, so we know you can handle a sibling group. Not everyone can." There's an awkward pause. "Also, I understand you're a mixed-race family?"

"Yes. I'm white and my husband is black. He's Jamaican."

"That's perfect. Devon and Makayla have a white mom. They have different dads, but both dads are black. It's so important to place kids in families where they look like they fit."

Whether Tina knows it or not, this is an issue close to my heart. My stepson, Sam, has a dark complexion like his dad. After taking in my freckles and fair skin, strangers often ask him if I'm his "real" mom. So, I get it. Kids shouldn't have to deal with that.

"When can we meet them?" I ask.

"We really don't like to showcase children. We used to do these adoption fairs …" her voice trails off without completing the thought.

"Anyway, the kids end up hurt and disappointed when they aren't chosen."

I understand, but I'm still surprised they're asking us to make such an important decision, a lifelong decision, without even meeting the kids first.

As though reading my mind, Tina adds in a sing-song, "Remember, we don't get to meet our birth children before we commit to them."

Coiling the phone cord around my finger, I venture, "But they're so little. Can't you tell them it's a play date?" As Tina's indecisive pause stretches, self-conscious words jumble out of my mouth in my rush to not be misunderstood. "It's not that I want to see what they look like or anything like that. It's just that we tried to adopt a little boy a few months ago. His name was Eli. It … it didn't work out."

"That's why you asked to be taken off the adoption list?"

"Yes." I sway into my desk chair, unable to put the grief of our failed adoption into words. Having to send Eli back into "the system" was devastating and I still haven't gotten over the heartbreak and the guilt. "We can't jump in again without at least meeting the kids first."

"Well," Tina says, drawing out the word thoughtfully, "let me talk to my supervisor and see if I can't arrange for a short, little visit."

We hang up and my fingers tremble with excitement as I dial my husband's extension. Delano and I are both employed by the same company. I work upstairs as a project manager and he works downstairs in the warehouse. I hear a forklift beeping in the background when he answers my call.

"You're not going to believe it," I gush. "I just got a call to see if we'll adopt a little girl and boy. They're two and three." As I go on, Delano takes it in stride, not surprised I'm once again talking about foster care and adoption. After all, it's how we met.

Back when I was single, long before meeting Delano, I'd scrolled through face after face of smiling foster children on the AdoptUS website. I was especially drawn to the sibling groups whose only wish was to be adopted together. I was still in my early twenties and single. I was afraid adoption agencies wouldn't consider me qualified to be an adoptive parent so I signed up to foster instead.

My longest placement—over six months—was for two sisters. Taylor was eight with the cheekbones of a runway model. Laila, six, had frizzy hair and spindly arms and legs. Both girls told me I was way too young to be a foster parent, and they were probably right. While my friends were out dating and going to parties, I was learning how to parent on-the-job.

We spent long hours on South Florida's beaches and went to many events hosted by the mega-church I fostered through. I drove them to school every morning because I didn't like the look of the bus stop, even though the case worker assured me it was safe. It was also my responsibility to supervise weekly visitations with their parents, and to comfort them after each visit when all they wanted was to go home to their mommy. Laila often wet the bed for the couple of days following these visits. I surprised myself with the ease at which I was able to manage cleaning up after this. However, my apartment didn't have a washer or dryer, so there was no escaping Saturday morning trips to the laundromat.

One morning, I was folding our clothes while the girls sat on flimsy plastic chairs eating gummy bears. They were watching a cartoon on the TV that was mounted on a wall in one corner of the facility. A friendly little boy with a toothy smile came running out of the office to watch with them. The manager, my future husband Delano, had a muscular build and a wide smile with perfect teeth. "That's my son, Sam," he said in a soft Jamaican accent. He pointed to the boy who was howling with laughter at the cartoon and had theatrically rolled out of his seat. Sam's mother had passed away and Delano was a widower. "He's six. About the same age as your daughters?" he asked.

"They're six and eight," I said. Not wanting to leave any false impressions, I added, "But, they're not mine."

His eyes widened. "I see you here every Saturday. You're so kind to them. Like they're your own children."

"They're sweet girls," I said, ducking my head.

The next time we saw Sam, I asked if he could spend the afternoon with us, knowing the laundromat couldn't be a fun Saturday for any kid. Delano agreed, suggesting we come by his apartment later that evening for dinner. That's how I found myself face-to-face with Jamaican chicken foot soup.

Sam put one boney chicken foot in his mouth, demonstrating how to suck the meat off. Taylor and Laila, who could never get enough to eat, followed Sam's example, slurping and smacking their lips. When I snuck my two chicken feet into Laila's bowl, Sam caught my eye and gave me a precocious wink. Later that evening, when we said goodbye, Sam stroked my long, straight hair and offered me the top of his head in return. I gamely ran my palm over his tiny curls. Seeing this, Taylor yanked me toward the parking lot with a scowl. It was the first of many "dates" Delano and I had with our kids in tow.

By the time Taylor and Laila returned to live with their mom, I had become quite attached to them. I'd always known they'd leave, but never expected it to hurt so much. I only took short-term foster care placements after that, because I couldn't bear to get my heart tangled up again.

When Delano and I married some months later, he and Sam moved into my apartment, and Sam took over my foster care bedroom. To foster again, Delano and I would have to reapply together, so I put that dream on hold and focused on my new role as Sam's mom. A year later, Delano and I had a child together. We named him Amias which means "loved." We went on to get licensed to foster children together, and I never stopped dreaming of blending adopted kids into our family.

Now, two years later, I'm clutching the phone, eagerly telling Delano about Devon and Makayla and how my adoption dreams may finally be coming true.

I look up when my coworker Pat raps on the glass of my office door. I end my call with Delano and wave her in. Frustrated energy hums around her wiry frame and she shoves a hand through her short, gray hair. "I just wanted to make sure you saw the request I emailed you yesterday?"

"Oh, it's all done," I say.

"Done?" Pat barks a surprised laugh.

I smile. "I know you're under a lot of pressure, so I took care of it first thing this morning."

As her body visibly unwinds into my guest chair, Pat says, "I'd say, 'Add it to my tab,' but I think I owe you more than a coffee for this one!"

...

Our visit with Devon and Makayla is in a musty room in the bowels of a Department of Children and Families (DCF) building. Not wanting to raise Amias and Sam's hopes, we've left them home with a babysitter.

Piles of shabby toys lie strewn across the floor, and there's a faded pink and white plastic kitchenette set against one wall. Devon and Makayla are already inside the room. We go in and sit on the floor while Tina and another DCF worker pull up folding chairs outside the door.

Makayla stands, holding a limp cloth doll, and stares at us with her mouth open. She has huge, round eyes. Purple barrettes that match her dress dangle from the ends of her long braids.

Devon grins at us, pink cheeks rounding against his honey-brown complexion. He's got the kind of face that can charm anyone, and he's sure out to charm us. He tugs at my sleeve, and I watch him move a chunky plastic truck along the floor as he makes putt-putt noises. I fiddle with my silver hoop earrings, enchanted, as he shows me how he can stack blocks into a tower. I glance at Delano to see if he's watching, but he's holding out a Barbie doll to Makayla.

"Here sweetie. Do you want this baby doll?" he coaxes.

"Wook, wook." Devon bumps a toy block against my face. I smile and reach up to steady him, surprised by how solid he is.

Delano pretends to drink from a pink plastic teacup before holding it out to Makayla. "No," she growls, keeping her distance. I can't help but feel drawn to this little warrior girl who refuses to make sweet with strangers.

When our short visit is over, Tina's colleague takes the kids by their hands and leads them out of the room. Makayla doesn't give us a backward glance, but Devon beams over his shoulder and waves to us for as long as he can. I wave back until they turn the corner and are out of sight.

"Makayla is normally very friendly," Tina says, worrying her beaded bracelet. "I'm not sure why she was acting like that. She might have been tired or hungry. I hope y'all won't decide not to adopt them because of this." She fixes us with an expectant look. They've accommodated our request for a visit—against policy—and now it's time for our decision.

Delano nods almost imperceptibly and I already know my answer. Devon is friendly and easygoing. Amias will love having him for a brother. Makayla is going to be a handful for sure, but I love her spunk.

As we walk toward the exit, Delano laces his fingers through mine. Tina goes over the next steps for Devon and Makayla to acclimate to the family before moving into our home. As she tells us they'll remain foster children for three months before the adoption can be finalized, my heart snags on a memory. We didn't make it through the same mandatory waiting period last time. Sending Eli back broke something inside of me. I can't go through that—can't do that to a child—ever again.

2

Delano strides through the garage, clenching a roll of paper towels in one hand. His accent is usually melodic, but when he's upset his dialect runs thick and fast. Right now, he's upset. He's sure one of our neighbor's dogs peed on the concrete floor. I point out that the garage door has been closed all day, but he pays me no mind. "Me keep telling the man to keep him dog over him house."

I sigh, knowing this will only fuel his war with our neighbors over their unruly Rottweilers who constantly defecate on our lawn. To my embarrassment, Delano scoops up the poop and flings it onto their front yard. I'm not particularly concerned about the dogs, because they're just a nuisance and not dangerous.

"Me can't take this," he rants. "Keri, you have to do something about this. You hear me? You-hear-me-Keri?"

The whole neighborhood probably hears him, but I've got more important things to worry about. I go back inside the house, through the kitchen, and to the living room. Standing outside of the door, I peek in. There's a loveseat, shelves, and toy bins against the walls. The room—heated by the Florida sun through two large windows—is toasty, but the kids don't seem to notice.

I watch two-year-old Amias pull a plastic Dalmatian puppy across the floor by its cord. Its tail wags as its red nose blinks, and it plays jaunty music. Devon jostles Amias, pushing closer to the action, and Makayla shows off dimples that I hadn't noticed before. Amias has a chocolate fingerprint smear up the side of his tee-shirt, and Devon has a white powder mustache.

After we'd agreed to adopt Devon and Makayla, DCF had wasted no time. We had two more short visits, and, less than a month after meeting them, here they are. Of course, our fostering license was in order, and there weren't many preparations to make: the house is childproofed and a tall, wooden fence surrounds our grassy backyard. When we moved in, the first thing we did was tear out the previous owner's above-ground pool. Sam had grumbled as we dismantled and carried one of his long-held childhood dreams to the curb. But, with

Amias beginning to toddle about, a pool seemed too risky.

Devon and Makayla are sharing what was Amias' bedroom. It's not a problem, because Amias co-sleeps with us. Delano and I are already planning to move into a larger house once we finalize the adoption. We'll need more bedrooms, and, judging from the toys scattered all over the living room floor, we need a playroom too.

I pick stuffed animals up off of the floor and place them in a plastic bin. Smoothing one doll's long, blond hair and straightening its dress, I say, "Makayla, this doll is …"

"Kayla."

It takes a moment to realize she's asking—well, more like ordering—me to call her "Kayla" instead of "Makayla." I put a smile in my voice. "Kayla, sweetheart, this doll is for you. Isn't she pretty?" She doesn't reach for the doll, so I set it on the shelf.

I ease onto one arm of the loveseat to watch them play. Kayla, not yet stretched tall like the boys, is chubby with eyes as round as marbles. Amias is three months older than Kayla and a year younger than Devon. He has looser, darker curls and a wide smile. He's a string bean, unlike Devon, who is husky. The tallest of the three, Devon has low, golden curls. Even so, at first glance, just as Tina had hoped, the three kids could easily pass for biological siblings.

…

On Devon and Kayla's first day of daycare since moving in, my eyes snap open before my alarm clock buzzes. The tasks for the morning are ticking through my mind. I don't wear makeup and I simply run a brush through my hair before pulling on jeans and a black, V-neck top.

Delano has left a load of folded laundry on the machine. I sort through and find pink shorts and a white t-shirt with a florescent pink flower for Kayla. I pick out a pair of jean shorts and a Blue's Clues shirt for Devon. After rousing everyone from bed, I pour myself a cup of coffee and gather the "little kids" in the living room to help with their buttons, zippers, and shoelaces. Sam, quite a bit older, takes care of getting himself ready in the mornings.

Amias and Kayla determinedly, albeit slowly, dress themselves. Devon holds out his shirt to me. "You're a big boy. You can do it," I say, with enthusiasm that would rival a brand-new preschool teacher. After a moment's hesitation, he pushes a foot through one sleeve of the shirt. His dark eyes, hooded by long lashes, watch me watching him.

Poor thing, he's almost four and he doesn't know how to dress himself. I motion him to me, and slip the shirt over his head. "See? Easy peasy." Devon puts his soft pudgy hands on either side of my face and rewards me with a bright smile.

I pick up his shorts and put them on his head like a hat. "Oops. That's not right. Hmmm. Do you know where they should go?" His sweet giggle burrows towards my heart. He snatches the shorts off his head and pulls them up his legs and on. "Good job," I say encouragingly. "Put on your socks next." When he turns away, I begin to straighten Kayla's plastic bow barrettes in her mounds of curly hair.

Then, Devon sneezes. One. Big. Sneeze. His hands hang limp at his sides as snot strings down over his lips and chin. He licks it. I gag and rush to get a package of baby wipes.

Sam snickers from the nearby table where he's eating cereal. "Awe, mom hates that stuff," he tells Devon.

I quickly clean Devon up so we won't be late.

Sam normally walks to the elementary school, which is a few blocks away. We wave goodbye to him as we pull out of the driveway and head for Little Rascal's, the daycare center where DCF has enrolled Devon and Kayla. It's close to our house, but I've never liked the look of it. From the outside, it's dingy, and the side alley has been poorly retrofitted into a concrete play area.

Delano waits in the car with Amias while I take Devon and Kayla inside. As I open the main door, I recoil from the sour smell of cleaning chemicals and dirty diapers. Devon tugs at my hand to pull away. I crouch to hug him and he stiffens in my arms. "Have a good day," I say, before releasing him. He turns and runs to the table where staff are serving breakfast.

I tuck Kayla's dangling braids behind her ears. She clutches my arm. "You're not goin' anywhere," she demands, screwing up her face. I kneel and point out a dollhouse and a reading area, but she refuses to budge. "You're. Not. Goin'. Anywhere," she punches out.

On second glance, the reading area isn't all that appealing. The vinyl bean bag chair has cracks, and the books look grimy and old. I spend some time trying to comfort Kayla and to get her interested in toys.

One of the daycare workers notices my dilemma and lumbers over. She pries Kayla's fingers off my arm and tells her they'll go have breakfast. Kayla looks at me with furious eyes. My stomach clenches at the thought of walking away. I look over and see Devon earnestly eating his cereal. "I'll be back soon," I promise as I give Kayla a hug and a kiss on her soft cheek.

Our next stop is Amias' preschool, King's Kids. It's a clean, spacious building with a modern playground visible through spanning windows. Unfortunately, they don't have a contract with DCF which is why Devon and Kayla can't come here too.

Amias' teacher, Ms. Angelica, is petite with auburn hair and a sweet smile. As I'm leaving his classroom, Amias plays one of his favorite games, teasing me that he might love "Miss 'Gelica" more than he loves me. His pants are twisted from dressing himself, and I tug on the elastic waist to straighten them. As I do, I fake cry and make a sad face until he smothers me with kisses. "I love you most, Mommy," he says.

Once at work, I try to focus on tasks I'm normally passionate about—updating project plans, writing business requirements, and reviewing vendor proposals—but I can't concentrate. Instead, I'm jotting down a mental to-do list: grocery shopping, a few things to pick up at Walmart, call the caseworker back to schedule our first home visit, fax documents to the adoption lawyer ...

...

On Saturday we wind our way through the Swap Shop, a sprawling indoor-outdoor flea market where vendors hawk everything from knockoff designer handbags to cell phones. We find a Caribbean hair shop and Delano haggles over a price. In a heavy Dominican accent, the friendly woman promises us braids that will last at least six to eight weeks.

As Kayla takes a seat on a tall stool, the boys head for the arcade and food court with Delano. Miffed, Kayla folds her arms over her chest and clamps her mouth into a frown. Her hair reaches down to her lower back, and it takes close to two hours for the woman to undo the current braids and then create new braids. When they're finished, with pink and purple beads on the ends, she holds up a mirror for Kayla to admire herself, but Kayla only scowls.

I leave a generous tip.

We meet the boys near the exit. They're all smiles, having played games and eaten carnival foods. Delano has a bowl of mango chunks that he's bought for Kayla. She eagerly takes them, giving him a huge smile.

I take Devon's hand, stopping his twirling, and we lead the way to the parking lot.

"Did you have fun?" I ask.

Devon bobs his head and his cheeks round with freckles as he grins up at me.

"What did you do?"

I'm pretty sure what he's saying is that he had a Coke slushy. His words are jumbled and somewhat incoherent, but I'm mostly able to work out what he says. Devon is a year older than Amias and Kayla, but his speech is babyish, like a much younger child. He can be hard to understand, but the more I talk with him, the better I'm getting at it. He pulls at my hand as he half walks, half bounces beside me like Tigger. I need to make sure Delano knows that Coke is full of caffeine and sugar.

The beads on Kayla's braids clink and chatter as she stomps past the lines of parked cars. By the time we reach our vehicle, she's tugging at the braids and scratching her scalp. I sweep her hands away and tell her how pretty they are. How pretty *she* is.

"Her ears are too hard," Delano says, and he's right. She's one stubborn girl.

The next day, Sunday morning, I sit on the couch with my legs curled beneath me and my coffee cup on the side table. My mind flits back to my early twenties, when foster care adoption was only a far-fetched dream. In the quiet of the house, I journal about how Devon is so gentle and sweet. I can sense the softness inside of him. Kayla is harder, like she's got a chip on her shoulder, and she acts much older than she is.

Kayla stalks into the room. One side of her hair is a frizzy mess. The other side is still braided, but her fingers are busy at work. I can't help but chuckle in resignation. "Someone didn't get much sleep last night," I say, and motion her to me. I push my journal beneath a couch cushion and cuddle her onto my lap to help her undo the rest of those "ouchie" braids.

After breakfast, I settle in to work on Kayla's hair. I sit on the couch behind her, and she sits on a pillow on the floor. Combs, gels, elastic bands, and hair bobbles litter the coffee table. I twist small locks of hair into simple three-strand braids while she watches *Elmo's World*. One of my friends taught me how to properly care for African American hair back when I had foster children, but I realize that I'll have to ask her about Kayla's hair, because it's curly with a fine texture.

Meanwhile, Devon is in the bathroom trying to use the potty "like a big boy." I'd been surprised that both Devon, almost four, and Kayla, two-and-a-half, were wearing diapers when they came to us. We took them to Walmart so they could pick out undies. Devon had chosen briefs with doggie paws but only reluctantly wears them. He prefers

GoodNites, diapers that pull on like underwear, but I only let him wear those at night.

Devon hasn't had any accidents at Little Rascal's, so he is at least partially potty trained. Delano makes sure that Devon uses the bathroom before he goes to bed, but he still has accidents most nights. It's odd. The sheets are pee-soaked, but his GoodNites are dry. Maybe he's too nervous to use the bathroom in a new house. I remember Eli also wetting the bed at night, and he was a few years older than Devon.

Sitting back, I admire my braids. Adorable. But Kayla does not think so. Despite what Tina told me, I'm finding that Kayla hates getting her hair done, pretty barrettes, dresses, or anything "girly." On our Walmart trip, she'd picked out superhero undies from the boy's aisle for herself. Following Amias' example, she wears them backwards so she can see the picture that's meant to be splashed across her bottom. I'm not sure why she was in diapers when she came to us, because she hasn't had a single accident.

Four braids later, I stand to check on Devon. There's an encouraging smile already on my face as I turn the corner into the bathroom.

I see Devon sitting on the edge of the bathtub. His arm is elbow deep in the toilet. Horrified, I move toward him.

Then, I see the poop in his hand.

I clap my hand over my mouth, and my stomach lurches.

3

Delano does most of the cooking in our household, and tonight he's made white rice and Jamaican Bully Beef. It's a combination of corned beef, thyme, peppers, and onions that reminds me a little too much of canned dog food. The kids love it, but I'm eating a sandwich.

"What do you have for homework?" I ask Sam.

He plucks a morsel of Bully Beef off the green, vinyl table cloth and pops it in his mouth. "Ummm, spelling sentences."

Devon shovels Bully Beef into his mouth as fast as he can and asks for more.

Glad Sam won't need my help, I mentally organize my evening to take the little kids for a walk around the neighborhood after dinner. The weather is nice, and it would help them to get their energy out.

I've been all smiles, accepting congratulations on our pending adoption, but, in truth, settling into our new routine these past weeks has been exhausting. How did I ever imagine that going from one toddler to three, literally overnight, would be easy? Teeth-brushing, shoe-tying, snacks, potty breaks, boo-boos, baths—three times everything. Of course, it's also three times the cuddles at bedtime, three times the hugs and kisses, and three times the sweet sound of being called "Mommy."

"Slow down, Mon," Delano says, scooping another serving of food onto Devon's plate.

Without warning, un-chewed corned beef spews out of Devon's mouth, down his shirt, and across the table.

"Not again." Sam shoves away from the table, hand over his mouth. Unfazed, Kayla continues eating and watches the scene unfold like it's dinner theater.

"Me keep telling you. You too craven, Mon," Delano huffs.

I place a hand on Delano's arm. I try to squelch a gag, but my throat involuntarily clenches with the effort. I whisper, "Stop. You'll hurt his feelings. He didn't mean to." Delano wipes Devon's face and pulls his shirt over his head and off. To him, this is just Devon being greedy.

Kayla has issues with food too. Once, I found her sitting crisscross-applesauce on the pantry floor with her fingers in the peanut butter jar. And, in the evenings, she lounges in her booster seat, snacking and keeping Delano company while he washes dishes. He affectionately calls her his "little foodie." It's like a cherub's arrow straight to his heart, because he loves to feed people. Unfortunately, Devon's gorging is much less endearing than Kayla's grazing, because it sometimes ends in vomiting.

Delano cleans up the kitchen while I take Devon to the bathroom. I fill the tub with warm water and two capfuls of bubble bath. Devon's easy smile returns as he scoops bubbles on top of his head and slides beneath the water, holding his breath. He comes out smelling fresh and clean, as good as new.

The kids play calmly until bedtime. I tuck Devon and Kayla in for the night. Their bedroom has two twin beds across from one another with a large window over Devon's bed and a dresser against the back wall. I draw the blackout curtains tightly across the window. The nightlight sends stars cascading across the ceiling. "Let's do Goodnight Moon," I say.

"Good night, poster," Devon says.

"Good night, toy box," I say.

We pause to give Kayla a turn, but she doesn't say anything.

I say, "Good night, doll house."

"Good night, dresser," Devon says.

"Good night, Kayla," I say.

Lying still in the darkness, Kayla doesn't respond.

I kiss them both before leaving the bedroom. It's Devon who starts the wailing for tonight and then Kayla echoes it. Back and forth they go. Devon is hollering a sort of mewing sound and Kayla is calling, "Mommy, mommy." It's as if they think that I've left them, but I'm standing right outside of their bedroom door. They can see me.

Devon and Kayla have fussed at bedtime since they moved in which is totally understandable given the circumstances, but recently its escalated into this hollering and screaming. Delano uses the TV, as only a father can, to tune them out. He glibly promises they'll be famous singers when they grow up because screaming exercises their vocal cords. It's a Jamaican old-wives' tale, but not knowing how to comfort them is beyond distressing, and I'm not heartened by the supposed silver-lining.

Standing helplessly at their bedroom door, it's all that I can do to not go back in. My resolve almost melts, especially listening to

Devon. Kayla sounds just plain mad, but Devon wails more like a pitiful, broken animal. I determine to wait them out. They've got to learn that screaming and yelling isn't the way to get what they want. But instead of calming down after a few minutes as I expect them to, they feed off each other, only getting louder and louder. Then, I hear a banging on the front door.

It's our neighbor, no doubt looking to score some cheap points in the ongoing feud over his poorly behaved Rottweilers. "I'm gonna report y'all for beatin' those kids," he spits out as Delano comes up behind me. Smoke from our neighbor's cigarette wafts through the door like an ill-mannered trespasser. "Yeah, we hear 'em screamin' all the time. I know what you people are doin'. You damn people are sick."

Without a word, Delano swings the door shut in his face.

Unease nips at my heels as I walk back toward Devon and Kayla's bedroom. As distasteful as our neighbor is, I can't fault him. I've never heard kids scream quite like Devon and Kayla do, or for as long. What if he does call the police? To be cautious, I leave a voicemail for our caseworker, Laquita.

Into the phone, I say, "They're fussing, and, well, my neighbor is threatening to call the police." Devon and Kayla's voices punctuate the background of my message like exclamation marks. "I guess, he thinks we must be abusing them." The moment the words are out, I want to call them back, but I can't. I quickly end the message, not wanting to cause undo alarm.

"Hush now," I say, as I kiss Kayla's forehead and she quiets. Devon hugs his purple Barney, loved threadbare, and I tuck the comforter in around them both. "Hush now and go to sleep," I tell him. His whimpers tug at my heartstrings as I settle on the floor next to his bed. "It's okay. I'm here." I pat his back and knead my neck.

Letting them scream it out isn't an option. I'm going to have to find another strategy.

...

During our bi-weekly home visit, Laquita asks how Devon and Kayla are doing at Little Rascal's. I make a face, and she says, apologetically, "I know. I know. At least it's close by."

"That place is really run down." We're sitting at my dining room table drinking iced tea. "Kayla is upset at first when I drop her off, but then she's fine. They keep sending home notes about Devon. They're having problems with him because he doesn't stay on his mat during nap time."

"Maybe he's not the kind of kid who needs a nap?"

I nod my agreement. "I'm going to see if they'll let me send his Barney in with him. Or maybe they'll let him have a book during naptime."

"That's a good idea. I'll contact the daycare and see what else I can find out." Laquita jots down a few notes on her pad. "How are the kids getting along at home?"

"They're doing great," I gush, going on about how nicely the kids play together, how we read every night at bedtime, and my plans to take them to the Miami Zoo this weekend.

"Tell me about what happened the other night with your neighbor," she says.

"He has something personal against us." I wave a hand dismissively, then tell her about Devon and Kayla's you-have-to-hear-it-to-believe-it screaming.

Laquita leans back in her chair and asks if Devon and Kayla are having any other behavioral problems at home.

I describe how Kayla grazes and Devon gorges. How I've caught Devon playing with his poop and how he wets his bed.

She nods understandingly. "I know it seems disturbing, but what you're describing is all pretty typical for kids who've been severely neglected."

I shift uncomfortably in my seat. "They were ... neglected? This is the first time I'm hearing anything like that. I was told they were never abused—"

"Well, they *have been* in foster care," Laquita interrupts, with just a pinch of condescension, but it's enough to chasten me. "Don't worry. These types of behaviors go away once kids feel secure in their forever families."

I nod. Of course, she's right.

Laquita stows her note pad in her bag and stands. "So many people are looking to adopt kids like them. Young and not having a long history in the system. You're really lucky to get them." We walk toward the door. In the foyer, she turns and touches my arm. "You're doing great. After the adoption is finalized, they'll feel safe and won't need to act out anymore. You'll see."

I close the door behind Laquita and rest my forehead on the cool metal. I listen to the clinking of toys and muffled voices from the living room as I turn her words over in my mind. Severely neglected? I try to push away the foreboding, but my heart is raw from our failed adoption of Eli. Uncertainty creeps up my body and settles over me like a sticky goo.

I'd first come to know about Eli when I saw him profiled on a local TV news segment called "Forever Families." He was a wiry boy, close in age to Sam. He liked football and wanted a family with other kids and a pool. When I called for more information, the adoption worker explained that Eli had been in foster care since he was three. His birth mom neglected him and an uncle had sexually abused him. He had five brothers and sisters, but it was such a large sibling group they weren't being placed for adoption together.

The whole process took only a few short weeks and then Eli was put in our home as a pre-adoption placement.

I was all in.

Eli was too. Right from the start, he called us Mom and Dad.

Sam and Eli became fast friends, sharing a bedroom and walking to school together each morning and afternoon. They played football in the backyard and took turns riding Sam's bike around the neighborhood.

Then, like a pulled thread, the adoption unraveled.

After school one afternoon, Sam burst through the door. "Mom, Mom," he yelled, rushing through the house to find me. "This woman …" He leaned on his knees panting. "This woman. She's coming. Eli did something bad. Real bad."

Alarmed, I put Amias on my hip and hurried through the house. A scowling woman I'd never seen before was at my front door. "Is that your son?" she asked, jabbing a finger at Eli who was dragging his book bag on the ground behind him as he came slowly up the sidewalk.

"Yes. He is. What happened?"

"Your son flashed his privates at my boys."

"I'm ... I'm so sorry," I stammered, sucking in a shocked breath. "He's never done anything like that before."

"I wouldn't be so sure of that," she said. Turning towards Eli, she added loudly, "Next time, I'm calling the cops." As she stalked away, Eli stumbled off the sidewalk into the lawn to give her a wide berth.

Eli admitted to exposing himself, but said he didn't know why he did it. When I told the caseworker about the incident, I was shocked to learn Eli wasn't only a victim of sexual abuse, but he'd also gone on to molest his younger siblings. I realized then, that this must be the real reason why they couldn't be adopted together.

Delano and I were devastated. We faced an unthinkable choice. How could we adopt a child who would put our two other kids at risk?

But, how could we send him back? We grappled with the dilemma, trying to find a way to make it work. Trying to find a way to keep everyone safe.

I worked my way up the chain of command at DCF and even sent letters to the state inspector general and governor. What solutions are there for kids who desperately need a family but can't safely live in one?

They had no answers.
And so, we had no choice.
We had to send him back.
Demoralized, I'd given up my dreams to adopt—until now.

I take a steadying breath, drawing optimism deep into my chest. Devon and Kayla may have been neglected, but that's nothing the love of a forever family can't heal. I just need to know more about their backgrounds, and I'm pretty sure I know where to find some answers.

...

When Kayla and Devon first came to live with us, each had a small bag of personal belongings and what are colloquially called "Blue Books." Florida's foster kids all have them—aqua-colored accordion folders with pockets and two-prong fasteners to secure medical records and court documents. As children move through the system, the books are passed from caregiver to caregiver.

Devon and Kayla's Blue Books have been on my desk since they moved in, but I've only given them a cursory glance. When Tina said that they were "never abused" and "practically perfect," I'd believed her.

On Saturday morning, while everyone is asleep, I carry the Blue Books to the kitchen table. Despite the early hour, the bright sun cascades through the windows, promising another warm Florida day. Since Devon is the oldest, I pick up the first of his two thick books. Clipped inside the front cover, I find a grainy, black-and-white computer printout photo of Devon. His grin is so wide and his eyes so happy that I smile back. The picture isn't dated, but he's probably about two-years-old.

Curious, I flip open Kayla's single, much thinner Blue Book. She looks to be about 18-months-old, with impossibly round eyes. She has the same startled, dazed look that she had the first time we met her in that shabby DCF visiting room. The contrast between Kayla's picture and Devon's is disconcerting.

Going back to Devon's Blue Book, I'm surprised to find extensive details about their birth mother, Sarrah. I scan through the early case summaries and learn that Sarrah was physically abused as a pre-teen and was neglected by her parents. Eventually, they lost custody when Sarrah was 16. She became a chronic runaway, bouncing around the system for the next two years—four group homes and nine foster homes—and dropped out of high school. At 17, Sarrah became pregnant with Devon. DCF placed her with Ms. Price, a registered nurse and seasoned foster parent with children and grandchildren of her own.

Amias toddles into the kitchen rubbing his eyes. He crawls up onto my lap and I cuddle him while I continue to read.

Devon was a Valentine's Day baby, born at the same premier labor and delivery hospital where Amias was born. Sadly, I imagine Sarrah—an unwed, teenage mother, herself a foster child—may not have had quite the same "premier" experience I did. After the birth, she and Devon both went back to live with Ms. Price. Shortly after Sarrah's 18th birthday, Ms. Price came home from work to find them both gone. Sarrah had "aged out" of foster care and had every legal right to leave and take her son with her. She had been the foster child, not Devon.

Ms. Price was worried about Devon and requested a well-check. I read the resulting report from the Sheriff's Office.

```
2002 - Case 13092
Devon was found to be in good
condition, alert, with no marks or
bruises. Sarrah reported she left
her foster home because she wanted
to be on her own. She resides in an
efficiency apartment. She reported
she was working and able to take
care of Devon. A referral was made
for daycare. No other services were
offered. The risk was found to be
low. The case was closed with no
indicators.
```

Unexpectedly, I find myself rooting for Sarrah. She appears to be pulling her life together for herself and Devon. I go to the next case summary, but, with only the year listed, I'm not sure how much time has passed. Let's see. Devon could be as young as three months or as old as ten months.

```
2002 - Case 141902
Devon and his mother have been
living at a motel. Today, the mother
left Devon alone while she went out.
Another resident heard the baby
crying. Devon's diaper was clean and
dry when he was found. The mother
returned within thirty minutes and
stated she had been in the parking
lot talking to a friend. There are
no clothes or formula for Devon. The
mother of Devon has been arrested
for child neglect.
```

With no one to bail her out, Sarrah was in jail for a month before all charges were dropped. By that time, Devon was in foster care and back living with Ms. Price. I marvel at that bit of unlikely fortune. The next documents are medical reports and notes from home visits that the caseworker made with Ms. Price. I'm happy to read that Devon was healthy, happy, and doing really well.

Still, the story isn't quite adding up for me. Sarrah left Devon alone for only 30 minutes. It's not unheard of for parents to leave kids unattended in a hotel room to run to the lobby, to grab something out of their car, or to switch a load of laundry—and they don't lose their children forever. Not for only that.

I'm finished skimming the documents in the second book when Devon and Kayla wander into the kitchen. Stacking the books on my desk, I promise myself that I'll return to them soon.

As butter sizzles in a skillet, I use an upside-down cup to press holes out of slices of bread. I place two pieces of the bread in the pan and crack eggs inside of the holes. It's a special breakfast I remember my dad making when I was a kid. The story about Devon in the hotel room fidgets in my mind as I slide the toasty egg-in-a-hole slices onto plates and put them on the table for Devon and Kayla. I return to the stove to make more for Amias and Sam.

Then, I remember. A few months ago, I profiled several foster families for an article in a local newspaper that I write freelance for. Using my computer, which sits on a desk in the corner of the kitchen, I pull up the online edition of the newspaper. Sure enough, there's the story of Phyllis Price, undoubtedly the Ms. Price of the Blue Books.

Going back to the stove, I think back to my interview with Phyllis. She was Jamaican, with the soft accent of someone who, like Delano, has been in the States for years. For confidentiality reasons, I didn't get to meet Devon or know his real name. In the article I'd given him a pseudonym.

Phyllis had told me about how she'd been volunteering at the shelter the night police brought Devon in. When she'd told me how Sarrah had "abandoned" him in a hotel room, I'd imagined him dehydrated and filthy after being left alone for days. I'm not sure why she didn't correct my assumption, but she must have known it was only 30 minutes and that he was physically fine. When Phyllis realized who this shelter baby was, she volunteered to foster him. By the time I was interviewing her, Phyllis had already had Devon for two years and wanted to adopt him. However, DCF had a rule that siblings must be adopted together, and Phyllis couldn't afford to adopt both Devon and Kayla.

This *can't* be a coincidence. We were approached, out of the blue, to consider adopting. Then Devon ends up being the same little kid who I wrote an article about. He's even been living in a Jamaican home. Surely this adoption is meant to be. A bit overwhelmed by emotions, I turn away from the stove. I cross the kitchen to where the kids sit eating breakfast and place a loud, smooching kiss on Devon's cheek. He startles away. Disconcerted, I press my lips to Kayla's forehead and she loops her arms around my neck.

4

As promised, Laquita contacts Little Rascal's. They tell her that Devon has been throwing tantrums, hitting other kids with toys, and urinating on the bathroom walls. He won't lay down during nap time. He wanders around trying to play with the other children and, when they are asleep or ignore him, his feelings get hurt and he sometimes kicks or hits them.

Laquita schedules an appointment to have Devon evaluated for possible ADHD. It's an overreaction. He's adjusting, and the daycare needs to be more patient with him. But, I do as I'm asked and take Devon to the appointment. From my many years as a foster parent, I know how important it is to not fight "the system" and cooperate with the caseworker.

Devon swings his thick legs and flips through a picture book and I notice his green and white Velcro sneakers are on the wrong feet. How odd. I put his sneakers on him myself this morning. I reach over and change them to the correct feet.

"Do you want me to read that story to you?" I ask.

He shakes his head.

As we're escorted back to an exam room, I hold Devon's hand and murmur, "Don't worry. We're just going to talk. Nothing will hurt." After shaking hands with the young, fresh-faced doctor, I sit down, and Devon sits next to me.

"Hello there. You must be Devon," the doctor says.

Devon nods, and one corner of his mouth flickers. Then he goes wild. He twirls in place. Flops like a fish on the floor. Tries to climb the wall, literally. Knowing the doctor wants to evaluate Devon's behavior, I don't attempt to corral him. After a couple moments of trying to coax Devon into talking to him, the doctor pulls out his prescription pad and says, matter-of-factly, "He obviously has ADHD."

As we step outside after the appointment and walk toward the parking lot, I stuff the prescription in my purse and take Devon's hand. He snatches it back away. I take his hand again, more firmly this time. "Why were you acting so wild in there?" I'm genuinely curious.

Devon shrugs.

Over the weekend, I Google the medication on the prescription slip. It is a stimulant, and I really think Devon is too young for it. Besides, I've never seen him act like that before. Naughty, yes, but he's not hyperactive. I close the browser window, ball up the prescription, and toss it into the trash. What Devon needs is stability, consistency, and love. I'm sure of it.

On impulse, I reopen the browser. This time I search for information on why a child would play with feces. I click the first result. Possible reasons jump off the page: surviving satanic ritual abuse or being a psychopath. I hurriedly click on the back button. I scan through other sites until I find one that says playing with feces isn't uncommon for foster kids. Relief floods me.

Completely normal.

It's completely normal.

That night, Amias and Kayla snuggle close on one side of me, in my king-sized bed. Devon is on the other side of me, craning his neck to see the pictures on *Stinky Face*, the board book I'm holding. The kids giggle at the ape-boy who has a shock of red hair and is wearing orange striped pajamas. I read, "Mama, what if I were a big scary ape? Would you still love me then?" I flip to the next page where the illustration shows what Mama would do if her son was a "big scary ape." She would make him a cake decorated with bananas. I read, "Mama says, 'I love you, my big, scary ape.'"

We read *The Rainbow Fish* next. It's a shiny, hard-cover edition that Kayla brought with her when she came to live with us—the one beautiful thing she had. She especially loves the shimmery foil scales and traces her fingers over them on each page.

When we finish reading, I take Devon and Kayla to their bedroom. I rub my cheek to Kayla's cheek. "Look at that. Another freckle jumped off my face onto yours." She giggles and hugs me around the neck.

Crossing the bedroom, I tuck Devon and his Barney in under the covers and kiss both of them on their foreheads. Sinking to the floor with my back against the wall, like I do most nights now, I settle in to wait for them to fall asleep.

When I emerge a while later, the house is quiet, other than the murmur of the cricket game that Delano is watching in the living room. I find Sam in his bedroom, hunched over his desk. I peer over his shoulder. "Homework?"

Sam shakes his head. He's drawn "Life with My Mother: An Almost True Story" in bubble letters and is coloring them with markers. Sam has big plans to be a famous author. He's going to write about the first time he watched me—his new, white step-mom—peel sunburned skin from my shoulders. He was horrified. He has other chapters planned about how I'm like a human lie detector no matter how clever he is, and how I make him write sentences as a consequence for misbehavior. Having been raised in the Jamaican culture of corporal punishment, he finds this to be shocking. He's a funny kid with a big personality. I leave him to it.

Carrying Kayla's single, slim Blue Book into my bedroom, I turn on the bedside lamp. Amias is asleep and I curl into bed beside him and begin to read:

```
2003- Case 309773-01
Sarrah gave birth to a baby girl.
She agreed to voluntary protective
supervision. She designated Rachel
Sellick to be the non-relative
placement for her daughter.
```

I furrow my brow. Didn't Tina tell me Kayla was in a *good foster home* since birth? I'm familiar with non-relative placements from my foster parenting training. It's when a parent chooses a friend to take their child instead of having them go into foster care. It can be risky because there's almost no monitoring by the State. How well did Rachel take care of Kayla?

Next, I find a report from Kayla's Guardian Ad Litem (GAL). GALs are volunteers who advocate for children within the court system. She describes Rachel's house as unkempt and says that Kayla had no bedding. The next document is a court order:

```
Change of Placement and Status
A recent background check on Rachel
Sellick's friend Ms. Lansky revealed
a past charge for child cruelty. Ms.
Sellick has been advised to not
leave Makayla in care of this
friend. Today, the Child Advocate
learned the child was being left
```

DENIAL

> with Ms. Lansky and immediately
> removed the child from her care.

I wince. No wonder Kayla's such a tough cookie. It's not documented anywhere here, but I'm pretty sure I've already seen the most indelible record from Kayla's life before she came to live with us. It's a faded brown scar on the inside of her right knee, shaped like the tip of a clothes iron. I can count the small round steam holes. I don't know how it happened, but it sure doesn't look like it could have been an accident.

A judge signed the order to move Kayla into foster care at the end of April, a few days before she turned two. Where was she living during the months between when she left Rachel's house in April and when we first met her in November? I had no idea about this gap. I flip through the last few pages, mostly medical forms, but don't find the answer.

To make room for the Blue Book, I scoot the books on my nightstand over. There's my Bible and the book I'm currently reading, *I'm Chocolate, You're Vanilla: Raising Healthy Black and Biracial Children in a Race-Conscious World*. The others are suspense novels. It's my favorite genre, but I always read the last chapter first to make sure that there's a happy ending.

Under the covers and snuggling Amias to me in the darkness, I'm haunted by what I now know about Devon and Kayla's early childhood. It's especially painful to imagine because of how Amias is so attached to me and I to him.

When Amias was born, the doctor detected an irregular heartbeat during the labor and Amias was sent to the NICU. I'd immediately climbed out of the hospital bed, pulled my gown around me, and headed down the hall with them. As we walked past the nursing station, I heard someone say, incredulously, "Isn't that the woman who just gave birth?" One of them called, "Ma'am you shouldn't be walking around." But I was not going to be separated from my baby. Not for a minute.

The doctor cleared and released Amias from the NICU the next day. When we returned home, I fell into the rhythm of attachment parenting, at the time not knowing it was a thing—carrying him in a sling, foregoing a stroller, breastfeeding on demand, and co-sleeping. Delano and I were always at Amias' beck-and-call, even when his call was nothing more than a whimper.

I can't help but compare that with how Devon and Kayla were cared for, or not cared for, as infants. When they cried, did anyone come? How did Devon feel when Sarrah suddenly disappeared from his life? How does a baby even process that? Does Kayla cling to my arm at Little Rascal's because she's literally afraid I won't come back for her? It's on these deeply disturbing thoughts that an uneasy sleep finally comes.

The next morning, I'm feeling optimistic again by harkening back to my foster parent training. Children are resilient. Even if they've gone through terrible abuse and neglect, they can thrive and heal with the love and permanency of a forever family. Children act out because they are feeling unsafe. This is why consistent parenting is so important. That's why they do much better after they are adopted.

...

If Devon thinks of anyone as "mom," it's Phyllis, and that's one connection I can keep intact for him. She can be one less person in his life who has up and disappeared.

I invite Phyllis over for dinner and Devon is so excited that he brushes his teeth and changes his clothes all by himself. He presses his forehead and fingers against the bay window watching for his "Granny." That's what Phyllis has suggested he call her going forward. Amias and Kayla pay him no mind since they don't know Phyllis. They are busy playing with building blocks.

"She here! My granny is here!" Devon dashes for the door when she pulls into the driveway.

Phyllis is short and solid with cropped hair, round glasses, and high cheekbones. "You being good in school?" is the first thing she asks.

Bobbing his head, Devon looks at his feet, thin lips quivering as he fights to suppress a shy smile. Suddenly, he takes off running into his bedroom. He returns, panting and holding up a coloring page. It's a fat caterpillar on a tree branch. In the sky above floats its future self—a butterfly with hearts adorning its wings. Devon has colored it with purple, pink, and green.

"Very nice. Thank you." Phyllis takes the paper, folds it in half, then half again, and slips it into her pocketbook.

Delano comes out of the kitchen and hands Phyllis a tall glass of fruit punch clinking with ice. "I'm fixing brown stew chicken and rice and peas," he tells her. They exchange words in Patois. In more formal settings, Delano goes out of his way to speak in very dignified, "proper" English. He only speaks Patois with other Jamaicans like Phyllis, but bits and pieces carry over into all of his conversations, because it's a dialect made up of non-standard English grammar and British vocabulary. I'll never forget the time he was lecturing Sam, "You must always carry a rubber with you. Do you hear me? Never you go to school without a rubber." He meant a pencil eraser and I was quick to intervene, telling Sam to call it an eraser, not a rubber.

Phyllis clucks her approval of dinner, and Delano disappears back into the kitchen. The hearty scent fills the air, as Phyllis and I sit on the sofa. Devon stands with his small fingers on Phyllis's leg. He's telling her about daycare, at least I think he is. His speech is more unintelligible than usual and I'm struggling to understand him.

Phyllis pats his back and says, "Go play."

He looks at us as though unsure what to do.

"We'll watch you," I reassure him.

Devon reluctantly heads over to where Amias and Kayla are playing. He casts furtive glances over his shoulder to make sure we're watching. We are.

"Him looking good," Phyllis says.

"He's so cute and sweet. And he's a good helper too."

When I tell her about Devon's morning sneezing, she snorts. "Him still doing that?" She doesn't seem surprised about the screaming at bedtime or the potty issues either.

I'm confused. There's nothing about these behaviors happening at Phyllis's home in the Blue Books. That's why I'd assumed they only started after Devon moved in with us. Why didn't she tell the caseworker? I can't think of a polite way to ask, so I don't. Instead, I shift the conversation to something else. "Why did Sarrah leave?" I ask, in a hushed voice so that the kids won't overhear.

Phyllis gives a half shrug. "I came home from work and they were gone. No note. Nothing."

We sit quietly for a few minutes watching the kids play. Amias sits on the floor holding the base of a tall, thin tower to keep it steady. The higher up it goes, the more it sways. Still, Kayla, who is standing, adds blocks to the top. Devon runs a toy car in loops on the floor in front of where he sits. I ask Phyllis if she has any baby pictures of Devon that I could make copies of.

Phyllis shakes her head. "Sarrah took everything when she left.

She didn't want me to have nothing."

I glance at Amias' yellow baby book, which is sitting on the nearby bookshelf. It has pictures of him laying on my chest mere minutes after he was born. I know his first word and when he said it. I have the exact dates when he rolled over, crawled, and took his first step. Even for Sam, I have a small baby book with a handful of pictures and a bit of hair his mother saved. Someday, Devon and Kayla are going to ask for their baby books and mementoes and all I'll have to give them are those scrappy printouts in their Blue Books.

No. I shake my mind free of the thought. I refuse to accept that. I'm going to take so many pictures that I'll need entire bookshelves to store all the photo albums of happy family memories we're going to create.

5

The boys are sporting button-down shirts and pressed jeans. Kayla is wearing a dress with a burgundy velvet bodice and white voile bottom. Delano is wearing a dark suit, and I have on dress slacks and a rose-colored top. As the courthouse elevator opens and we shuffle out, we look every bit the beautiful "forever family" I've always dreamed of being.

In reality, Devon is clutching at my pant leg, hiding behind me from Kayla's fierce glower. They don't seem to have a natural sibling bond, which makes sense as this is the first time ever that they've lived together. More than once, over the last four months, I've watched Kayla chomp down on Devon's back and him smack her with toys.

But none of this can dampen my spirits. We made it. Adoption day is finally here. The one thing I'm sure of is that everything will resolve itself after the adoption is finalized. This is our beginning.

Delano walks ahead with Sam and Amias, but I pull Devon and Kayla aside. I kneel down to their level.

"Her bit me." Devon shows me a forensics-worthy impression of teeth on his right forearm. "Her did it."

Kayla clutches *The Rainbow Fish* in her hands. She pinches her lips together and shakes her head.

When Devon had first shown me the bite mark in the car on the way over, I wasn't sure who was telling the truth. Now, looking at his proffered arm, it's obvious that he's at least been keeping the bite mark fresh with his own teeth.

"Her did it," he sniffles.

Kayla glares at him.

"Kayla, go with Daddy," I say. After a gentle nudge in that direction, she trails after him.

"I didn't do it," Devon says, with a note of hysteria.

I pull Devon into my arms. He stills. "No one's in trouble. This is our special day. Remember?" He looks at me with that fawn-like, shy smile I've come to adore. "Let's go inside so you can become mine forever," I say, and take his hand. He skips down the hall beside me.

Laquita meets us at the courtroom door with congratulations on our big day. I invited Phyllis to the adoption hearing also, but she said it's best for Devon to not have any further contact with her if he's going to adjust to his new family. I don't agree, but it's her decision to make, and there is nothing more I can do.

Inside the courtroom, Delano and I arrange the four kids sitting between us at the large conference table, and Laquita sits on my other side. Kayla opens her book on the table top and the foil scales of the Rainbow Fish shimmer.

"What do you have there, Makayla?" Laquita asks.

Kayla lifts the front of the book so Laquita can see the cover.

"Ooh, that's one of my favorites."

"She brought it with her when she came to us," I say. "But, do you know what's strange?" I reach over and lift the first pages of the book, just enough for Laquita to see that "Adriana" is written in marker on the inside front cover.

Laquita begins nodding her head. She turns her face toward me, and says, "That's what that family who tried to adopt them before you called her."

"What?" I exclaim, then cover my mouth apologetically when the judge looks up. He's sitting at his desk in one corner of the room, flipping through paperwork. In a near whisper, I ask, "Someone else tried to adopt them?"

"No one told you?"

I shake my head. It wasn't anywhere in the Blue Books either.

"The mother wasn't able to have children of her own and had always wanted to name a little girl Adriana. She said Kayla didn't know her name, so they started calling her Adriana."

"When was this?" I ask.

"A few months before they were placed with you."

I think of how Kayla was so particular about not wanting to be called "Makayla." There's no way she didn't know her own name. I'm reeling from this new information and want to know more. I ask, "What happened? Why didn't they end up going through with the adoption?"

Laquita leans her head closer to my ear and whispers, "One day, the daycare saw welts all over Devon's legs. They called the caseworker, and she came and picked them up right from daycare."

I suck in a breath.

Laquita pulls back and gives me a knowing look, then leans

close to my ear again. "Devon and Makayla never went back to that home after that day. The mother was heartbroken. I heard they got a divorce over it."

Our conversation ends abruptly, and Laquita straightens in her chair as the judge stands from his desk and moves toward the conference table. He's a short bald man. On the paperwork that's passed to me, I recognize his name from the Blue Books. This is the same judge who signed the order terminating Sarrah's parental rights. He begins the proceedings by asking why we want to adopt Devon and Kayla.

I'm a shy introvert and I don't like speaking in front of groups, but I've prepared for this. "Devon and Kayla have been living with us for almost four months. We love them and want them to be part of our family."

The judge nods and looks to Delano. "And you, Sir?"

"Devon and Makayla are like our other children whom we dearly love. God has blessed us by bringing them into our family. We are honored to be their parents," he says, ceremoniously.

The judge nods, and begins, "Adoption is forever. Today Devon and Makayla are becoming your children, the same as birth children. There is no difference." He gives a lengthy monologue that he's clearly intoned many times before. "You cannot return an adopted child any more than you can return a birth child," he concludes, warning that if we ever try to, we'll be prosecuted.

I'm so offended. Why would he even say something like that? At an adoption hearing? It's just plain rude.

The judge flips through the files as the courtroom waits and watches in silence. I'm also adopting Sam today. I'm his mom without the paperwork, but want him to understand how committed I am to all of my children—adopted, step, and birth children alike. The judge signs off on all three adoptions.

We meet with our lawyer in the hallway, and he hands us new birth certificates for the kids. It's a bit surreal. On them, I'm listed as their mother and Delano as their father. With these, no one would ever know they aren't our birth children. The lawyer reminds us that we'll receive Devon and Kayla's new Social Security cards in the mail. It's a closed adoption and these completely new identities will keep Sarrah from ever finding them.

Devon and Kayla have been classified as "special needs" by DCF solely because they're bi-racial, which makes adoptive homes for them harder to find. Because of this they're qualified for Medicaid until they're eighteen, adoption fee reimbursement, and a small stipend. We have good health insurance through our jobs, so we won't need the Medicaid. I think of declining, but the kids are tired and I let it go.

After accepting congratulations, I take Devon and Kayla by their hands. Delano carries Amias, who has fallen asleep, and Sam hefts the diaper bag onto one shoulder. We walk out through the courthouse doors, into the bright sunshine, a forever family.

6

A few months before the adoption, Hurricane Wilma was forecast to decrease in intensity as it came ashore. Instead, it sucker-punched South Florida. Like so many others, we were woefully unprepared. We were without power for a week and I developed a painful abscess on my stomach. I walked to an emergency Red Cross vehicle and stood in line for hours. The nurse said it was only a boil and gave me a black tar like ointment that she promised would clear it right up. The boil healed, our electricity got turned back on, and life went back to normal. But, I decided I was never going to go through hurricane season again.

After that, my identical twin sister, Becky, and I dreamed up the idea of moving to the same neighborhood and raising our kids together. She and her husband, Jason, have two children, Jacob and Abby, who are close in age to ours. At the time, they were living in New Jersey. Becky and I looked for an affordable city with jobs and a good place to raise kids. Delano insisted that we couldn't move anywhere cold, so I told him a little white lie: "It never gets cold enough to snow in Charlotte." With that, we put a pin in it.

Then, Tina had called about Devon and Kayla, and we put our moving plans on hold. As soon as the adoption was finalized, we listed our house. Now, I'm spending every spare moment packing and cleaning.

My knees ache from kneeling on the marble tile as I lean into the oven and scrub the inside. Last I checked, Sam is hiding in his bedroom to escape babysitting duties, while the little kids chase through the house, over the sofa, under the table, and in and around the cardboard obstacle course of moving boxes. They're like a litter of puppies—playfighting, squealing, and nipping.

Looking up from the stove, I still my hand and listen. The house is quiet. Suspiciously quiet. I grab a paper towel to wipe my hands and hurry toward the living room. I find the kids in my bedroom. Kayla is crouched behind Amias on my bed. She is holding the black marker that I've been using to label moving boxes, poised over Amias' back. They're both wearing boy's superhero undies—backwards as usual—and "tattoos" cover their arms, bellies, backs, and faces. Devon scurries over to my side, his eyes as wide as my mouth is open. I can literally taste the astringent smell of the Sharpie. My face contorts between laughing and crying. Then I start to panic that the ink might seep into their bloodstream. I call the poison control center and the operator actually snickers as he tells me that they'll be fine.

Plopping my little ink slingers into the tub, wearing their undies like bathing suits, I scrub at the marks with soap and a washcloth. Devon begins picking at the edges of the wallpaper while watching me out of the corner of his eyes. I brush his hand away from the wall as I scold Amias and Kayla. Soap doesn't work and I ask Devon to hand me the toothpaste. Dubiously, he holds out the tube. "You're such a good helper," I tell him.

The grit of the toothpaste helps fade the "tattoos," but they don't disappear completely. The worst of the marks are on Amias and Kayla's faces because I can't cover them up with clothing. I spend our last few days in Florida explaining: No, my kids aren't covered in bruises. It's only marker. They did it to themselves.

...

Our new home in North Carolina is in a small, diverse neighborhood close to playgrounds, schools, and the city's bike trail. It sits next to Becky and Jason's house and we create a stepping stone path to connect our front doors. My kids love to play at "Auntie Becky's house." They never knock and she never locks her door. "You're *always* invited," she insists.

They spend many happy hours next door playing with their cousins, Jacob and Abby. They ride scooters inside the house when it rains and Auntie Becky doesn't complain when the glass in her picture frames gets broken by a soccer ball.

Becky and Jason get a spaniel puppy and tell my kids that, of course, he belongs to them too. The cousins all agree to name him Ben 10 after their favorite cartoon. Devon asks, "Season 1 or Season 2?" They agree to "Season 1" and Becky and Jason submit the official AKC paperwork with the dog's full name as "Ben 10, Season 1," but everyone calls him Ben for short.

We soon fence our backyards together to create a double-sized yard perfect for soccer, stomp rockets, and an unexpected snowman.

That year's snow melts quickly, leaving behind a mucky mess just as we're setting out on an off-season vacation in Myrtle Beach.

We rent a resort suite that is large enough for our communal family. The hotel has an indoor lazy river and swimming pool, indoor and outdoor hot tubs, and direct access to the beach.

Becky and I sit poolside, wrapped in towels, watching as Sam gathers the little kids in the shallow end of the indoor pool. They crouch with their fingers ready to pinch their noses as he counts down, "Three. Two. One. Go!" They all duck their heads under the water—except Sam, who stays poised just above the water's surface. Watching. Waiting. The little kids are wearing life jackets and their bodies bob, face down. Kayla's long curls fan out around her.

Sam's timing is uncanny. The moment the little kids start to gasp up out of the water for air, Sam slips underwater. Jacob floats comically on his back, unable to roll back over or move to a standing position with the lifejacket swallowing up his tiny frame. Amias, Kayla, and Devon point and jabber excitedly as they watch Sam's incredible feat of holding his breath underwater so much longer than they can. When he finally springs up, they yell and splash at him and call for a rematch. Then another. Sam wins every time. As I watch, I find myself wishing they always played together this nicely.

Earlier this morning, we were on the beach and the kids were burying Uncle Jason in the sand, an activity he was enjoying every bit as much as they were. Becky and I were lounging on beach chairs and sipping Starbuck's Iced Chai Tea Lattes beneath floppy sun hats.

Spitting sand out of his mouth, Jason had called over to my sister, "Hey, Beck. Remind me to bring the big garden shovel next time we come." I shook my head imagining the potential disaster of the kids swinging a metal shovel bigger than themselves over his head.

They built a sprawling sand castle too, running back and forth to the water's edge for buckets of wet sand and water. It was an idyllic holiday at the beach, until Amias started frantically wiping at his eyes. He stumbled toward me, crying that Devon had thrown sand in his face.

Devon was squatting and piling sand over his feet. He was pretending to not be paying attention to Amias' hysterics. "Devon," I'd said sternly, "do not throw sand."

"I didn't do it," he whined.

Before long, Amias had scurried back to the castle and Jason said to Devon, "Buddy, can you help fill up this moat?"

Devon eagerly ran for the shoreline. I watched as he happily carried buckets of water up to fill the moat. That's one of the paradoxes I've noticed about Devon. He uses baby-talk and acts much younger than his age, but he's surprisingly industrious.

I resumed my conversation with my sister and let the kids' voices and laughter be carried away from me in the beach breeze. Before long, Amias was crying and stumbling toward me again. I didn't see what happened, myself, but I heard Jason say, "Bud, you gotta be careful."

I couldn't hear Devon's reply over Amias' sobs.

Then Jason said, "I know you didn't do it on purpose, but you need to be careful."

Amias' eyes were poufy, red, and watery. "Cry it out," I encouraged him while holding his hands away from his face. I called Devon over and told him to sit next to me in time-out.

Devon insisted that he had not thrown sand in Amias' face, even accidentally. There was a breeze. It was possible that Devon was telling the truth and the wind had blown the sand into Amias face. Before I could make up my mind, Devon began wailing loudly and kicking sand into the air. I told my sister I was going to have to take him back to the hotel room to stay with Delano.

I took Devon by the arm to lead him up the beach, but he went limp and flopped onto the sand. I really had no choice. I couldn't let him think he could get his way by throwing a fit. I carried him as he thrashed in my arms. I was so embarrassed. All the way up the elevator, he carried on. Down the hall, he bawled and tantrumed in my arms.

The moment I swiped the keycard and swung the door to the suite open, Devon's body stilled. His wailing stopped other than his hiccupping sobs. I looked at his flushed face in astonishment. I set him down and led the way to the sitting room. Delano had hissed his teeth, clearly thinking I was overreacting. I'd left them, unsure of what had just happened.

Back on the beach, I'd described to Becky the complete transformation Devon had made as soon as we entered the suite. "Maybe he thought Delano would spank him," she said.

I shrugged, but didn't think so. Delano doesn't have knee-jerk reactions like that. He would give Devon several chances before reaching that point. Devon has sat through enough of Delano's mind-numbing lectures to know that.

That sand-incident happened several hours ago and, now, the kids are all playing happily as if nothing happened. I unwrap my towel and drape it over my chair. "Are you going in?" Becky asks, looking up from her paperback.

"I'm going to take the kids to the deep-end to practice swimming." I wade into the pool and the kids rush toward me eager to take a turn.

Kayla unsnaps her life jacket and wraps her arms around my neck as I carry her deeper into the water until it's up to my chest. She pushes at me. "Let go. I can swim. Let go." At her insistence, I do. She paddles her arms furiously but still sinks toward the bottom of the pool, all the while smiling up at me with her eyes wide open. I sweep her back up into my arms. "I can swim," she pouts, and tries to pull away from me again.

Next, Amias lays on his back with his eyes shut. My fingertips support his back, and I tell him to relax and pretend he's sleeping. His lithe body doesn't float naturally. "You don't have any blubber," I tease him. "That's why you can't float."

When it's Devon's turn, he wraps his arms and legs in an octopus hug around my body. "I won't let go of you. I promise," I say, trying to extricate myself so he can practice floating on his back. He shakes his head and digs his fingernails into my skin. I want to show him that he's safe, but, after several minutes, I realize he's just not ready. As I carry him back toward the wading pool, I let myself enjoy the unexpected closeness. Back in the shallow end, I secure his lifejacket once again and he heads over to play with his siblings and cousins.

Standing back by my chair I wrap myself in my towel. "Did you see Baby Amias?" I ask my sister. "He's so skinny he can't float."

"He's four-years-old, not a baby," she says, laughing at me.

Later that evening, Becky and I leave the kids with our husbands and sneak away to the hot tub. Before we reach the elevator, the door to our suite whooshes open. Kayla calls after us, "Wait for me, Mommy. Wait for me."

I motion to her. "Come on."

A smile darts across her face. Her purple flip-flops snap as she rushes toward us. She's holding the straps of her orange and yellow swimsuit for me to tie in a bow behind her neck. Curls have escaped her ponytail and fuzz at the edges of her face and nape. I push the elevator button, and Kayla looks up at me with old-soul eyes and a reprimand: "I told you. Girls stick together."

7

On Sam's 13th birthday, the little kids chorus, "Happy birthday to you. Cha, cha, chaaaa," in a cacophony around him. It's tradition, and the more off-key the better. With five kids aged five and under, plus Sam, my sister and I invent what we playfully call "speed birthdays"—store bought cupcakes, frenzied present opening, and singing Happy Birthday—all in 30 minutes or less. Speed birthdays, like all messy events, take place at Becky's house.

Delano hands out juice boxes and the kids wiggle in their seats as they wait for their cupcakes. Going in age order, Uncle Jason starts with Abby, who is the youngest. She immediately begins licking the frosting and I reach over and swipe her wispy blond hair back behind her ears. Jason passes the next cupcake to Jacob who grabs it with an impish grin.

"Don't feed them to the dog," Jason warns, as Ben circles around the kids' toes, hoping to be passed a treat. Jason gives cupcakes to Kayla and Amias. "Here you go, Bud," he says, handing the next one to Devon while eyeing Sam mischievously. With a flourish and peal of laughter, he smashes a cupcake into Sam's face. The kids roar with laughter and Sam's chair clatters to the floor as he chases after Uncle Jason.

After the ensuing chaos calms, Delano sneaks out of the front door to go home and the kids go upstairs to play. Becky takes a cup of tea and sinks into the sofa, while Jason flops into a nearby armchair. I clear up the paper plates and crumpled juice boxes. Jason winks at me. "Wish my wife was a little more like her sister."

"Oh my God, I forgot to tell you," Becky says to me, ignoring Jason teasing about her dislike of cleaning. "I was at the grocery store this morning and the cashier looked at me funny and said, 'Weren't you in here earlier today?' I realized it was you she'd seen."

Jason snickers, but I groan. How embarrassing.

I wipe frosting from the table with a sponge as Becky continues. "When I told her I have an identical twin sister, she was like, 'There are two of you?'"

There's a crashing sound and pounding of feet down the stairs Kayla hurtles around the corner with Devon on her heels. "It's not true," Devon cries. "Her's lying on me."

"He," she jabs a finger at Devon, "wants to play."

I raise my hands to quiet them. "Why can't he play?"

"He picked his nose," Kayla says, with all the indignation of a teenager.

Devon swings his head from side to side in a wide arc. "I did not. I did not."

"He's gross," Kayla wails.

When it comes to telling the truth, all bets are on Kayla. But what I say is, "He's not gross. Kayla, you need to say 'sorry.' And Devon, go wash your hands, then you can play."

"But I didn't," Devon insists.

I flip on the bathroom light. "It's not a big deal. Just go wash them."

Devon stares, unmoving and unblinking. Kayla has her arms crossed over her chest with her mouth clamped shut, and I realize she's not going to say sorry.

"Okay, let's go home, then," I say.

Devon melts into a heap and beats on the laminate floor with his fists. I haul him to his feet and walk him toward the door. "What about Amias?" Kayla demands as she trails after Devon and me across the stepping stone path back to our house.

"Amias isn't part of this fight."

I plop Devon onto a kitchen chair and point to another where Kayla sits. As the kitchen timer ticks out five minutes, Kayla clamps her mouth shut, but Devon continues to blubber and fuss.

When the time is up, Kayla mumbles an, "I'm sorry."

"Okay, you can go back over," I tell her. She scrambles out of her seat and hugs me around the legs. "We'll be over in a few minutes," I say, and she rushes out letting the front door slam behind her.

I tell Devon, "Go wash your hands, then we'll go back over too."

He doesn't move.

"Come on, I'll help you."

Devon screws his eyes closed, juts his chin into the air, and brays.

I look at him, not understanding. He'd rather not go back to

Becky's house than do something as simple as wash his hands? "Do you hear this?" I call to Delano who is in the living room watching TV. "All this because he doesn't want to wash his hands."

"If you cyan 'ear, you mus' feel," he calls back in response.

I've heard Delano say that one too many times as warning of a spanking: "If you cannot hear, you must feel." But Devon keeps his fussing low and Delano is not disturbed enough to come deal with him.

Over the months, Devon's behavior at Becky's house only grows more concerning. He sneaks around and goes through cabinets and drawers. Of course, Becky and I know some of this is normal with kids. But, with Devon, it's different. He doesn't rummage around in a drawer and leave it open with the contents dribbling out. He's sneaky. No matter how fun the fun is, he steals away on his own. Then he startles if we walk in on him. He slides tampons, a stray earring, and other "treasures" into his underwear and takes them back home to his bedroom. Becky catches him eating out of her trash can. After that, I don't let him go next door to play unless I'm there to supervise him.

One morning, Amias and Kayla are next door and Sam is at school. Delano is watching Devon, who is sitting at the table coloring with crayons. I walk into the kitchen to pour myself a fresh cup of coffee, and Devon looks at me with pleading eyes. I can read them as readily as written lines of a book.

"You know why you can't go," I answer. "I'll take you over after I'm done working, when I can keep an eye on you."

The house is quiet, other than the hum of my computer booting up as I settle into my office chair. Fortunately, when we moved to North Carolina, my boss asked me to continue working remotely. I'm working from home full-time, but I cannot watch the kids at the same time. For this reason, Delano isn't going to look for a job until after the kids are in school. It doesn't make sense to pay for daycare for three kids.

The login screen on my computer flashes, bringing me out of my thoughts. In focused work-mode, I make good progress on several projects before realizing the time. I head downstairs for lunch and find Devon playing quietly in the playroom. He comes out holding a drawing of a bright rainbow with a family beneath. Dad is wearing a green box on top and blue rectangles on his legs. Amias stands next to Kayla, whose hair is a halo of loops. I laugh and point to it. "Look at Kayla's hair. It looks just like her!"

Devon grins. He's drawn himself with short, light brown hair. I have long, dark hair and a pink dress.

"What's that?" I ask pointing to a round scribble on my torso.

"Your coffee."

"I love it," I say, putting my arms around his shoulders and giving him a squeeze. I make Devon lunch of a PB&J sandwich, a handful of chips, and some grapes. I bring it to him and pick up his drawing from the table. "Can I hang this on the refrigerator?"

He nods, his mouth full of sandwich.

"I love that you drew my coffee," I say, as I use a magnet advertising a local urgent care to affix it to the stainless-steel refrigerator. I grab the sponge and rub at a smear near the handle. With all the little fingers around our house, no matter how hard I try, it's impossible to keep it shiny.

I glance up at Devon. At first, I'm unsure of what I'm seeing.

Is he?

He is.

He's pushing his fingers into his mouth.

Now he's vomiting all over the table.

8

Resting my hands on my belly, the kids take turns feeling their baby brother kicking. "He wants to get out and play soccer with you," I tease, and they giggle. I re-adjust myself on the couch, far enough along to be feeling uncomfortable. In one corner of the room, cable news is muted with the closed captioning running across the screen. I like the setting because it's usually difficult to hear over the bustle of the household and I have a bit of a news addiction. I figure closed captioning must help the kids learn to read when they're watching cartoons too. Jason thinks that's preposterous and it's become a running joke between the two of us.

"I remember when you were in my belly," I say, and pull Amias, onto my lap kissing him up until he squeals. I spin my well-worn tale, one that's become a favorite of theirs: "Sam was in Monica's belly but she died when he was a little boy and it was very sad. When Daddy married me, I became Sam's mommy."

I wiggle a finger at Devon and Kayla, "You weren't in my belly either. You were in Sarrah's belly. She loved you so much," I make an exaggerated frown. "But she was a teenager and didn't have a job or a place to live. She didn't have any way to take care of you."

Kayla bounces next to me and eagerly adds her favorite part. "There was a whole lot of people fighting over who'd get to adopt me!"

"And me," says Devon, one finger screwed in his nose. "They was fighting over me too!"

Kayla scowls. I narrow my eyes at her in a silent warning: Be nice. To Devon, I say, "Of course, they wanted you too."

He sucks his finger into his mouth.

"Devon ..." I swallow thickly. "Devon, go wash your hands."

All this talk has piqued Kayla's curiosity. "What does Sarrah look like?" she asks.

"I bet she's pretty like you," I say, but in truth, I have no idea.

After the little kids are in bed, I ask Sam to lug the Blue Books out of the attic where I've stored them in a plastic tub. Flipping through,

I find Sarrah's full name and date of birth. I'm amazed, but thankful, that DCF didn't redact this information.

A few clicks are all it takes to find her. Sarrah has shoulder-length, light brown hair. Her face is heart-shaped with clear, porcelain skin. Cropping the picture to make it look a little less like the mugshot that it in fact is, I print two copies to frame.

Kayla loves hers and proudly displays it on the nightstand by her bed. Devon carries his around with him for days, and then it disappears somewhere into his bedroom.

...

Devon has a boil and Delano has been applying a poultice of honey and flour to draw out the pus, which usually works. But, this morning, when I felt the warmth of infection radiating across Devon's belly, I knew that he needed a doctor. "Only Americans does that. No one needs to see no doctor for that," Delano had called after me as I'd bustled Devon out the door to urgent care.

It turns out, the sore I contracted during Hurricane Wilma, wasn't an innocuous, quick-healing boil like the nurse had said it was. It was MRSA, which is insidious and resistant to treatment. In our family, Delano is the only person who has not been affected. The MRSA has spread next door too, and Becky, Jason, and both their kids have been infected. Sometimes we'll go months thinking we've finally dealt with the MRSA once and for all and then a new boil will swell up on one of us.

Now watery pus dribbles from the swollen, purple abscess on Devon's belly. The doctor prods at the taut, inflamed skin with two gloved fingers feeling for the real sickness, the hard mass lurking beneath the surface.

As the doctor prepares his instruments on a shiny steel tray, Devon's whimpering turns into begging. Eyes wild and possessed with fear, he begs, "Please, please. It will get better by itself. I promise. I promise."

I put my arms around him and soothe, "It'll only hurt for a minute and then it will feel so much better." Flailing for how to make this horrible moment better, I add, "We'll get ice cream after."

He freezes like a deer in headlights. "Two scoops?"

Without warning, the doctor presses against the sides of the boil. Devon shrieks and thrashes wildly. Thick, yellow pus shoots out in a viscous arc. Nurses rush to hold Devon's arms and legs as the doctor presses over and over. The sharp smell hits my nose and I gag, my already sensitive reflexes heightened by my pregnancy. The doctor doesn't stop until bright red blood dribbles out of the puckered, deflated sore. Now that the infection is drained, Devon doesn't flinch as the nurse puts on a bandage.

Devon and I stop by Baskin Robbins on the way home and he orders three scoops in a dish: chocolate, strawberry, and cherry.

After the short ride home, I lug my pregnant belly up the stairs and follow a banging sound into Devon's bedroom. Delano has pulled Devon's platform storage bed away from the wall and I don't have to look to know what he's found. He points at the crumbs and wrappers between the bed and the wall. "What this, Devon? What this?"

It's a rhetorical question—a waste of time. We all know Devon sneaks to the pantry and takes crackers and other snacks to hide in his bedroom. During one middle of the night forage, he took a swig of apple cider vinegar thinking it was juice. He spit it out with a yelp and woke me up. That's when I put a lock on the pantry door. It's just a hook and eye lock, but it's high enough that the kids would need to stand on a chair to get to it.

Delano gets upset whenever he finds food and wrappers in Devon's room because of the bugs it will attract. More concerning, we sometimes find medicine blister packs with the paper peeled and the foil indented and scratched in Devon's stash.

"It wasn't me …" Devon's eyes dart around the room. "Not me. I promise."

I pick the picture of Sarrah up from the pile and dust off crumbs before setting it on the dresser.

"Why you so craven, Mon?" Delano demands. "Bugs-gonna-come-for-you. They'll-eat-you-up."

"It wasn't me. I *promise*."

"Then, who? Who did it?"

With my finger tip I push back an unwrapped tampon and uncover a hoop earring. I pick it up and look for anything else that needs to be saved before Delano cleans up the mess.

"Maybe a mouse …" Devon tries.

Delano snorts. "You the mouse."

9

Labor pains wake me at midnight, but I can't go to the hospital yet. I wrap up projects for work and reply to client emails. I email my boss, put Sam on the school bus, and send the little kids next door. Uncle Jason is taking the day off to watch them. Only then do Delano and I head to Carolina Medical.

I didn't take any drugs during my 32-hour labor with Amias, and that's precisely why I'm getting an epidural this time. Delano says a mother can only really love her baby if she feels the full pain of labor. Not true. The instant Brandon is in my arms, I'm smitten. Only with great reluctance do I hand him to a nurse so we can both get cleaned up.

As Delano helps change the sheets on my hospital bed, Becky bursts into the room. She's left school in the middle of teaching a class to rush over. She swoops Brandon from the nurse's arms. "I'm your second mommy," she coos. Perhaps it's an identical twin thing, but we really are more like second moms to each other's children than aunts.

The first night that I'm home and sleeping in my own bed, I wake up in the dark, nearly blind without my contact lenses. My breasts burn and my nightgown is soaked with milk. Is Brandon on my right or left? I can't remember. I touch the body on my left and run my hands up and down *long* legs and *long* arms. Who is this? It's not Amias or Brandon. In a panic, I flip on the light. Amias? Amias! In that instant, my brain registers that he is no longer a toddler. It's incredibly disorienting and I keep touching him as if it's a dream. I'm hardly able to believe it.

Becky laughs when I tell her. "You're the only one who thought Amias was still a baby. He's four. Now that you have a baby again you realize how big he is."

I guess she's right. And it's not only him, Devon and Kayla seem to have grown big overnight too. Devon's babyish behavior begins to really stand out to me. He's five and still wets his bed and wants help getting dressed. He uses baby talk and blubbers all the time. He's so immature compared to Amias and Kayla. Why didn't I notice this before?

I tell the kids that their new brother has a "glass" head and they must be careful not to hurt him. I let them take turns holding him while they're sitting on the couch, but only when Delano or I am next to them. They are fascinated, but Sam shakes his head and says it's like having Amias as a baby all over again: way too much work.

My mom lives in Vermont and she books a flight to come meet her new grandson. With clear skin and shoulder-length, brown hair, she likes to describe as "baby-fine," people often ask if we're sisters. She loves that. I'm glad she's come, but I don't necessarily need her help.

I swear, Delano is so nurturing that he would breastfeed Brandon himself, if he could. When Brandon fusses in the middle of the night, Delano eagerly gets up to burp and rock him. He insists on changing all of the diapers too. He says I don't do it properly, a ridiculous statement, but one not in my best interest to contest.

The first morning after Mom arrives, I curl up on the couch nursing. There's a small spiral of thread pasted to Brandon's forehead with saliva. Before Mom can wipe it away, Delano stops her. "No, Grandma, leave it. Him was hiccing-up."

Mom looks baffled, but I let my heavy eyes drift closed. I learned long ago to pick my battles. Most of Delano's Jamaican home remedies are wonderful, like warm lime and honey for coughs and ginger tea for sick tummies. I'm not, however, a fan of how he believes it's better to suck mucus from a baby's nose with his mouth than to use a nasal aspirator. That's just gross. Thread and spit? Not something to worry about.

After Brandon finishes nursing, Mom lifts him out of my arms and sits in the rocking chair humming. She rubs his back waiting for him to burp and I drift back into a light sleep.

Before long, the kids zip down the stairs and race over to Grandma. Kayla giggles shyly. Amias nudges her for space and clutches the arm of the rocker. "Grammy, want to walk our dog?" he asks.

"I'd love to go for a walk," Mom says. She's an exercise addict, but I'm not sure how much cardio she'll get with all those little kid legs with her.

Devon hurries over to the other side of the rocker and taps Mom on the arm. She smiles at him and compliments him on his Diego pajamas.

The three kids talk over each other in an effort to get Grammy's attention. "Chatty, chatty," Delano says, shooing them and handing my mom a burp cloth.

"Let me hold this sweet baby for just a minute more," Mom tells the kids. Devon taps Mom's arm again. Then again. Once he has her undivided attention, he shifts awkwardly from foot-to-foot. "Ummm, those new?" He points at her pink slippers.

"They are!" Mom exclaims as if he's won Jeopardy.

"I haven't seen 'em before," Devon says. "I like 'em. I could tell they're new."

Mom stands up and hands sleeping Brandon to me. "Are you coming for the walk too, Devon?" she asks.

"I'll get your shoes," Devon says, and rushes toward the garage. He returns with her white sneakers and my mom sits next to me to put them on.

"Do the kids need to get dressed first?" she asks me.

Devon hovers over her and is right in her face. "Are they new too?"

I shrug. "I'm not too worried about it," I say, knowing it's warm outside.

"I haven't seen these before," Devon says.

I wave him away, "Go put your shoes on." He always vies to be the center of attention. In fairness, they all do. I know that. But there's something about the ingratiating way Devon does it. Lately, it rubs my skin like sand on bed sheets.

Mom stands next to me and smooths a hand over Brandon's curls. She brushes her lips to his forehead. "You're such a natural with babies." She kisses my forehead too.

Devon is back. His shoes are on the wrong feet, but I don't worry about fixing them. I walk them all to the front door and watch the kids race across the path to Becky's house, still in their pajamas, to get Ben.

…

The day before Mom is scheduled to leave, we go to Starbucks. The kids stay home with Delano, except Brandon, who we take with us. "I keep meaning to tell you about what Kayla did on our walk," Mom says. "She walked right in front of me. I tripped over her and she was furious … *with me*."

"She's feisty, but also really sensitive. She was probably embarrassed."

Mom nods her agreement. Brandon is sleeping with his tiny

body curled against her chest. "Devon made a beautiful card and bookmark for me. He's such a good boy. I wonder if he has a little developmental delay with his fine motor skills though," she muses. "He was really having a hard time using his fork last night."

I purse my lips recalling how Devon was eating his macaroni with his hands. I'd told him to use his fork and he'd fumbled it and dropped it on the floor. My mom had very patiently helped him. "He was pretending because he wanted your attention."

Mom looks at me thoughtfully. "I've also noticed he doesn't always make eye contact." I open two packets of natural sugar and pour them into her hot tea for her. She uses her free hand to stir it in.

"He doesn't make eye contact when he knows he's in trouble," I say, drolly.

"He does seem to be in trouble more often than the other kids." Her tone is careful. Insinuating.

I know why. Devon's immature and naughty behavior grates on me, especially when he acts like a baby for attention. Mom's right, though. Something is off. "It's like there's a 'mental disconnect' with him," I tell her. "He doesn't understand the relationship between actions and consequences. If I give Amias and Kayla a time-out, they get it. Devon doesn't. He always goes right back to the same behavior. And he's so stubborn about it."

"Maybe he really doesn't understand. He's only five, right?"

"Maybe, but Amias and Kayla are younger and they both understand." I know this isn't as innocent as my mom thinks it is. It's something about the tilt of his head and the look in his eyes. I'm certain that he does understand. Sometimes, it feels as if he's doing these things on purpose.

Mom pats Brandon's back. "He might be on the spectrum. That might explain a lot."

10

At Devon's kindergarten orientation for SCA Grammar School we walk the path from the bus lot to his classroom three times. I want to make sure he'll know the way in the morning and won't be nervous. He's excited to be starting school, especially because Amias and Kayla can't go and are jealous.

His classroom has large windows across one side. Colored letters and numbers square dance across the tops of the walls above colorful pictures of animals and shapes. Shelves burst with books and bins of educational toys. Devon goes doe-eyed shaking hands with the pretty, blonde Ms. Lizzie. She's a bubbly first-year teacher and all Devon can talk about when we get home.

Before going to bed, he picks out an outfit from his new school clothes: an orange and yellow Curious George tee-shirt and matching orange shorts. He arranges them on the floor as though dressing a paper doll. He climbs into bed and falls asleep hugging his Blue's Clues backpack like it's a teddy bear.

The next morning, Devon meticulously tucks his shirt into his shorts before eating his boiled egg and toast for breakfast. I ask Sam to tie Devon's shoes because I'm busy packing their lunches. He squats in front of Devon and I hear him moan. "Always on the wrong feet. Now, today, on the right feet? I knew you been playing with Mom. You gotta stop that stuff now. You're a big boy." Sam ties Devon's shoes and sing-songs, "Over, under, around, and through, meet Mr. Bunny Rabbit, pull him through."

Devon loves school and eagerly tells me all about it each day as I walk him home from the bus stop. After having a snack, he pulls out his homework and sits at the table without me prompting him. Amias likes to "help" Devon with his homework and then pronounce that he, too, is ready for kindergarten.

With Devon at school, Amias and Kayla get along well and my days at home are quiet and manageable. Delano is glad that I have a little more time for him too. Our blended family has settled into a busy normality and I'm breathing a contented sigh, when SCA Grammar calls.

"Devon was standing in line with his class, waiting to use the bathroom ..." The principal's words send the scene unfurling in my mind. Devon eyes the fire alarm pull lever as he works up his courage. He takes a deep breath. He pulls the lever and startles in surprise when the alarm screeches. Ms. Lizzie looks over at him, and he jams his hands into his pockets. She corrals the students into a line and they follow her outside. I imagine Devon's excitement at seeing the fire trucks and hearing the sirens. "Pulling the fire alarm is very serious and causes a major disruption," the principal finishes.

I am mortified and I know Delano will be, as well. Apologizing profusely, I assure her that this will not happen again.

I'm standing on the sidewalk, as usual, when Devon dismounts the afternoon bus. I haven't said a word and he's already insisting, "I didn't do it. I didn't touch it." As we walk the block home, he prattles on. "I just want to see what it feels like." His eyes dart between me and the ground.

I'm skeptical. I really am. But maybe it *was* an accident. Worst case, he was simply being a normal, curious kid. I tell Devon not to touch the fire alarm unless, of course, there's a real fire.

A few weeks later Ms. Lizzie calls to "share her concerns" about how Devon has been climbing the classroom bookshelves. According to her, he has a short attention span. He wanders around while the other students do their seat work. "He's active and needs to be moving. I don't mind as long as he stays safe."

I bristle at her naiveté. "Devon can sit still. He's never been hyperactive."

"Well, I don't mind if he walks around," she says sweetly. "As long as he stays safe."

That afternoon I greet Devon at the bus stop with my hands on my hips and my voice firm. "You need to sit yourself down during seat work just like all the other kids." I tell him, "Glue, Devon. Pretend like you have glue on your bottom and don't you get up out of that seat. Do you understand me?"

He bobs his head up and down.

I've always questioned Devon's ADHD diagnosis, but I'm beginning to wonder. I decide to make an appointment for a psychological evaluation, but it takes several weeks to get in to see a Medicaid provider.

Slender and perfectly poised, Monica Stevens is a real-life Neiman Marcus mannequin. She rents an office in one of those shared business centers with a common lobby. She explains that she'll meet alone with me first while Devon sits in the lobby. There's no receptionist, but she brushes aside my concerns and assures me that he'll be fine looking at the picture books while we talk in her office. I'm wary, but she does this all the time. She's the expert.

Offering me a seat in front of her large desk, Ms. Stevens leaves the door to her office open a crack. First we go over, what she calls, Devon's "social history."

Was he full-term? Yes

Did his mother get prenatal care? Yes

Were there complications? I don't think so

At what age did he first crawl? I don't know

What age did he first walk? I'm not sure

When did he say his first word? I have no idea

I shift uncomfortably in my seat. For Amias and Brandon, these answers would be on the tip of my memory. Realistically, there's no way for me to know these details about Devon, but I still feel embarrassed and negligent.

Ms. Stevens asks if Devon had any developmental delays, and I assure her I wasn't told about anything like that. She asks me to describe his current behavior at home, in school, and in social settings. This I can do.

Once the interview is finished, Ms. Stevens explains that it will be difficult to make any definitive diagnoses without details of Devon's early childhood development. I knit my brows together thinking of other diagnoses—diabetes, asthma, a peanut allergy—don't you either have a diagnosis or not? She hands me a stack of forms to fill out while she works with Devon.

Then, rounding her desk, Ms. Stevens reaches for the door. As it swings open to the waiting room, I see Devon. He's bent over, his neck craned under the water dispenser. He is sucking on the spigot. "Devon!" I blurt, jumping up and rushing towards him. I yank him away. "What are you doing?"

"I was thirsty ..." he whispers, a prominent lisp in his voice so it comes out sounding babyish as "tirsty."

"Well, use a cup," I snap, pointing to the paper cup dispenser. Mortification washing over me, I turn to Ms. Stevens. "I'm so sorry. Do you have something I can clean this with?"

Devon curls his shoulders in as though shrinking into himself and hangs his head.

"I'll get it taken care of later," she says, looking at Devon empathetically. She writes, "Out of Order," on a piece of paper and tapes it to the dispenser. With that, she leads Devon into her office and the door clicks shut.

I rummage in my purse for a pen. Whole pages of the forms, I can't fill out. I simply don't know the answers. Drawing lines through the sections labeled "Maternal History," "Paternal History," and "Early Childhood," I write "Adopted" in the margin in glossy purple ink. I'm better able to respond to other questions like: "Is he/she able to dress himself?" I go on to rate statements like, "Makes friends easily?" on a scale of one to five. I wonder, do cousins and siblings count?

When Ms. Stevens brings Devon out 90 minutes later, I've long finished the paperwork and am desperate for a coffee. "Devon was very cooperative and did an excellent job," she says, adding that the report will take several weeks to complete and she'll mail it to me. Leaving her office and walking towards the car, I'm pleased with how comprehensive the assessment was and optimistic that we're on the right track to get some answers.

A couple of weeks later, at our first kindergarten parent-teacher conference, I perch awkwardly on a child-sized plastic chair listening to Ms. Lizzie gush about Devon. He's her favorite student. I glance warily at the bookshelves spanning the back wall of the classroom. Beaming with pride, Ms. Lizzie tells me about her new behavior plan for Devon and how "it's done absolute wonders." She explains that when he's having a hard time or has too much energy, she calls the assistant principal to watch her class. Then, she and Devon go for a walk. Usually, they walk through the hallways, but a few times he's wanted to go outside, so they go to the playground.

I tell her, "Devon needs to sit and behave himself like any other child. Taking him out of class for a special walk is rewarding his bad behavior."

She's taken aback by my negative response and insists, "He's very well behaved after he goes for a walk. And it's not every day."

...

Everyone else is asleep and the windows are inky black when I tear open the manila envelope that's come in the mail from Ms. Stevens. It's a 10-

page document titled "Psychological Evaluation."

The first few pages document the social history that I provided:

```
Mrs. Williams reported her primary
concerns include Devon's defiant
behaviors, tantrums, and his "mental
disconnection." She feels there is
poor attachment to her.
```

Following this, I find descriptions of the assessments that she gave Devon. My eye catches on "Draw a person." Curious, I flip ahead and read:

```
Devon drew a stick figure in the
upper left corner of the paper. The
drawing appears developmentally
immature and suggests depressive
tendencies.
```

I do a mental eye roll thinking of Devon's beautiful, detailed drawings hanging on the refrigerator. I wonder what Ms. Stevens would make of those.

Going back, I read the other test results. First is an IQ assessment for children. Devon scored in the sixth percentile for Verbal Comprehension. This single score is in the mentally handicapped range but his composite IQ score is in the normal range. How can that be?

The next section lists "Adaptive Behavior Domains" like life-skills, play, and communication. Devon scores below his age on everything. His socialization skills are at a two-year-old level. I haven't known if he's developmentally delayed or if his babyish behavior is purposeful. Now I know and I resolve to be more patient.

Next is the autism evaluation. The results are:

```
Very Likely.
```

```
Mrs. Williams endorsed the following
occurred when she got him: did not
reach out to be picked up, did not
become upset when left unattended in
her crib, did not cry or become
```

DENIAL 59

> upset when held, did not cry when
> handed from adult to another adult.

What is she talking about? Devon was almost four when he came to live with us. He wasn't in a crib. And Ms. Stevens is calling Devon a *"her."* She must have cut and pasted this from another child's evaluation. Frustrating. And completely useless. Shaking my head, I dismiss the autism finding.

I skip to the page with the diagnoses.

> Attention-Deficit/Hyperactivity
> Disorder (ADHD) 300.02
> Generalized Anxiety Disorder 313.81
> Oppositional Defiant Disorder
> Pervasive Developmental Delay, NOS

I'm not sure what all of this means, but I'm definitely going to contact our pediatrician, Dr. Adebayo, to talk about getting a prescription for ADHD medication.

In the last section of the evaluation, I find Ms. Stevens's recommendations:

> Lecturing Devon may not be very
> beneficial.

Ms. Stevens and I agree about that. Another recommendation reads:

> Anytime Devon can "see it, hear it,
> feel it and do it," the better. Pair
> meaningful visual aids with items in
> any list.

Finally, something I can work with.

I slide the evaluation back into the envelope, switch off the light, and walk through the house to my bedroom. My mind races with ideas, making it a struggle to fall asleep.

The next day, Devon and I sit at the kitchen table with a stack of index cards, markers, and pencils. He munches on Goldfish crackers as I explain. "This is going to be your special, *What to Do When I'm Upset,* book. We're going to write down some steps for when you get upset." Devon's favorite color is green, so I pick out a green marker. On the first card, I use bold block letters and say the words out loud as I write: "Do 10 jumping jacks."

Devon smiles, orange cracker mush clinging to his teeth. I pass the card to him. "I'm not good at drawing, but you're a great artist, so can you draw the pictures?" He eagerly takes the card. On the next cards I write more activities: Count to 10, Stretch as far and wide as you can, Find everything blue in the room, and Climb up and down the stairs 3 times.

Working together, we make ten cards in all. Once Devon finishes the drawings, I punch a hole in the corner of each card and secure them together with a ribbon. "Want to practice?" I ask.

Devon "reads" the first card, sets the booklet on the floor in front of him, and begins his jumping jacks. He counts to ten and flips to the next card. "Do I stretch standing up or laying down?" he asks.

Shrugging my shoulders in an exaggerated motion, I say, "What do you think?"

"Standing."

He finds lots of blue things—the spines of several books, a toy car, Brandon's baby blanket, and the tee-shirt that Kayla is wearing. He methodically circles the room to be sure that he hasn't missed even one blue item. I listen to him thud up and down the stairs as I pack up the art supplies.

A few minutes later, Devon hurries towards me with a huge smile on his face. "Done. I'm done."

"Great job," I pat his shoulder. "What do you think? Will this help you calm down when you're feeling upset?"

"Yup!"

"Let's put it on the bookshelf so you know where to find it when you need it."

Devon disappears into the playroom and I put on a fresh pot of coffee. Relief and satisfaction pulse inside me. This is it. *This* is going to work.

Then the unmistakable shatter of cascading Legos interrupts my thoughts. Devon jogs out of the playroom chased by the sound of Amias' outrage. "What happened?" I ask.

"Amias tooked my piece."

"Amias, come here," I call.

"But *I* gotted upset." Devon says, shooting a look toward the bookshelves.

And then, I understand. "If you got upset, I guess you should try out your book."

Devon eagerly rushes over and snatches it up. Setting the cards on the floor in front of him, Devon begins his jumping jacks. After he's gone through the whole sequence, he says, "I'm still upset. Can I do it again?"

11

Leaning back in my desk chair, I jot notes on a legal pad. Our sales guy is explaining via conference call why our software is not a fit for a particular organization. My mind is already cranking out solutions and workarounds. I love these types of challenges and have several ideas to make it work. When he finishes, and asks for my thoughts, I eagerly launch in.

I'm halfway through my list when my cell phone jitters on my desk. I glance at it and see "SCA Grammar" on the caller ID. "Would you excuse me for a moment?" I say. I mute my work phone and answer my cell.

It's the principal. "Devon brought a knife to school today in his backpack."

I gasp, sure I must have misheard her.

"It was a butter knife, but we have a zero-tolerance policy on weapons," she says. "We're giving him a one-day suspension."

My mind reels. He's in kindergarten. It's a butter knife, not a gun for goodness' sake.

I snap in a breath, realizing this is a misunderstanding. Of course, it is. Relief washes through me. No five-year-old takes a knife to school on purpose.

I rush to explain. "Over the weekend my children had a picnic and they used Devon's backpack. I'm sure that's why the butter knife was in there. It was just an accident."

There's a beat of silence between us.

"Regardless of how the knife ended up in the backpack, Devon was chasing other students with it, and he was threatening to cut them. I'm going to need you to come pick him up."

12

In the fall all the kids start school, except Brandon. Amias and Kayla are both in kindergarten at SCA Grammar. Devon is in first grade and has started medication for ADHD. Delano has taken a job as a school bus driver. The schedule is terrible, at least for me. He leaves in the morning before the kids are up, and gets home after dinner.

    Devon's teacher, Mrs. Sutton, wears pleated mid-calf skirts and hose, and is not willing to put up with any nonsense. Within days of starting the new school year, Devon is out of his seat, disrupting the class and not listening. When Mrs. Sutton refuses to take him for a walk, he goes by himself. That earns him a call home.

    The second time Devon takes himself outside for a walk during school, the assistant principal chases him around the building and herds him away from the busy road. Another call home.

    Ms. Lizzie set a bad precedent in kindergarten and I know I've got to nip this in the bud. I ask Mrs. Sutton to email me the next time Devon starts acting up, and she does. The school is a few miles away, and I drop everything to rush over. I feel it's important to catch Devon in the act so I can know for sure that he's connecting his actions with the consequences.

    I sign in, then hurry down the hall with Brandon on one hip. My hair is tangled in one of Brandon's fists as I peer through the door's window into the classroom. I watch Devon stand in the front of the class while the teacher writes on the board. He mimics her and looks over his shoulder to make sure the other students are watching. With exaggerated motions he sticks his bottom out and pretends to write in the air with an imaginary marker. The teacher deftly ignores him, literally teaching over his head.

    I rap on the door with my knuckles and Devon stares at me as though not able to reconcile my presence. I beckon him to me with one finger. He stumbles in his rush to obey. He follows me through the silent hallway asking, "Where are we going?"

    Once in the minivan, I spank him. He kicks and flails, although I suspect it hurts my palm far more than his bottom. Holding his chin between my thumb and forefinger so our faces are close enough that I smell the peanut butter on his breath, I say, "From now on, this is what's going to happen every time you misbehave in school."

As I step out of the minivan with a sniffling Devon, and heave Brandon onto my hip, I see a spindly woman who is standing a parking spot away. She peers across a car hood at us. "What could he possibly have done to deserve that?" she asks in a shaky voice.

"You don't know what you're talking about," I say curtly. Taking Devon's hand, I walk him back towards the school. What business is this of hers?

The woman's voice prickles across my skin like nettles as she calls after us, "I just don't know what any child could do to deserve that."

Mrs. Sutton continues to email me when Devon acts up. After I show up and take him to the parking lot for a spanking a few times, days, then weeks, stretch by without a call from school. He starts bringing home some papers with smiley faces and check pluses. He gets invited to a classmate's birthday party.

Things are better for Devon at school, but, at home, he's spinning out of control. He hurls crayons like daggers, smears apple juice on the table, and wipes boogers on the walls—and on his brothers and sister. He breaks toys and fusses about everything. He may as well be in a perpetual time-out.

I'm tired of hearing my own voice:

"Devon, stop."

"Devon, don't."

"Devon, you're going to hurt someone …"

Delano doesn't see any of this. His biggest frustration is coming home after work to a messy house. My life begins to feel like quicksand sucking at my ankles. I normally thrive on stress, but am finding it harder to fit everything into a day. I pull all-nighters a couple times a week. It's a cycle I manage for days, even weeks. But, when it catches up to me, I crash hard. Unbearable pain stabs through my eyes. I vomit, every heave sending blinding pain through my brain. During the worst episodes, I go to urgent care and get a shot to put me to sleep. When I wake up, the pain is gone, but the cycle starts again.

…

"Let's go, guys. Five-minute pickup time," I call, and the little kids reluctantly emerge from the playroom. Sam clomps down the stairs from his bedroom. They're all unhappy to have to help clean, but it's what we do every evening. "Daddy's almost here," I warn. I load cups and cereal bowls from breakfast into the dishwasher while Amias picks up Legos and action figures. Kayla hangs up a sweatshirt and straightens shoes on the shelf in the garage. Sam uses a disinfectant wipe on the surfaces of the downstairs' bathroom.

Meanwhile, Devon begins to twist on his back in the middle of the living room floor, pumping his arms and legs in the air like a toddler. "I don't want to clean," he wails. I offer him the *What to Do When I'm Upset* book. He jumps up and snatches it out of my hand. Shredding and tearing, he flings the pieces into the air. They float to the floor and he jumps up and down on them.

Scrambling over to a toy bin, Devon grabs Amias' favorite Megazord and holds it up menacingly as though to hit Kayla. He won't actually do it, but she is frightened and darts away.

"My Megazord!" Amias yells.

Devon smashes it down against the tile floor and the pieces fly apart. I'm not sure if Devon really meant to break it, but he definitely enjoys hearing Amias squawk.

"Stop that right now," I order, taking Devon's arm and leading him toward a chair for time-out. He uses his body weight to make me drag him like an anchor. I pick him up and sit him in the chair. "Don't move."

I'm two steps away, and Devon darts back into the living room.

"I'm warning you," I say crossly. "Come sit in this chair right now."

Devon jumps on the couch.

I storm towards him and try to grab him, but he climbs up onto the back of the couch and dashes by me. I reach out for him, but I don't even come close. I look stupid. I feel stupid. I'm not doing this. I'm not chasing him around the house.

I sit down on the time-out chair myself, and pull Brandon onto my lap. "That's fine. If you don't want to do your time-out with me, we can just wait for Daddy to get home." Devon narrows his eyes and makes a punching motion at Brandon. Brandon shivers in my lap, and I hug him tighter to me.

Devon's tantrum ends abruptly a few minutes later when he hears the garage door open. He immediately begins picking toys up off the floor and putting them away.

Delano enters the house and hisses his teeth. He stomps into the kitchen and snatches up the broom. "Nobody never cleans nothing," he fumes.

"We cleaned," I try.

"Nobody cleans nothing."

"You don't understand," I falter. "Devon's been throwing a tantrum." But Devon is crouched by the bookshelf and is carefully straightening the spines of each picture book, belying my words. His head is angled in our direction, and I know he's watching and listening to our interaction.

Delano vigorously sweeps together the remnants of Devon's torn up book. "You can't even keep the house clean," he mutters, supposedly under his breath, but it's meant for me to hear. He chucks his chin towards Devon. "Him the only one who helps clean."

Bursting into tears, I rush upstairs. I turn on the shower to mask the sound of my sobs. With my back to the bathroom door, I sink to the floor and hold my head in my hands.

13

With three kids in elementary school, I schedule parent teacher conferences back-to-back. I meet with Amias' teacher first and hand her a shopping bag of tissues and cleaning wipes. She pats her dark helmet of hair as though it's out of place. "Thank you," she gushes. "We can never have too many of these."

  She invites me to sit at the side of her desk and passes me samples of Amias' work. As I flip through the folder, she tells me how he became upset one day when he heard another student use the "F-word." There was a lot of confusion because the other child insisted that he had not cursed. Amias very reluctantly whispered in her ear the word he'd heard. "He thought 'fart' was the F-word," she says, laughing. I smile sheepishly, but not surprised. Neither Delano or I use curse words, so Amias would think that.

  My next stop is across the hall to the other kindergarten class. Kayla's teacher has a long, messy ponytail and, with three rather rambunctious boys of her own at the school, she's frazzled as usual. She places the bag of extra classroom supplies I've brought on one of the low art tables at the back of the room. "I'm concerned about Kayla's progress," she says. "She's struggling with even basic letter sounds and counting to ten." Kayla keeps to herself but doesn't have any behavioral problems.

  My final conference is with Mrs. Sutton. "Well, let's start with the positive," she says. "Devon's behavior has dramatically improved from the beginning of the year. I really appreciate how engaged you are. And Devon is always good one-on-one." She goes on to explain that he has a hard time waiting his turn. When she's helping other students, he jumps up and down and calls out. "He also needs repeated prompts to complete his morning work." She points to the morning to-do list that's hanging on the wall next to the chalkboard at the front of the classroom.

  I imagine Devon sitting at his desk. Every time he looks at the list, he could easily be distracted by any number of things going on in the classroom. I reach into my purse for a pen and say, "Let me make a laminated copy of the list. You can tape it to his desk. He's actually pretty good with lists." I copy down the information and leave Mrs. Sutton with her bag of extra classroom supplies. I've tucked a Starbucks gift card in there as well.

Later that afternoon, Devon sits at the kitchen table staring down at his notebook and pencil. It's dusk outside and nearly dinner time. "I met with Mrs. Sutton today," I tell him. "She said you always interrupt her when she's trying to help the other kids. Why can't you wait your turn?"

He shrugs, but, when I don't remove my expectant gaze, he mumbles, "I need her help."

"The other kids all need her help too, right? She can't spend all her time helping only you."

Amias and Kayla are also sitting at the table, working together on a math sheet. Even though they're in different classes, they usually have the same homework, a life saver since Devon requires most of my attention. "One … two puppies, three … four cats. That's four pets. Right, Kayla?" Amias asks.

She nods distractedly.

He continues counting the remaining pets: "Three hamsters. That's seven. Seven pets." Amias writes "7" on his worksheet. Kayla peers at his paper and copies the "7" onto hers. Seeing that she's gotten the same answer he has, Amias says, "Let's do the next one."

To Devon I say, "If Ms. Sutton is busy helping someone else, I'd rather you draw a picture on the side of your paper than interrupt her."

He opens his eyes wide and starts shaking his head.

"No really. That's better than hollering and jumping up and down."

"Her won't let me," he says.

"Here's what I want you to do," I say, warming further to the idea. "Next time you need help and Mrs. Sutton is helping someone else, I want you to draw a little picture on the side of your paper. Or on the back. Do you understand?"

"Her will put me in trouble for that."

"Don't worry. I'll email her about it tomorrow." Returning to the kitchen to continue making dinner, I tell him, "Okay, get to work on your homework now."

Amias and Kayla have finished their math page and packed their papers, folders, and pencil pouches into their bookbags by the time I walk over to check on Devon's progress. He hasn't even started.

"Devon. Do your work," I say firmly and read the instructions to him again, "Practice writing the days of the week three times."

"I don't know 'em," he says sulkily.

"Sunday, Monday, Tuesday ..." Amias chimes from across the room where he's dribbling a soccer ball with his knees.

I shush him. "Devon knows the days of the week."

"You can't make me," Devon pouts and clutches his hands in his lap. As usual, he is persistent enough to outlast me, and I eventually cave. "You can write them one time, instead of three."

He ignores me.

I write "Sunday" on the paper to give him a running start. "See, only six more to go." I hold the pencil out to him, but he doesn't reach for it.

"Keri, Brandon is hungry," Delano hollers from the living room where he's watching a soccer game.

Giving up, I shove Devon's notebook into his backpack. I walk to the refrigerator and take out the bottle of mustard. I love nursing, but my body can't manage it any more with all the stress I'm under.

I've been breastfeeding on demand, a tenant of attachment parenting, and can't imagine weaning Brandon cold turkey. It seems so mean. It's probably just my imagination, but I feel sure it will hurt his feelings. He won't understand, and will think his mommy is rejecting him. I can't do that to him. I just can't. I squeeze a bright yellow glob of mustard onto the tip of my finger. I reach down the front of my shirt and smear it on my nipples.

Going into the living room, I scoop Brandon out of Delano's lap. We sit on the couch, and he latches on as heartily as ever. He immediately rears back with his mouth scrunched at the tart taste. "Oh, what's wrong, Baby?" I sing-song. I offer him the other side and after having a taste he curls his lip and begins to push at me, pushing me away.

"Come." Delano says, lifting Brandon out of my arms. As they head toward the kitchen for some cornmeal porridge, warm tears drip down my face. I catch Devon peeking around the corner, watching, and guilt compounds my sadness. Even after all this time, my attachment with Devon is nothing like what I have with the other kids. Wiping the tears from my face, I determine that I have to do better.

At the next opportunity, I am *the* perfect after school mom. Milk, crackers, cheese, and a Cutie—all of Devon's favorite snacks.

I am patient.

I am enthusiastic.

I am fully-focused.

Devon puts his head down on the table and takes a nap.

I explode. "Oh. My. God. Do the work."

I walk away so frustrated that I'm shaking.

Devon begins to wail, "It's your fault. I wanna do my homework. You won't let me." It's as if a winding knob attached to the side of my head has been turned tighter and tighter for days. And, now, the string has snapped, and my brain is spinning and tilting inside my skull. "It's your fault. It's your fault." The words whirl round-and-round, faster-and-faster.

14

The faint sound of the kids' voices draws me toward the surface of wakefulness. Toys clink. I feel the scrub of the sofa against my skin. My arm tingles like I've lost circulation. I'm sticky hot and my whole body is leaden.

    I try to open my eyes.
    I can't.
    I can't move.
    I panic.
    My heart races.
    Am I in a coma?
    Am I paralyzed?
    I try to move my arm. My finger. I channel all my energy into moving one finger.
    I scream. No one notices. No one helps me.
    "Help!" I scream with everything I can.
    Can't they hear me?
    My chest caves inward as I feel something—an arm?—wrap around my throat and cut off the air. I can't breathe and panic surges through me. I claw at my throat trying to suck in just one breath …
    Suddenly I jerk off of the sofa.
    My eyes fly open.
    Devon and Amias are playing quietly on the carpet nearby. My skin is sticky in the eerie still of the house. "Didn't you hear me?" I pant.
    Amias looks at me curiously. "You were sleeping, Mommy," he says. Seeing the terrified look on my face, he comes over and puts his arms around my neck.

15

The school year ends, and, with Delano home for summer break, Devon's behavior dials back down. Becky and Jason, both teachers on a school schedule, are home too. They often watch the kids playing in the backyard or biking on the sidewalks while I work.

Kayla is set to repeat kindergarten in the fall. She doesn't know her numbers or letter sounds. And it's not only Kayla who struggled during the past school year. Sam, now in high school, got Cs and Ds in his classes. He swears he isn't smoking pot, but I'm suspicious. Once upon a time, I would have morphed into a helicopter-mom—monitoring his phone calls, friends, and homework. I simply haven't had the bandwidth. Not for him. Not for Kayla. Not for any of them. Only for Devon.

Hoping it may not be too late for Kayla, I've scheduled an appointment with our pediatrician to talk about learning disabilities. While we wait in the exam room, I complete a NICHQ Vanderbilt questionnaire. Kayla swivels on the stool, holding the reflex hammer. Dr. Adebayo opens the door and laughs heartily at the sight of her. He's a tall, first-generation immigrant from Trinidad. In a thick rolling accent, he asks, "Are you the doctor now?"

She taps the reflex hammer against her palm. "Yup."

Dr. Adebayo pats the exam table. Kayla scrambles up, and he claims his stool.

Once, I brought Kayla in with a soaring fever. She couldn't tell us where it hurt, but he said it was one of the worst cases of strep throat that he'd ever seen. Dr. Adebayo told me kids who have been neglected sometimes struggle to identify feelings of pain. He has an adopted daughter too, and she can't tell time even though she's in her early twenties. Dr. Adebayo says, sometimes, a child's frontal lobe doesn't ever fully develop if they were neglected at a young age, which can cause the types of issues I'm experiencing with both Devon and Kayla.

"What joke do you have for me today?" Dr. Adebayo asks Kayla.

She knew he'd ask. He always does. "What did the banana say?"

He thinks for a moment. "I give up."

"Bananas can't talk," she deadpans.

He slaps his knees. "You're so funny. Are you going to be a comedian when you grow up?"

"A police."

"Wow. You're not going to pull me over and give me a speeding ticket?" Looking into her ears, he asks, "How are your brothers doing?"

She shrugs.

"How about Devon?"

She purses her lips like she's an adult, like she's seen me do a hundred times. "Bad."

Dr. Adebayo arches a dark brow and I clarify. "He's still throwing the tantrums, although less often now that his dad is home for the summer."

"The higher dosage didn't help?"

I shake my head. "It doesn't seem to make much difference."

Finished examining Kayla, Dr. Adebayo swivels to face the computer. "Your husband still talking about taking him to Jamaica?" He pecks on the keyboard.

I widen my eyes in mock exasperation. "He'd like to."

"He's right about that. Your husband and me, we're from the old country. A month. That's all it would take. These kids' behaviors change fast with a little discipline. But this is America, so you have to try medications and hope they'll work." Dr. Adebayo says Kayla may have the inattentive component of ADHD and offers to let us try a low dose medication.

The next morning, I hand Kayla a cup of water and the small pill along with her breakfast. To my relief, and surprise, she's able to swallow it on the first try. A little while later, we sit at the kitchen table with a handwriting pad and a pencil. "Let's start with your name," I say, and draw the letters out on the first line. Kayla picks up the pencil. Slowly and carefully, she copies each line and curve.

Perfect.

I have her write a few more lines of words and, again, they are neat and even. "This is beautiful!" I exclaim, and she beams.

I dig around in her backpack and find some papers with her normal penmanship—a scrawl of wildly uneven and illegible marks. I stride into the living room and Kayla scurries after me. I hold up the before and after writing samples for Delano to see. "We should be on a commercial for this medication." Pride captures Kayla's entire face.

"I told you. Her need to put her mind to it," he says.

Groaning, I take Kayla's hand, and we go back to the table.

"Very good work, Kayla," Delano calls after us. "Very good. You just need to practice. That's all it takes. Practice."

As I watch Kayla write—her attention and focus transformed by the ADHD medication—I wonder why Devon's medication seems to have no affect at all on him.

Delano's recliner groans. Moments later, his voice echoes down the stairs. "Devon. Devon. Why you go in my bathroom?"

Leaving Kayla to continue practicing her writing, I hurry up the stairs after Devon to mediate whatever trouble is about to happen. Delano stands by the open toilet. His arms are crossed Popeye-style over his chest. It's the bathroom at the top of the stairs, the one that only Delano uses. He's obsessive about the house—and especially the bathroom—being immaculately clean. After a few years of listening to him complain, I decided to be pragmatic and let him have this one for himself. The kids and I share the master bathroom.

"What you use my bathroom for? And you don't even flush?"

Devon shakes his head wildly, like his eyes might bounce out of his head.

I tap my foot in annoyance. Delano doesn't care when Devon throws tantrums with me, but, oh my God, an unflushed toilet: life shattering.

"Me know it was you. It's a little tiny poopie. Who else do little poopies?"

"Maybe it was Brandon," Devon tries.

It could be any of the kids, but Delano and I both know that only Devon is sneaky like that. He's probably got a granola bar or some crackers stuffed down his underwear right now.

"Or maybe it was the mouses," Devon says.

Delano snorts. He flushes the toilet and closes the door, shutting us out.

After this, Delano wakes up several times a week to find his toilet used and unflushed. Why not flush so Delano would never know? It seems as if Devon is enjoying the cat-and-mouse game.

16

Devon and I bend over the dining room table, absorbed in our latest 1,000-piece puzzle. It's a beautiful Disney character image, but this brand is less precise than I prefer. It's too easy to slot pieces into the wrong place. I'm working on the background, filling in from the edges, and Devon is working on Alice. He sorts through the box, searching for the last piece to complete her skirt. There's just a sliver of the blue skirt missing and it'll be on the knob of an otherwise gold piece, but Devon won't move on without finding it.

I notice his persistence and say, "You're my best puzzle helper," and he definitely is. The other kids only show up to puzzle with me when I'm almost done because they want to put in the finishing piece. That's when I tell them the tale of the *Little Red Hen* who doesn't receive any help from her barnyard friends until she's finished making her bread and "needs help" eating it. I've told them that story way too many times.

Kayla and Amias are kneeling at the coffee table. Amias arranges Fruity Cheerios into groups while Kayla munches on a handful from the box. He counts each group then pushes them together to show her how they combine. "One … two … three … four … five." Amias looks at her expectantly. Kayla pops more Cheerios into her mouth. Undeterred, Amias walks her through the entire math problem again.

"Look, Mom." Devon eagerly holds out the piece.

"You found it!"

He presses it into place.

"What part are you going to work on next?" I ask.

"The rabbit."

"Oh, I have some pieces for him," I say, and sweep a pile his way.

As bedtime nears, we make our way upstairs for baths. I sit in a rocker in my bedroom while the kids take turns showering. My feet ache, and I stretch my legs to rest them on the side of my bed while I cradle the phone to my ear.

"You need a break," Becky says.

"Delano's not back yet. He'll be too tired for me to go out."

"Where is he?"

"Washing his car."

Becky grunts her disapproval. "He can watch the kids on a Friday night so you can go to the movies."

"The principal called me back today about Kayla. I think they're going to let her go to first grade." I say.

"That's great."

"He said they'll do some math testing—"

Panicked shrieks peel through the air. My phone tumbles to the floor, and I sprint toward the sound. I fling open the shower door.

Devon clamps his mouth shut.

"What's the matter?" I blurt.

Water cascades over his body. He's not hurt. Not even upset. There's no blood. No spiders or bugs. I hate when he plays these games with me. "Get out. You're a big boy. No one's keeping you in there." I spin on my heel and return to my bedroom and find my phone.

"What happened?" Becky asks.

"It was just Devon," I huff.

"What's wrong with him?"

"Nothing. He just *wants* to scream."

Devon begins to call, "Let me out of the shower. You won't let me out of the shower …"

There's no way I'll be going to the movies tonight. Becky and I end the call.

"Let me out of the shower," Devon calls.

Brandon seems oblivious to Devon's relentless voice as he sits on the floor playing with his toys. I guess he's used to it by now.

"You won't let me out of the shower. Let me out. Let me out of the shower …" I try to ignore him. That's what they taught us to do in foster parenting class. Ignore junk behavior. "You won't let me out of the shower. You won't let me out of the shower …" My nerves crawl as the words worm their way through my brain. I begin to pace. Over and over, he calls, "You won't let me out of the shower. Let me out of the shower."

When I'm unable to bear it for another second, I rush back into the bathroom and yank open the shower door. Spinning the water off, I throw a towel at him.

"Get. Out. Right. Now."

Devon hugs the towel to his chest. I watch his lips peel into a grin.

PART II
DEPRESSION

17

3 years later

I hold Brandon's hand and watch as the kids climb the steps onto the morning bus. Devon, now in fourth grade, is stocky and a head taller than Kayla and Amias who are both in third grade. "It's turn-it-up-Tuesday," he calls to me in a sing-song as he waves goodbye with a grin. That's his catchy way of letting me know he's decided to make trouble. Sighing, I take Brandon's hand and we head for home.

After school Devon cheerfully tells me about the sloppy Joe he had for lunch and how he played kick ball at recess. Sounds like he had a good day. The little kids all sit at the table watching *Duck Tales* while they wait for their afterschool snack. They sing along to the theme song as I place paper plates of apple slices with peanut butter in front of them.

I glance at the clock. Sam is at the high school, and they have a different bell schedule, so he'll be at least another hour. And it's still a long time until Delano will be home from work.

Devon finishes his snack and sits watching the cartoon as though transfixed until a commercial comes on. Then, like a bomb, he explodes. Picture books crash against the walls. Super hero action figures zoom through the air and land in a heap on the floor. Brandon cowers behind my legs and trembles.

Demanding that Devon stop, I text Becky with one hand and try to reassure Brandon by patting his head with the other.

Amias complains, "I can't hear." Kayla has the remote, and she turns the volume all the way up. In turn, Devon ratchets his voice up to screaming.

It's so loud, I don't hear the front door open. Becky takes in the situation—the mess, the noise, and Brandon Koala-bear-clutching my leg. "Come here, Brandy," she says, gathering him into her arms. She flips off the TV and tells Amias and Kayla to come to her house to play, and they trot out the door after her.

It's now just Devon and me, and I weigh my options as he careens around the house. Spanking won't work. At Devon's age and size, it will turn into a wrestling match. If I threaten a punishment, like being grounded this coming weekend, he won't care. Unsure of what will work, my muscles tense. The only thing I can think to do is to corral him somehow. I drag the large box from our new over-the-range microwave into the middle of the dining room floor. I say, "Get in the box."

Devon looks at it dubiously, and I think he's going to refuse. But, perhaps because of the novelty of it, he climbs in. Looking comical, he sits with his shoulders and head sticking up out of the top. He picks at the edges of the flaps. I don't care. He's contained, and so what if he rips apart a cardboard box? I begin to clean up the books, toys, and other mess. The last thing I need is Delano complaining when he gets home from work. Devon watches me, expressionless and quiet. When I'm finished, he whines, "Let me pee. Let me pee …"

"Go to the bathroom. Wash your hands and come right back." I reach into the refrigerator and pull cheese, milk, and a stick of butter out. The cardboard scratches across the tile as Devon tries to scoot it across the floor. Minutes slough by as my cheese sauce begins to thicken on the stove top. There's only the sound of the slash of my whisk against the pan and the scratch of cardboard. My heartbeat has slowed to normal and I don't dare look at Devon and risk breaking the spell.

He begins to holler, "You won't let me pee. You won't let me pee."

"I told you to go to the bathroom!"

"You won't let me pee. You won't let me pee …" he chants over and over.

"Devon," I snap. "I said, go to the bathroom." I knead my neck, already painful to the touch, a migraine in the making.

"You won't let me pee," he continues on as though he hasn't heard me, but I know he has. He stands, and I see a dark stain spreading from the crotch of his jeans down the leg.

There's a moment of silence.

Our eyes lock.

"You made me pee my pants! You made me pee my pants!" he screeches.

I stare at him, stunned. Something is very, very wrong.

A burnt smell brings my attention whirling back toward the

stove. I grab the handle of the pan and drop it into the sink. It clangs sharply, only adding to the raucous noise that Devon is making.

It'll be cereal for dinner. Again.

18

One morning, Devon noticed tiny air bubbles in the milk around the edges of his cereal bowl and became hysterical. He insisted Sam had spit in it. I set a new, clean bowl on the table in front of him, and I poured in Honey Nut Cheerios and milk. "Here you go. No spit."

"But I had Fruit Loops," Devon said.

"That was the last of them. They're all gone." I put the cereal box and milk back away.

Devon howled, almost melodically, as if he was enjoying the sound of his own voice, which I'm pretty sure he does. "There's spit in my cereal. There's spit in my cereal …"

At my wits end, I dumped the cereal in the trash—bowl, spoon, and all.

Since then, Devon uses "spit bubbles" as a regular excuse to throw tantrums, but never on the weekend when Daddy is home.

"Well, Sam probably did spit in his cereal," Mom says, when I tell her the story while I'm driving home after dropping the kids off at school. I'm fuming because the "spit bubble" hysteria made us late again.

"But what about all the other times?" I ask. "What about when *he watches* me pour the cereal and milk? He *knows* there's no spit then."

"Kids don't freak out for no reason," she insists.

"You don't know what he's like, Mom. Every day, he throws a fit. Every day. He makes himself throw up all over the table too."

"Are you sure? He's way too young to be doing anything like that," Mom says, her skepticism oozing through the phone. "I don't think that's even possible at his age. Why would he do that?"

"I don't know *why*. I don't know what's wrong with him. I just know he's doing it." I pause only long enough to take a sip of coffee. "He's destroyed his bedroom too. The worst part is the smell. He pees everywhere."

"What does the therapist think is the problem?"

Since the adoption, I've taken Devon to see two therapists. The first, looked at me in mystification. "How can he be stealing food if it's his house?" he'd asked. The second, did a few sessions of play therapy. Devon sure had fun, but they never talked about anything, and, ultimately, it didn't help.

The new therapist who we're seeing, DeShawn, is young and wears trendy clothes. Devon thinks he's cool. I think he might actually know what he's talking about. At our last visit, during the first 15 minutes of the session when Devon sits in reception, DeShawn had leaned back into his desk chair and steepled his hands. "Tell me more about his behaviors."

"Whenever he doesn't get his way, he screams and throws things. He even knocked a hole in his bedroom wall."

"What I've suggested to other parents in your situation is creating a safe space. It can be a bathroom, a closet, or a guest room. A space where you can clear out anything he can damage or destroy."

"Won't that teach him to hit things?"

"It's like running or using a punching bag," DeShawn had answered. "You want to teach him appropriate ways to channel his anger and frustration. Put some pillows and stuffed animals in there for him to punch and kick."

Now, I tell my mom about how I've set up the closet under the stairs as a safe space. "I hung *Finding Nemo* wallpaper and put a soft rug and pillows in there for him."

"That sounds nice. He must love that," she says.

"He goes in there to read and play. But when he's throwing a fit, he refuses to use it as a safe space. So, what good is it?" I turn onto the wooded street leading to our neighborhood.

"Hmmm. Well, does he listen to Delano?"

When I'd told Delano about my plan for the safe space, he'd said, "Kids in Jamaica, them don't do those things. Him needs discipline." And by discipline, I knew that he meant spanking, which only escalates the situation. I don't let Delano spank Devon anymore, and that choice comes at a high price. Delano says, if I'm going to do things the American way—with time-outs, therapists, and medications—I'm on my own, and he means it.

I tell my mom, "Devon never throws tantrums in front of Delano. He thinks I'm making this stuff up." I sigh heavily. "I'm home now. I have to go. I have to work."

"I know you're frustrated," Mom says. "But Devon needs to know you love him. When he's misbehaving, give him a hug and some special time with you. I promise it will make all the difference."

I feel hollowed out and empty inside, my will to keep trying gone. Sitting in the dark of my garage, I text Becky about my conversation with our mother. She responds: "This isn't about him not getting enough hugs. She has no idea what we're dealing with."

That evening, my mom's words flay my back as I bend over Devon's bed to kiss his forehead. He lies as still as stone. I run my hand through his tight, thick curls. The sun has brought out the highlights, and each curl is like a miniature golden halo.

"Look at all those freckles," I say, brushing my fingertip over his nose. "I might have to start calling you 'Freckle Face.'"

Devon's eyes crinkle in a smile. I switch off the light and the solar system glows on the ceiling above his bed. I leave the bedroom, pleased we've had a moment of positive connection.

…

"You're wasting your time. Nothing wrong with Devon. You must want to spend time alone with that man," Delano says, not for the first time.

I consider my unkempt hair, chipped fingernails, and flabby middle and don't bother responding. Lately I don't have time for jewelry or anything more than a t-shirt, yoga pants, and flip flops. I'm overwhelmed and desperate for help.

I lift the couch cushions and run my fingers under them. I call in the direction of the stairs, "Devon, come on. Let's go." I peel back the vinyl tablecloth from the kitchen table. Beneath is a shelf littered with playing cards, a word search book, several action figures, math flash cards—and there they are—how in the world did my keys end up under there?

Delano stands. "Me gonna take Devon this time."

I pinch the bridge of my nose and squeeze my eyes tight. I say, "Fine, go ahead," but I know it will be a wasted session. Delano scoffs at the very idea of therapy. He doesn't believe in anything having to do with mental health or therapy. He doesn't even believe this is a behavioral problem. He believes this is a parenting problem—a problem with *my* parenting.

Deciding to make the most of these unexpected couple hours of time, I hunker down to get some work done. I've made good progress when Delano bursts into the house. "Did you call the man?"

"I sent him an email to let him know you were bringing Devon."

He looms over me. "Show me the email. Devon sits on the floor by the garage door, watching us while he takes off his shoes.

"This is stupid. What's wrong with you?" I click on an internet browser and navigate to my Gmail account. Delano scrutinizes my actions over my shoulder. Annoying, since I know he couldn't send an email to save his life.

"Devon told me you spend the whole session talking to the man while he sits in the reception," Delano says.

I scrunch my face as if it's a joke. "That's not true," I choke out an indignant laugh. I click on my sent folder. Delano scans the innocuous two lines of the email. Grunting, he nudges me to move over, but I click the lid shut. "No way. This is my work computer. You could mess something up." There's no secret email, no inappropriate conversation. But, none of that matters. Delano doesn't believe anything is wrong with Devon, so he's sure something else must be going on.

"Tell me the truth. Why do you want to see that man? What's really going on here?"

"Devon's lying."

He looks at me with incredulity. "Tell me, why would Devon lie about something like that? Does that make any sense?"

I have no answer for that.

Delano goes on badgering me. "Him should only talk to Devon."

"That's not how therapy works. Therapists always talk with the parent," I insist. "You don't understand. I can't control him. I need help."

"Send him to him room until I get home."

I bark a laugh. "And what if he refuses to go?"

"You need to start acting like the parent."

I shake my head. I'm finally getting a little help and he wants to sabotage it. "You know what DeShawn told me? When I explain to Devon how I know that he's lying, I'm teaching him to be a better liar next time." I pause, waiting for the epiphany that DeShawn's advice is helpful to hit Delano like a brick. When it doesn't, I plunge forward. "Devon hides his behavior from you on purpose. He's really, really bad."

"Nothing wrong with Devon," he scoffs.

Delano is annoyed because I have to spend so much of my time dealing with Devon. That's what this is really about, but these types of confrontations leave me drained. I pull my cell phone out from where I've tucked it into the top of my bra and press the contact for DeShawn's office. I ask the receptionist to cancel our next appointment and tell her that we won't be coming back.

19

Shrieks stab like ice picks into my eardrums. Glancing between the cell phone on my lap and the road, I feel a surge of triumph when my call connects to Delano's cell phone, unbeknownst to Devon.

"Mom," Amias garbles out, holding his hands over his mouth. "He's blowing snot bubbles."

I scrounge around on the floor for a plastic shopping bag, afraid Amias, who is grossed out easily like me, is going to vomit. My eyes catch sight of Devon in the rearview mirror with snot ballooning like a semi-transparent marble from one of his nostrils. I dry heave. I struggle to catch my breath as my throat constricts. "Kayla, give Amias your Goldfish bag."

I glance over my shoulder in quick bursts trying to watch the road. Kayla's hand is in the Goldfish bag, and she shakes her head no. Amias gags, and Devon's shrieks curdle into peals of high-pitched laughter.

Not noticing a red light until the last minute, I slam on my breaks. Devon smacks into the back of the front passenger seat. "Stop trying to kill me! You're trying to kill me," he shrills in mounting hysteria.

"I *told you* to put your seatbelt back on," I holler.

Not five minutes ago, Devon was trying to climb out of the window. I'd had to pull over to set the child safety locks on the doors and windows and force him to buckle his seatbelt. He was out of his seatbelt again as soon as I started driving. And, he'll just keep unbuckling. I'm out of options. I have to get home.

Devon flings himself first against the driver side of the minivan, then the passenger side. He raises his fist in a threat and Brandon shrinks back into his booster seat, his teary eyes pleading with me through the rearview mirror. Watching Amias, Kayla, and Brandon squeezed together in the back seat—like bunnies trapped in a cage with a rabid animal—fury fills me and spews out. "How dare you act like this? *How dare you?*"

Devon lays on the seat and with his legs in the air, kicks my headrest. My body jolts forward with my chair. Finally, I slam to a stop in the garage. Rounding the minivan, I open the sliding door and wedge my body into the middle seat to cage Devon so the other kids can squeeze past. His sharp nails dig into my arms and neck as he tries to climb around and over me. I call after the kids, "Lock yourselves in my bedroom," thinking, at least that way, they'll have access to a bathroom.

Devon, moments ago desperate to get out of the vehicle, now anchors his feet against the side of the door. He holds the armrest as if in a death grip. Frustrated tears stream down my face as I wrangle him. He screams and kicks. He's maybe 70 pounds, but his frenzied fighting makes it difficult to hold onto him. I half carry, half drag him into the house and drop him onto the living room floor, none too gently. I get in his face. "Sit! Just sit!" All I have is my greater physical strength and the power of fear. Maybe if I yell louder than he does, he'll be scared enough to stop.

My pulse thrashes. I'm certain I'm on the verge of a nervous breakdown. Hope sparks when I remember my phone. I hurry back into the garage and find my cell phone where it has slid under the brake pedal. My connection with Delano has dropped. I call him back. Out of breath, I ask, "Do you see how bad he is now?"

He chucks his tongue. "I turned off the phone."

"You did what?" I hiss.

"I'm almost home anyway. Why do you make him go on like that?"

Furious, I jab the end call button and go back inside. Devon hasn't moved. He wails, but with no words and no tears.

My fingers shake. I can't think straight over the unrelenting noise he's making, as I try to make a pot of coffee. I spill the grinds, and they scuttle across the counter and floor. I grip the edge of the sink. The urge to clobber Devon is so strong that I'm barely maintaining control.

Then I hear the garage door rumble open and, just like that, the only evidence of Devon's tantrum is his sweaty face. I look at him in disbelief. Delano walks in and sees the spilled coffee grinds. "Cha, Mon. Come. Sweep the floor," he barks.

Devon gives me a smirking look and runs for the broom.

Defeated, I go upstairs to the shower, the only place where I can have any privacy. The water is steaming hot, and I heave choking sobs until I can't breathe. After the water begins to cool, I get out and wipe the fog off of the mirror. I lean forward and rest my forehead against it. The face that stares back at me from the mirror has blotchy skin and eyelids that are swollen into fat cushions. The narrow slits of my eyes are so dramatic that they don't look real. I have a fleeting hope that Delano will see them and understand my distress. But he won't. He doesn't believe me.

No one believes me. No one believes me because my life is like a bad movie with an over-the-top script. I'd be the first to say this could never happen in real life. But it is.

A few weeks ago, I made the mistake of telling Devon's teacher how unbearable his behavior has become at home. I knew from the look on her face she thought I was exaggerating. I wasn't. My sanity revolves around the school's schedule. I count down the minutes until I can drop him off int he morning and then watch in trepidation as the clock careens toward 3:45. But I didn't tell her that. I did tell her about Devon's tantrums lasting hours—no, *literally,* hours—I'd assured her.

She'd cocked her head, whether in curiosity or accusation, I wasn't sure. "Is there anything going on at home?"

Yes. Yes there is.

I'm losing my mind.

20

"I'm glad you called the police!" Devon calls, between hiccups of laughter. "I'm gonna tell on *you*. You're a bad mother. They'll take you to jail!"

Right about now, that's not sounding so bad. I watch the street from between the blind slats. They're furry with dust. My laptop sits untouched on my desk and work is piling up in my virtual inbox.

When the officer arrives, I open the door before he has time to ring the bell or knock. As his boots clomp down the hallway, I'm acutely aware of the damning silence around me. Where is the screaming child? Where is the whirling tornado of books and toys?

Feeling like a fool, I insist that Devon has been completely out of control. He was chasing his brothers and sister with a baseball bat. They were terrified. I had to send them next door to my sister's house. How old is he? He's eight.

The officer looks at me like I'm one of those crazy people who calls the police when McDonalds runs out of chicken nuggets. "Ma'am, since he's only eight, there isn't much we can do." He can't seem to wrap his mind around a parent who has called 911 for *this* and turns toward the door.

My desperation clutches after him. What Devon needs is a talking-to by a big, stern police officer. "Please. Can you at least talk to him?" I plead.

The officer agrees and follows me back to the living room. With some effort, he gently coaxes Devon out from behind the couch by assuring him that he's safe now.

He's safe now? I look on, devastated by the direction this is going in.

The officer soothes: "You need to listen to your mom, Buddy." Devon looks at him with syrupy eyes and a trembling upper lip. The officer pats him on the back and stands to leave. "Can I count on you to help your mama pick up this mess?"

Devon hurries to obediently begin cleaning up the toys scattered across the floor.

As I stand at the window watching the police cruiser disappear down the street, the tendrils of Devon's laughter string through the air and tighten like a noose around my throat.

Later that evening, while I cook dinner, I tell Delano what happened with the police officer. The gas stove has left its black fingerprints caked up the sides of the dull aluminum pressure cooker and it rocks and shrieks on the burner as we talk.

"Why didn't you make the man take him shoes off?" Delano huffs. "You made him track dirt all over the house."

I flip the release button on the pressure cooker and steam hisses out, but my safety release lever snapped off long ago. I storm from the kitchen. I am living a nightmare. It's bad enough that Delano won't help me. He doesn't have to make it harder.

I jam the kids' shorts, shirts, and socks into plastic grocery store bags. From the bathroom, I grab our toothbrushes, my contact lens case and saline. I snatch up my work laptop and shove it into the case. Medications. Cell phone charger. Purse. What am I forgetting? Nothing I can't pick up at Walmart.

As I pass by the living room, I glance at Delano. He's lying on the couch with one arm flung over his eyes. He wants me to think he's asleep, but I know he's not.

"Go get in the van," I tell the kids, loudly enough for Delano to hear. He doesn't open his eyes or act as though he cares.

Driving aimlessly, I circle my problems: I can't go on living like this. I'm barely making it through each day, and I can't handle the added pressure that Delano heaps on me as if this is all my fault. As if I can control Devon, but won't. As if this is by choice. I pull through a Chick-fil-A drive-thru and hand out waffle fries and chicken nuggets. Waiting in the Dunkin' Donuts' drive-thru, I call my mother.

Her voice crackles through the bad signal. "I'd love for you to come visit. But, are you on your way now?" she asks.

"I need a break."

"Honey, did you forget that I'm on vacation in Maine?"

"Oh," I say, my chest beginning to cave in on itself in despair.

"You can come here," she adds, hurriedly. "I'm staying in a cottage by the beach. The kids would love to play in the ocean with Coby."

"Is there enough room for us?"

"I'll make room. Just come."

Some 16 hours later, we wind our way along a narrow dirt road. With a steady supply of DVDs, the kids have all done well. We pass quaint cottages set back from the road before reaching a mailbox with the right street number. My eyes burn. Shivering from way too much caffeine and no sleep, I pull in and turn off the engine.

Mom rushes out, and the screen door of the breezeway slaps closed behind her and her big dog, Coby. Mom squeezes the kids into hugs and the dog jumps on them, almost knocking them over. Sam picks a red Frisbee up off of the gravel driveway and sends it sailing through the air. The kids and Coby race to fetch it.

Mom hugs me and prickles race along my arms. Being touched makes me want to sluff off my skin. Have I always been like this? I don't think so, but I can't pinpoint when it started. I concentrate trying not to pull away because I don't want to hurt her feelings.

"Why don't you go take a nap," Mom says, leading me toward the cottage. "I'll take the kids to the beach. I'm sure they're sick and tired of riding."

I fall in and out of sleep, restless and haunted by my fear of becoming trapped in the coffin of sleep paralysis. Hours later, when voices float up the stairs, I drag myself fully awake. I trudge downstairs, taking in the cottage. The walls are nothing more than studs open to the exterior clapboarding. The cross rails are makeshift shelves crowded with beach glass, shells, and an assortment of ceramic lighthouses.

The kids are at the table, and Mom is serving hot dogs, baked potato chips, and corn on the cob for dinner. My stomach turns at the smell.

"Honey, do you want some supper?" Mom asks.

"I feel sick." I flop into a worn, blue-striped chair.

"Did you take some medicine?"

"Migraine pills."

"Don't touch that, Sweetie," Mom says, and guides Amias' hand away from a shiny white sea shell. "Grammy is renting this place. If we break anything, I'll have to pay for it."

The kids finish eating and go back outside to play with Coby and to swing in the hammock. Mom washes the dishes then goes outside with them.

Later, when mosquitos chase the kids inside for showers, I set up an assembly line of sorts: watch TV while waiting your turn, shower, brush your teeth, go upstairs to read in bed with Grammy. It's always easiest to go by age since any arbitrary order will surely cause bickering. After Brandon showers, I send him scurrying upstairs to my mom. Kayla needs my help washing sand out of her hair. Her curls spring out wildly, and I start to comb out the knots but she's anxious to get upstairs so I only make a halfhearted attempt.

"Your turn, Amias," I say. He and Devon are glued to the boxy TV that squats in a corner of the room. Its rabbit ears and fuzzy black and white screen are a novelty to them. "Amias," I call more firmly. He distractedly takes the towel from my hand.

The bathroom door clicks closed, and I go to the kitchen for coffee. My mom only drinks decaf, but, when she learned we were coming, she bought me real coffee and half and half. When I return to the living room, Devon is fingering a large sea shell. "Remember what Grammy said: no touching."

He places the shell back on its perch and circles the room looking at the other knickknacks. I sit in the striped chair, and try to relax. Devon strokes a glass mermaid.

"Use your eyes only," I mimic my mom's earlier admonitions and tone.

Devon slowly circles the room again looking at the trove of treasures. His hand snakes out like lightning and grabs a ceramic lighthouse. He raises it above his head, his eyes a challenge. I jump up and hot coffee splashes across my legs.

"Put that down," I order.

He narrows his eyes and shakes his head. As I move toward him, he stumbles backwards over the ottoman, but stays on his feet. "I'm gonna break it," he taunts.

21

In one quick motion, I grab Devon's wrist and pry the lighthouse from his fingers. He thrashes and grunts as I wrangle him onto a kitchen chair. But he springs back up from the seat. I grab at his shirt.

There's a gasp. I look up. Mom is standing halfway down the stairs with one hand over her mouth. "What's going on?"

"He's trying to break that." I motion with my chin toward the lighthouse. Devon howls and kicks his legs and I struggle to contain him, taking blows to my arms and chest.

"I can't handle this," Mom says tearily. "He's just a little boy. I can't …"

Devon stills beneath my hands and tears begin to trickle down his face. I look at him. How has he managed to summon tears? "What do you want me to do?" I demand. "Let him break everything?"

"I … I … don't know. But, I can't do this. It's too much." Mom turns and rushes back up the stairs.

No doubt happy that my mom has taken his side and not wanting to lose the upper hand, Devon saunters into the bathroom to shower.

Later, lying in the darkness, I swat at mosquitos. I'm sardined between Brandon and Kayla, but feel utterly alone. There's no way that I can control Devon here. If he did this on our first day, it's only going to get worse.

Kayla stirs next to me. "It's hot," she moans.

I adjust the rotating fan her way. She flops around, and I whisper, not wanting to wake the boys, "Do you want me to tell you a story?"

I feel the motion of her nodding.

"Once upon a time, I was sad because I didn't have a little girl of my own. Only boys. Then I found out that I was pregnant with you."

Kayla giggles, "That's not true."

"Who says it has to be true? This is *my* story." I smooth her hair away from her sweaty face "You ordered me to eat lots of chocolate and you told me what movies to go see. Miss Bossy, Bossy. Then, one day, you decided you were ready to come out. Out you came … and your hair went poof!"

"It did not," she whispers, and pets my cheek affectionately.

The next day, I sit on a large boulder hiding behind my sunglasses while the kids play in the salty waves and collect sea shells with my mom. I watch for signs of the tide turning but only see white capped waves breaking over and over against the jagged, rocky shore. After dinner I load up our things and set my GPS for home.

22

Dice crash against the clear, plastic lid of the Boggle tray as Amias shakes it far more robustly than necessary. He sets it down and shoves his wire-rimmed glasses up with one finger. At this point, they're irreparably twisted, because he's all in on everything he does, especially hurling himself headlong across the soccer goal.

I hand out a lunch of cereal, apple slices, and cookies. Devon flips the timer. Our usual rules apply. Only words three letters or more count, except for Kayla, who can make one and two-letter words. Each word is one point.

I try to get Brandon to eat his cereal but he wrinkles his face. "It's yummy," I say, putting the spoonful in my own mouth. I really need to make time to start cooking again. Lately, I'm doing a terrible job feeding the kids healthy food.

"Time's up. Pencils down. Pencils down," Amias hollers. "I'll go first," he announces. "Cat."

Devon slashes the word off of his list. "Not fair," his voice scrapes across my skin.

"Cat*s*," Amias continues. No one else has that one. "The."

"Ehhhh," Devon wails and my skin crawls.

After Amias finishes, Kayla reads her words. "I—A—An—It."

They tally up their points and Amias has won. I snatch an apple slice from his plate and pop it in my mouth. It's tart and crunchy. "Take a break now, and eat your lunch."

"See," Amias tells Kayla, "Mom eats after Brandon and *me*."

"She eats after me too," Kayla insists.

"I eat after all of you."

"Not Devon," Amias whispers loudly to Kayla.

"Shush." I tell him. Devon hangs his head, and I summon my very best maternal instincts. "Of course, I eat after Devon too." I walk up behind him. Panic grips my throat like it might strangle me. He's already eaten his apple and cookie. I stare at his bowl of corn flakes and my stomach turns inside out.

With four sets of eyes looking at me expectantly, I paste on a smile. As if in slow motion, I reach for Devon's spoon and scoop up some of his cereal. All I can see is the shine on his upper lip. I lift his spoon to my mouth, and my stomach lurches. I put it into my mouth, anyway. My throat shrinks to a pin hole, but I force myself to swallow.

"See?" I say, swallowing down an involuntary gag. My hand flutters to my mouth. I walk, as casually as I can, towards the bathroom.

23

I startle awake. Without my contact lenses, everything is an inky blur.

Feral eyes loom up and over me, mere inches from my face.

I gasp.

Devon jumps back. "I ... I ... need to use the bathroom," he stammers then scuttles back out of my bedroom.

I sit. Pant. My heart jerks in my chest. Feeling light-headed and beginning to hyperventilate, I grope to switch on the light. There's the creak of Devon's bed frame, then only the booming silence of my own pulse.

Why was he standing over me like that? How long was he there? Every scary suspense novel I've ever read spins through my mind. I don't dare close my eyes, don't dare even blink, until morning.

24

It's a gloomy day, and clouds hide any sunlight that might otherwise evaporate the dread that's settled over me. Popping four extra-strength Tylenol, with lukewarm coffee I don't have the energy to microwave, I slump at my desk, unable to concentrate and work.

Why was Devon in my bedroom? What if I hadn't woken up? Devon is so angry, hates me so much. What if he had gone for the baseball bat while I was asleep?

I shake my head, but it's as if my brain isn't working right anymore. I can't make sense of anything. I know I'm being irrational, but I can't free myself from this paranoia. Why didn't I change the Boggle rules? Why didn't I tell them all words counted with no canceling when two players found the same one? That would have been so simple.

Had I been happy when Devon lost the game?

I watch despondently as large drops of rain slide like tears down the windows. It's not the sort of thing you tell anyone, not even yourself, and awareness sinks into my gut like wet cement.

…

Desperate for sleep, I secure a pressure-mounted baby gate loosely in Devon's bedroom door frame. How has my life come to this? In the weeks since I woke up to find Devon standing over me, I've barely slept. I'm afraid of a child not even half my size. Satisfied with my jerry-rigged alarm, I say goodnight.

It takes only a few minutes. Predictably, Devon calls, "I gotta go poopie."

Sure you do.

I trudge upstairs to take down the gate. Devon dilly-dallies in the bathroom, making me wait. After getting him back into bed and resetting the baby gate in his doorway, I settle back in downstairs with my laptop and watch the news. Brandon curls beneath a blanket beside me. About an hour later, I hear the gate clatter onto the hardwood floor in the hall.

"It wasn't me. I promise. I didn't get out of bed," Devon shouts.

I get a few semi-restful nights of sleep before Devon figures out how to move from his bed to the door, scale the frame, and jump out. Delighted, he shows Amias and Kayla his new trick. They tell me about it in hushed whispers. They're scared of him wandering the house while we sleep too, and the fear edging their voices spurs awake my inner dragon.

I call a family meeting, sans Delano. Skewering Devon with my eyes, I say, "Amias and Kayla, you have my permission to punch Devon in the face as hard as you can if he tries to hurt you. Or, if he tries to hurt Brandon. You won't get in trouble for self-defense."

Devon's eyes bug out at me.

"That's right. You better think twice about going after them," I say, with exactly zero sympathy. I tuck the kids into bed with kisses on the foreheads, secure Devon's gate, and collapse onto my bed still fully clothed.

In the murky place between sleep and waking, I watch Devon climb onto the half wall at the top of the stairwell. A grin contorts his face as he stabs an accusing finger at me. He taunts me. Threatens to jump.

I sigh wearily, giving up. "If that's what you want to do, jump."

His socked foot slips, and he falls in slow motion. The sickening crack of his body on the ceramic tile snaps me awake.

I lay in bed, tears blurring the ceiling fan from view. This isn't how adoption is supposed to be. I'm supposed to love my son, but I don't even like him. The absolute certainty that God will now punish me—by taking one of my other kids from me—swallows me like a body bag.

I begin to neurotically check and re-check bicycle helmets and seatbelts. When the kids are with Becky, I call and ask, "Are they at your house? Are you sure? Send me a picture." When they take the bus, I call the school to make sure that they make it safely into their classrooms. Eventually, I start driving them myself every single day to be sure.

Dread balls in the pit of my stomach, and I'm nearly paralyzed with fear.

25

Brandon twirls in a pink glitter hula hoop while Devon crouches on the floor near the TV watching the antics of *Curious George*. I rest my head on the back of the couch trying to block out the irritating squeaking of the monkey talking to The Man in the Yellow Hat in what feels like episode 500 of the day. As yet another new episode is beginning, Amias rushes in and snatches up the remote. He flips through the channels.

"I was watching that," Devon says.

"That baby stuff?" Amias says glibly. "Power Rangers is on."

"Not fair." Devon pounds his fist into the carpet. Then, Amias holds the remote high, moving it side to side as Devon jumps for it. "Gimme. Gimme."

"You all like *Power Rangers*," I say wearily.

Amias sinks into a chair, eyes glued to the TV, and grips the remote. Devon flops around and moans, but I ignore him. *Curious George is* a baby show and Devon has been monopolizing the TV for hours with it. *Power Rangers* is a favorite of all the kids, including Devon. The boys have each claimed one Ranger as their own: Amias is Red Ranger and Devon is Green Ranger. Kayla says the whole thing is stupid. They try to make her "be" Pink Ranger, but she hates pink.

Devon and Amias both begin to mouth the dialogue along with "their" character on TV. I rest my head back against the couch. I hold my eyes barely slit open to keep watch. I want so badly to sleep just for a few minutes.

Before I know what's happening, Devon streaks by and karate chops Brandon in the throat. Brandon drops to the floor clutching his neck and sucking hard for breath.

I fly across the room and pull Brandon into my arms. I pin Devon with my eyes. "Why would you do that?"

"I ... I was playing with him."

My fingers clench and unclench like talons. I have to get him out of my sight.

"I didn't mean to ..." His voice sounds like he's sobbing, but I don't see a single tear.

"Go to your room. Right. Now."

Devon is rooted in place, but, when I stand to go for an ice pack, he shoots for the stairs. I return with a bag of frozen corn and cradle Brandon in my arms. He has a red mark on his throat, but he calms once he's over the shock. Meanwhile, my anger mushrooms into indignation. Devon has got to realize how unacceptable his behavior is and that there are consequences. Time-out in his bedroom is not going to make this stop.

"Let's get dressed to go to the playground," I say. Amias and Kayla scamper upstairs to change out of their pajamas. Brandon follows them.

"Devon, get dressed," I call, loudly enough for him to hear me from his bedroom. Then I add, "You can do your time-out at the playground and watch while everyone else gets to play."

I don't see Devon push Brandon down the stairs.

I only hear the yelp.

And a sickening thud.

26

Amias and Kayla saw how Devon pushed Brandon, with one big shove, from behind.

"What's wrong with you?" Sam growls at Devon.

"I didn't do it!" Devon spits out. "They're lying on me. They're lying."

My face flames. "Shut up! You. Shut. Up."

Devon stomps back up the stairs, smacking the wall with his palm.

Brandon sprawls on my lap and gulps sobs. I rub my hands over his body and look into his eyes to make sure they can focus. He doesn't seem to have any serious injuries. I look at the stairs stretching up high in front of me, and mounting horror slams through me. He could have been killed.

The front door swings open behind me. I look up and see Becky who is frantic. "Is Brandy okay?"

"Devon pushed him down the stairs," I wail.

Devon's dresser drawers crash and splinter above us. Becky shakes her head and purses her lips. "Let me take him so you can deal with Devon." She picks up Brandon and carries him toward her house. Amias and Kayla dash after her.

Sam stands in the foyer, fuming as I pound up the stairs and yell, "That's it." I'm pissed. This has got to stop. I grab Devon. He thrashes and fights me. I dig my fingernails into his arm not caring if it hurts.

I drag him.

He writhes.

I thrust him into the minivan.

I slap Devon's hands as he tries to twist the seatbelt away from me as I hook him in.

Sam rides next to Devon with his hand over the seatbelt latch. Devon thrashes back and forth. My heartbeat slams in rhythm with his shrieks. Each second stretches like a rubber band threatening to snap. Vehicles loom in my peripheral vision. "Mom. Mom!" Sam cries in alarm as I repeatedly slam my breaks.

We pull into the parking lot of Eastside Mental Health Hospital. I unlock the doors, and Sam releases Devon's seatbelt. Devon hurtles himself out through the door and bolts toward the emergency room entrance, shrieking as though he's escaped a torture chamber.

That's when I know. This is a mistake.

27

By the time I pass through the sliding glass doors of the hospital, Devon is flanked by two male nurses. They are leading him toward a set of steel doors with the words "Authorized Staff Only" painted on them. Devon squawks, but I see the jubilant spring in his step. Surely, they must too. Grinding my teeth, I turn away.

The receptionist sits inside a bulletproof fish tank of a room with a round speaker. She points us to the waiting rooms. There are two, and I pick the empty one. It's probably empty because it's the sick room, but I don't care. I can't handle small talk or the effort needed to avoid eye contact right now.

After half an hour, I approach the receptionist again and clear my throat, but she doesn't look up. "Do you know how long the wait is?"

"At least four or five hours."

I'm shocked. "I have other kids I need to take care of. Can you call me when the doctor is ready to see us?"

"No, Ma'am." My emotional distress bounces off her like she's a rubber ball.

"I don't live far from here," I add hopefully.

"You are not allowed to leave until intake has been completed."

Scrubbing my hands over my face, I fist my hair, the sharp sting on my scalp a center for my tornado of emotions. Delano is probably not home yet, and I doubt he'd help me anyway. I text Becky and ask her to come pick up Sam and bring my phone charger.

My body sags with relief when she arrives with an extra-large coffee. My throat tightens with distress as I tell her, "The kids have homework. I need to pack their lunches. They should be in bed by now."

"They can sleep at my house," Becky says. "I'll take care of them." I usher Sam out of the door with her and promise to call when I know something. As they walk away, I hear Becky tell Sam they'll go through a drive thru to get him some dinner.

Back in the waiting room, I sit on a plastic chair next to an outlet and charge my phone. I lean my head back against the wall and try to rest, but pop an eye open every few minutes to make sure that I'm still alone. The smell of old sweat and feet is almost more than I can handle. I scrounge around in my purse for my roll-on perfume and swipe it across the skin just under my nose.

When Brandon calls to say goodnight, he cries and I do too. "Go snuggle-buggle with Auntie Becky and I'll come for you when I get home."

"Mommy, I can't sleep without you." He sniffles, and I grow even more incensed with Devon for putting us in this absurd predicament. Yes, I let Amias change the TV channel when Devon was watching something else and, yes, that wasn't fair. But fair or not, I am the parent and I can make those decisions. His response was totally disproportionate.

"Please, Mommy ..." Brandon whimpers.

"I'll be home as soon as I can. I promise I'll come get you no matter how late it is." I can't bear to hang up on him. I listen to Becky comforting him before she ends the call.

I call Delano and hear the shower running in the background. As I explain what's happened, he grunts, disgusted—not with Devon—with me. He cannot fathom Devon having any behavior bad enough that we'd need to go to the mental health hospital. It's my bad parenting. I don't even have to read between the lines. He comes right out and says it.

I check in with the receptionist again. "The psychiatrist hasn't seen your son yet. Don't worry though, he's had dinner and is comfortable."

Well, thank God for that. Just what I was worried about.

She continues, "He watched TV, and staff's putting him to bed."

"So, the doctor won't see him until morning?"

"They'll wake him up whenever the psychiatrist makes his rounds."

"Even if it's in the middle of the night?"

"Yes, Ma'am," she says.

It's past midnight when a young intake nurse calls me back to a small room with bare walls and a computer on a portable stand. She motions for me to sit and pulls a stool up for herself.

"What brings you and Devon here today?"

"He karate chopped his four-year-old brother in the throat and pushed him down the stairs."

"Has he done anything like this before?" Her voice is flat. Uninterested. Just doing her job.

"Not this, specifically. No. But he has terrible tantrums," My words race out. Now that we're doing this, I might as well tell them everything. "He screams for hours, throws and breaks things, spits at me, and pees on himself when he's mad."

Her eyes don't leave the computer screen. "When did these behaviors begin?"

My thoughts trip and stumble as they run back over the last year, then further back, back to the beginning. "I guess since we got him. He came to us when he was three. We adopted him when he was four. He hoards food and gorges. Makes himself throw up." I pause as the nurse's fingers click across the keyboard. When she catches up, I plunge on: "We thought it was because he was coming out of foster care and he'd stop after he'd been with us for a while. At first, he was small enough for me to manage. I could pick him up and put him on his bed or in a chair. Today, I realized he's dangerous. He could've seriously hurt his brother." Urgency punctuates my words. "He's four. Brandon is only four."

"Has Devon ever had surgery?" she responds.

"No."

"Head injuries?"

"No."

"Is he currently on any medications?"

I fish the bottle of ADHD medication out of my purse, glad to have remembered to grab it as I rushed out of the house. After inspecting it, she updates Devon's electronic chart.

When we're done, I expect her to take me back to the ward, but she leads me toward the exit, instead. Her voice softens as she says, "Go home and get some rest. Devon's sleeping. The social worker will give you a call sometime tomorrow."

A shiver runs up my spine as I walk through the parking lot. Shadows taunt my frazzled nerves and I startle as they lurch toward me. I look nervously over my shoulder into the darkness, hurry to my vehicle, and quickly lock the doors.

At home, I find Delano snoring on his recliner. I trudge next door and let myself in. Amias, Kayla, and Brandon are all asleep in bed with Auntie Becky, arms and legs flopped over each other. Jason must be on the couch. Becky groans as I whisper an update to her in the darkness. I leave Amias and Kayla, but I pick Brandon up and carry him home. I'm able to get a couple of hours of sleep with his warm body close.

When my morning alarm goes off, my head pounds, and I struggle to get the kids ready for school. I put a sweatshirt on over my nightgown and drive them to school barefoot. I feel too unsafe to drive the few minutes back home. I pull into a parking spot at the school, lay back my seat and close my eyes.

It's early afternoon before the hospital social worker calls. "Ms. Williams, Devon has been excellent while he's been with us. We haven't witnessed any aggressive or inappropriate behaviors from him while he's been on the unit."

My stomach sinks. Just like Devon to make me look bad by being good. I run my fingers through my stringy hair and cringe at the broken strands I pull away.

She asks me to come pick him up.

As we drive home, Devon's cheery mood plucks my nerve-endings one-by-one. "It was fun," he says. "I got to eat as much as I want. The Jell-O is the best."

28

Devon throws himself on the floor and rolls under the kitchen table. His arms and legs flail. His shrieks pierce through my eardrums straight into my brain. He kicks the bottom of the table, lifting it off the floor over and over again. Every time the table legs crash back down onto the tile, the sound slams against the backs of my eyes.

This has been going on for hours. Hours of non-stop screaming. Hours of Devon's voice ricocheting through my brain. Hours of not being able to form thoughts.

Fingers shaking, I surrender, or at least I try to. I hand Devon the extra package of Pop Tarts he's been insisting he must have. Instead of taking it, he hurls it away as if I've handed him a coiled snake.

My heart is like the rapid fire of a machine gun. With shaking fingers, I text Becky: "OMG. I can't take this anymore. I want to die." I want to hurl Devon into a wall. This has got to stop. I close my eyes, for just a moment, rubbing my temples. My eyes fly open, a sixth sense, as Devon's spit backhands me across the face.

I jump up.

I dry heave.

I hysterically try to wipe the stringy mess off with my sleeve.

I spin on him. "Stop it! Enough! That's enough." I advance on him, my voice shrill. "Just stop it already!"

He flings himself backward on the carpet. I can't grab hold of him. He kicks my stomach and already bruised shins. A runaway train has slammed into me, and I'm careening forward. I frantically pump the breaks, but there's no stopping.

Just then, Becky rushes through the front door. Devon screams only louder as she pulls me into the bathroom. "You need to take him to the hospital," she says, jolting me out of my hysterics.

"It's a waste of time," I pant.

Devon beats on the bathroom door with his fists. "Let me in!" he yells. Pounding. Kicking.

"Someone is going to get hurt. Take him to the hospital. Now."

Once again, I find myself sitting in the waiting room for hour after wasted hour while Devon is coddled and watches cartoons, no doubt perceiving this as a reward for his behavior.

The next morning, my head pounds and nothing helps. I've been curled on the bathroom floor with a full-blown migraine when the on-duty social worker calls. Her words are no surprise, "You have a lovely, polite young man."

I picture him watching TV with empty Jell-O cups stacked like shot glasses on the floor by his feet, and bile rolls up my throat. My voice is shaky from the pain of my migraine as I tell her, "You don't understand. When he's home, I can't control him. He throws awful temper tantrums …"

"I understand things got tense at home," patronizing and judgmental, she spoons her words down my throat like acid. "I'm going to help you out. We can't admit Devon, but we can keep him here for 48 hours under observation to give you some space and time to calm down."

My politeness is on auto-pilot, and I find myself saying, "Thank you," but there's a humiliating hitch in my voice as I finish the call. Intense feelings of self-loathing sear my chest. *I hate you. I hate you. I hate you.* The mantra runs through my mind over and over, and I do hate myself.

When I arrive to pick Devon up from the hospital, he goes around and says goodbye to the nurses, janitor, and security guards like he's a celebrity. And they treat him like one, with broad smiles and high-fives. So much for learning his lesson.

Well, I've learned mine. We won't be coming here ever again.

29

Devon squats inside the closet in the shadowy darkness. He has a belt looped around his neck. I act nonplussed. It's a prop. And if he knows I'm alarmed, he'll be more likely to do it again. And again. "Stop being silly," I say in as carefree of a tone as I can manage. Reaching out, I take the child-sized belt away.

"Give it back. Give it back," he yelps, following me down the hall into the kitchen. "Take me to the hospital!" He stomps his feet and waves his arms and reaches for the belt as I hold it over my head. "I'm not stopping 'til you take me to the hospital."

Resigned to this nonsensical standoff, at least until Delano gets home, I carry my coffee into the living room. It's one of my favorite mugs, with a red dragon curling its long tail around the oversized creamy ceramic sides. I was born in the year of the dragon, but I sure don't feel strong. I'm exhausted from bracing myself against this mudslide of a life that's sweeping me over the edge of sanity.

I set the belt on the couch and sit on it.

Devon plunks himself in front of me on the ottoman and his knees bump against mine. He looks at me in silence for a long moment, then says, "Fine. Then I'll do this." He grabs at his eye and jerks. He holds up a spate of long dark lashes between his fingers and flips them into the air. "I'm gonna pull them all out. My eyebrows too."

I have no choice.

"He was just being dramatic," I assure the intake nurse at Eastside, with a purse of my lips at the utter ridiculousness of it. "He wasn't really trying to kill himself."

She shakes her head and frowns. "He's having suicidal ideations."

"Suicidal 'ideations' … what's that?"

"Thoughts of harming himself," she explains.

"You don't understand. He's not *actually* trying to hurt himself. He wouldn't even know *how* to kill himself with a belt."

The nurse looks at me, not responding, and clearly not understanding.

"He just did it because he wanted to come here," I say.

"Now, we don't know that, do we?" she chides.

The psychiatrist is also concerned about Devon's safety and decides to admit him. Devon has only ever been in the ER under observation and this will be his first in-patient admission. There's an open bed at The Pines, which is about a five-hour drive away. They tell me that he will be transported there by a police escort.

I ping pong between relief and disbelief. He's not that bad. This is crazy. I should go pick him up.

"At this point, it's out of your hands," the social worker says, in response to my reluctance. "Now that we've decided to admit him, it will be up to the psychiatrist to determine when he can be discharged."

After we hang up, her words are like indigestion twisting me up inside. My nine-year-old son has been *involuntarily committed to the psych ward*.

I hurry to Target and buy a teddy bear, comics, a word search book, and Spider Man pajamas. Weave in and out of traffic to get to the hospital. Rush through the glass doors. Rattle out Devon's privacy code. Then, I watch as the receptionist dials the phone with absolutely no sense of urgency to let a nurse know that Devon has a visitor up front.

A few minutes later, a nurse with thick cat's-eye glasses comes out and sorts through my bag. "Spiral bindings aren't allowed." She waves the word search book in the air, as though I've tried to smuggle in a pack of cigarettes.

Tears spring to my eyes. Tears? I'm a mess. I rip the pages off of the spiral binding under her cool supervision. I return everything to the bag and toss the now mis-shaped coil into the trash can. She leads me through the steel, double-locked doors and into the ward. The hallway is wide with windowed rooms flanking the sides. Several cots line the walls. A teenage girl, wearing brown scrubs, curls up on one. On another, a blotchy-faced young boy sits reading a book.

We enter the common room, where Devon is watching TV. His eyes light up when he sees me, and I smile. He runs over and grabs the bag out of my hand. As he sorts through the gifts, I look around. The ward looks boring, but not particularly unpleasant. There's a whiteboard with the status of each patient. "DW" must be Devon. He's on Level A, whatever that means. "TS" and "MJ" are on Level B, and there are a few patients on Levels C and D. The three other patients in the common room are wearing hospital gowns and sweatpants like Devon. They're docile, presumably drugged up. Devon does not belong here. This is *not* what I want for him.

A voice crackles over the speakers announcing that visiting hours are over in five minutes. I take Devon's hands in mine. "I'm so sorry, but maybe this will be good for us." His eyes wander back and forth between me and the TV. I tug his hands to get his attention. "If they can get you on the right medications, things will be better at home and at school." I'm weepy and feeling more affection for Devon than I have in a long time.

My stomach sloshes with guilt. I'm physically sick at the thought of sending him away, at having brought him here at all. I welcome the unexpected feeling. It's proof that I'm not a completely horrible mother, not a monster.

30

I wake already hyper-vigilant with dread coiled deep into my muscle memory. Then I remember. Devon is at The Pines.

A nurse calls for "consent to treat," and I have a brief intake call with a social worker. That's it. The psychiatrist doesn't call. The doctor doesn't call. Devon doesn't call. The lack of communication seems odd, but how do I know what to expect when my child is in a psych ward, especially one 250 miles away?

Trying to find my way back to normal, I make popcorn and root beer floats for a family movie night. The kids watch *Mr. Popper's Penguins*, and I watch them.

Brandon is a mini-Amias. When I compare their baby pictures, I often can't tell them apart. He doesn't have Amias' self-assurance and confidence, though. He's always worrying. When will you be back, Mommy? What if you forget me? What if I can't find you? He still falls asleep in my bed and is afraid of the dark.

Kayla's short curls are held back by a headband. Each year, I've cut it shorter as I've had less and less time to care for it. She's a mama's girl, and I can't even pull out of the garage to go to the grocery store without her ears perking up in time to run for her shoes. With what's happening with Devon, I worry that she'll become afraid we could send her away too.

Amias has a wide smile, where crooked teeth jockey for space. It seems as if he's been the least affected by the Devon-saga. More than anything, he finds Devon's behavior annoying because it interferes with his soccer and basketball games, and he can't have friends over to the house.

Sam is on the verge of being a young adult, but doesn't have his driver's license yet. I can't begin to take on the stress of teaching him to drive. He's been talking to an Army recruiter.

The kids giggle and squeal, falling all over themselves, as they watch the penguins' antics. Kayla's face dimples and she reaches over to tickle Brandon—at this moment, he's *her* baby penguin. I watch the kids slurp their ice cream floats and eat handfuls of popcorn, and a very different life shimmers in front of me like a mirage.

    Devon comes home a few days later and the kids sprint outside to meet him. They think it's so cool that he got to ride home in a real police car. Standing in the driveway, Devon pulls presents from a white plastic bag—partially used sample size toiletries, pamphlets for a zoo, and a disposable shower cap for Kayla. He hands me the manila envelope with his discharge documents. As he ambles into the house, I notice how slow and measured his words are. He seems frail and so very young.

    In Devon's discharge documents, I read his intake notes:

```
The patient's insight was poor,
judgment impaired and abstract
thinking impaired.
```

Scanning forward I find his diagnoses:

```
Axis I: Mood disorder, not otherwise
specified, attention deficit
hyperactivity disorder, and
oppositional defiant disorder.
```

    He's been prescribed two new medications and I wonder if that's why his affect is so calm. I keep reading:

```
Admission GAF: 22
Discharge GAF: 50
```

    By Googling "GAF," I learn that it's a scale of 0 to 100 that gauges a person's mental health. An optimal score is between 91 and 100. Devon was admitted at 22, which means, "seriously mentally impaired" with behavior considerably influenced by delusions or hallucinations, and acting grossly inappropriately.

    I scan the webpage for a GAF of 50 to find out how Devon's condition is improved after his treatment at The Pines. A GAF score of 50 means "serious symptoms" including suicidal ideations. I can't make sense of it. He was admitted 10 days ago for suicidal ideations and now discharged as "better" with the same exact issue?

    Dread slithers back into my veins and coils once again into my muscles. Devon's calm begins to feel less hopeful and more like the eye of a hurricane. Over the next couple of weeks, darkening clouds mount.

And then, pencils and notebooks are raining down as Devon throws them over his shoulder. He sing-songs, "I'm gonna rip up Amias' homework!"

I jerk Amias' backpack out of his hands.

Feigning hysterical laughter, Devon hurls himself backwards into a wall and sinks to the floor. "Are you gonna take me to the hospital *now?*"

I refuse to be provoked.

Devon skips through the dining room calling to me, "Hmmm, what should I break now?" I ignore him and repack Amias backpack. Just then, Brandon flies out of the playroom screaming. He stumbles, trying to pump his short legs faster than they can go. Devon charges after him with a marble, elephant-shaped bookend in his upraised fist and the parody of a grin on his face. "I'm gonna smash your head in," he calls after Brandon as if it's a joke.

Lunging for Devon, I yell, "Sam, I need help. Help." I wrestle the heavy bookend away while Brandon cowers under the kitchen table.

"Take me to the hospital. Right. Now," Devon demands as he twists and bucks to wrench himself out of my arms.

"Sam, help!" I shout, straining to contain Devon's wild thrashing. Sam thuds down the stairs. Amias and Kayla peer around the corner from the playroom and watch, wide-eyed.

Seeing Devon, Sam shakes his head. "Not again, Man. What's wrong with you?"

"Take him to the car," I pant. "I'm coming." I rush to find my purse as I text Becky to come for the other kids.

...

"You can't continue bringing him to the hospital." It's a social worker who I haven't met before. Jane? Nancy? I forgot her name as soon as she introduced herself. Her bittersweet perfume curdles in the air of the tiny, suffocating office. "In the last four months, you've been through the ER four times, and he's been admitted once." She looks down her nose at me.

My face burns. "I don't know what else to do. I know it doesn't seem like he could be dangerous, but he *really* is."

"Have you tried intensive in-home services?"

"What's that?" I ask, shaking my head.

"They provide crisis management in your home. Unfortunately, the waiting list can be quite long for these types of services. There's a new agency though, and they do take Medicaid. Let me find their card." She shuffles through her desk drawer and hands me a business card for Springbrook Family Care. "They're new, so they can probably get you in right away." She stands and opens her office door for me. "Please remember, the hospital is for acute care and stabilization of patients."

A week later, I finally have real help for three hours every weekday afternoon.

Delano hates it. "Is this what *you* want? People up in our house all the time?" he demands. But I refuse to cancel. I'm desperate. I can't control Devon. Worse, I can barely control myself. I'm afraid I'm one spit, one scream, one broken toy away from beating Devon. It's the ugly secret that's eating me alive: Devon's not the only one who's out of control.

Mr. Josh is Devon's favorite person on our Springbrook team. He's towering and beefy, and his voice booms and echoes through the house. He throws the football with Devon and Amias, but his go-to "therapeutic" activity is beaching himself for a nap on the playroom floor while Devon reads to him. That's fine with me, because Devon behaves whenever Mr. Josh is around.

My favorite team member is Aniya. Diet soda in hand, she keeps me updated on her trips to the gym as she works toward her goal to lose 50 pounds. Her generous smile, all teeth and enthusiasm, perks up the wilted and drooping mother inside me.

"You can call me Ms. Niya," she'd said, with a wink at the kids when she met them. She spends her assigned afternoons with our family trilling over crayon drawings and helping the kids with their homework. She watches them build Lego mazes for their pet hermit crabs. She often presides over hermit crab races, although I don't think any of the crabs have done more than climb over the walls of the Lego maze and certainly none have made it to the finish line.

One afternoon, Aniya pulls out the *Coping Skills* game. She holds Brandon on her lap and tells him they'll be a team. Amias rolls the dice, moves his red game piece three squares, and draws a situation card. "You feel confused by the directions your teacher gives," he reads.

"What coping skill will you use?" Aniya gestures toward the colorful game board which lists coping skills—like, "Ask for help," "Take a walk," "Take slow deep breaths"—next to whimsical illustrations of children.

Amias, who takes being called a "know-it-all" as a compliment, sits up straight and weighs his answer carefully. "I would ask the teacher for help. Or I could read the instructions, if there's a handout."

"Very good." Aniya smiles broadly and hands Kayla, who is sitting to Amias' right, the dice. "Your turn, Baby Girl."

Kayla blushes. "Can I go last?"

"Okay. Devon, here you go." Aniya hands the dice to Devon.

He earnestly grips the dice as if he's been tasked with throwing out the lottery numbers. He shakes and shakes … and shakes. Finally, he rolls seven and moves the green game piece. His situation card reads, "It's bedtime and I don't feel tired."

Aniya squints her eyes like she's thinking real hard. "That's a tricky one. What coping skill could you use?"

Devon stares at the board for several moments. He tentatively says, "Ask for help from the teacher?"

Amias groans, but Aniya shushes him.

Devon mumbles, "A handout …"

Aniya says, kindly, "Well, let's think about this. Is your teacher with you at bedtime?"

Devon's first individual therapy session is with our Springbrook clinician, Brianna. She's in her late twenties, and a smattering of freckles cascade like beauty marks across her bronze skin. She has shiny, coral colored acrylic nails, and her heels snap smartly on my tile floors. She asks Devon where he'd like to sit and talk. My heart stops as he leads her upstairs to his bedroom.

I imagine Brianna glancing into Kayla's bedroom with its soft rug and white poster bed. A few steps further and she'll look into Amias' bedroom and see posters of international soccer players and his sports trophies lined up on his dresser. At least Sam keeps his door closed. I don't have to worry about its teenaged boy mess and smell.

Then Brianna will reach Devon's bedroom with its door hanging ajar. There are four gaping holes in the walls. One is behind the door from the knob being slammed into it. Maybe she won't see that one. No posters are left on the walls. There's only a sheet and pillow on the bed. Lately Devon has been unraveling his berber carpet like a crimped ribbon on a present. A present just for me.

I should have thought to explain to Brianna that I can't afford to keep replacing Devon's broken stuff and fixing his bedroom, only for him to destroy it again. But there's nothing I can do now, so I sit and wait, nervously.

When they come back downstairs, Brianna doesn't bring up the condition of Devon's bedroom. Instead, we create a reward chart. I sit at the table, across from Devon and Brianna, and watch as she writes three goals:

```
1. Obeyed with no more than three prompts
2. Did not kick anyone or anything
3. Did my homework one day out of three
```

"Isn't this rewarding Devon for *not* being bad?" I ask. "I don't give Amias or Kayla a reward when they don't kick someone." They get rewards—Devon too—when they do something above and beyond normal expectations of behavior. Isn't that sort of "Parenting 101"?

"We need to help Devon develop habits of good behavior. Once the habits are formed, the rewards won't be necessary any longer," Brianna says.

Devon can't lose any stickers once he's earned them. I scan the chart and do a quick calculation. With three goals and four-hour time increments, he can earn 12 stickers in a single day. For 25 stickers I'm to take him out for ice cream. For 50 he gets to pick a family activity like going to the playground or the movies.

We start using the chart the next morning. Devon loves it, and why wouldn't he? I feel suckered every time I have to put a sticker on that stupid chart. Didn't kick anyone in the last four hours—sticker. Picked up my shoes—not the first time, not the second time—the third time mom asked me to—sticker.

Still, my interactions with Devon are calmer. He smiles more and screams less. Minutes turn into hours, then hours into days, and soon we've gone a week without a major tantrum.

While I may not agree with this parenting approach in principle, I can't deny that it is working. Devon earns his first reward in no time. As we lick our ice cream cones, he eagerly tells me all about how he wants to work in an animal shelter when he grows up.

As the days go by it's like being revived from a near-death experience. Hope dares to perk up inside me like a fern that's been protectively rolled up, unfurling into the sunlight.

Then the school calls.

31

Devon is sitting across from the principal's wide desk, nibbling on the skin around his thumbnail when I arrive. I sit down next to him and pull Brandon onto my lap. He's not feeling well, and I woke him from a nap.

"We had a serious incident with Devon this afternoon," the principal clips. "He was upset when his teacher called the class inside at the end of recess. He picked up a rock and smashed it into the gym door and broke the glass."

I glare at Devon, but my outrage ricochets off his infuriatingly blank face.

She continues, "His classmates were lined up at the door, and he walked up the line punching them. When his teacher tried to stop him, he punched her in the stomach." Her words suck the air from the room. "He's being suspended for two days, effective immediately."

Devon lurches up and careens into the front office. I dump Brandon off my lap and chase after him. Devon hurls papers and pencil cups off the desks. The school secretary flattens herself against a wall. Grabbing Devon, I push him down into one of the waiting room chairs. Not knowing how else to contain him, I sit on his lap.

Brandon crouches behind one of the administrative desks and peeks out. Tears roll down his face. I jerk forward as Devon beats my back with his fists and blats like a sheep. When the school resource officer strides in, Devon stops punching my back. Stops screaming.

She's dressed in dark slacks and a button-down uniform shirt. There's a radio on her sleeve. I don't see a holster. "Are you Devon?" she asks.

I feel him nodding, and he stills. I slowly stand, relieved to let the officer take over.

"I'm going to need you to calm down." Her voice is stern.

For a few seconds there's a silent standoff. Then Devon lunges at her, clawing the air wildly.

32

The officer deftly side-steps Devon. "You need to control him," she orders me. "If he touches me, I'll have no choice but to press charges for assaulting a police officer."

I grab Devon, shove him back into the chair, and sit on his lap again. The officer and school staff huddle and whisper, which infuriates Devon. He pinches my sides, digging in with his fingernails and twisting my flesh.

I hear the sirens first. The fire department has been mobilized to deal with a little boy's tantrum. *My* little boy's tantrum. They tromp in, decked out in full gear. They surround me, and I stand, backing away as they move in on Devon.

Brandon runs to me, and I hug him close. He trembles and I whisper, "It's going to be okay." But it's a lie. This is never going to be okay.

The firefighters put Devon on a gurney and stretch a strap across his lap. He wails, but doesn't fight them. As they wheel him away, I ask, "Where are you taking him?"

"To Carolina Medical, Ma'am," one of the men says.

"Can you take him to Eastside instead?"

"They'll transfer him by ambulance if they decide he needs to go there, Ma'am.

I sign Amias and Kayla out of school early, and we go home. I collapse onto the couch and wait. When Becky gets off from work a couple of hours later and can watch the kids, I head over to the ER.

I find Devon sitting on a hospital bed, watching *SpongeBob Square Pants*, munching on a cookie, and drinking apple juice. He's giggling. I snap off the TV. "No way. *You will not* sit here and watch cartoons after your awful behavior this afternoon."

Anger freezes in Devon's eyes as his face hardens like a petulant ice sculpture. I'm glad he's upset. This should not be fun. I turn on my heel and go find a vending machine. When I return, I sit in the visitor's chair. Devon crosses his arms over his chest, his lips a slash of displeasure as he stares me down. I stare right back.

Raising my eyebrows provocatively, I pop Peanut M&Ms into my mouth. I'm certain he can read the unspoken message in my face: If you want nice things like these yummy M&Ms, you'd better start behaving yourself, young man.

Long hours later, the hospital determines Devon is stable and discharges him. Another total waste of time.

Back home, I tell Delano what happened and he shakes his head in irritation. "If him can't behave in school, you should homeschool him," he says.

There are no words.

I should check *myself* into Eastside.

33

When I met Delano's mother, Mush, I didn't make a good first impression. While she was visiting, Sam told his third-grade teacher that he was afraid kids would laugh at his new braces and refused to take his hand off of his mouth. The teacher spent the morning using it as an opportunity to talk with the class about bullying. At lunchtime, Sam was hungry and took his hand off his mouth to eat. No braces.

Sam thought it was a funny joke, but his teacher did not. I did not either. I'd given him a bowl of Grape Nuts for dinner and sent him to bed. Mush did not approve of the punishment. She'd be fine sending him for a belt, but withholding a hearty meal is something she couldn't stand for.

"I told her, Mush," Delano hissed his teeth. "Spare the rod, spoil the child." That kicked off a fervent discussion about "the American way" and how it makes kids behave badly. I'd left them to it and found peace and quiet in my bedroom reading a book.

Still, I appreciate Mush telling me not to worry when Delano fusses at me. "He's always been a pain in the heart," she'd said, clucking her tongue. I often remind myself of those wise words.

While Mush lives in Canada and we don't see her often, she and Delano talk on the phone every Sunday afternoon about the family and news from back home in Jamaica, often for hours. Most of their conversation is in rapid Patois, and I have no idea what they are saying unless I enlist Sam to help me eavesdrop.

One Sunday, we get the devastating news that Mush has previously undiagnosed stage-four breast cancer and she has only months to live. That's what the doctors say, but Mush, like Delano, believes in miracles over medicine. As someone who believes in modern medicine, I insist that Delano travel to Toronto. He takes FMLA leave from work and travels on a one-way plane ticket.

Without Delano home in the evenings and on weekends when Springbrook isn't there, it doesn't take long for things to spin completely out of control at home.

"I don't know why you're showing out for your momma. Why you saving it up for when we're gone?" Mr. Josh drawls on his next scheduled afternoon. His large hand dwarfs the door knob as he prepares to leave.

Devon shrugs, looking at his white socked feet. The fabric is stretched and flapping a good couple inches beyond his toes.

"Let me tell you, none of them other kids I work with live in nice houses like this. They don't have none of those nice sneakers you got neither. I know your momma is nice."

"She's just bein' nice because you're here," Devon mutters.

I suppose there's some truth to that. Devon's on his best behavior when others are around, and so am I.

...

Devon refuses to come in the house after we get home from school. I shrug and walk inside, trailed by Amias, Kayla, and Brandon. Moments later, I hear banging. Opening the garage door, I see Devon slamming a bicycle helmet on the concrete floor.

"Get out of here. Leave me alone," he screeches.

No problem. I close the door behind me. What he's doing to the helmet is annoying, but not dangerous and the destruction is limited to 20 bucks. I check the time. Aniya will be here in a few minutes.

I hear the snick of a doorknob. Devon wails, "Let me out of the garage. You locked me in the garage. Let me out."

I set my teeth. That knob doesn't even have a lock. When the mechanism malfunctioned a while back, instead of buying a new one, Delano had moved a knob from one of the closet doors to replace it. No matter, Devon continues to yell that I've locked him in the garage.

Brandon, Amias, and Kayla are huddled together in the living room and anxiously call me over. "What is it?" I ask.

Amias shoves his glasses up on his nose. "It's Shelly. She's dead."

I press between them to take a closer look at the hermit crab. It's out of its shell and splayed, not moving, on the tile floor.

"What's wrong with her, Mommy?" Brandon asks.

I glance over at the Lego table and see Shelly's painted turbo shell inside the maze. It's pastel pink with a large paint chip peeled away revealing the unadorned, real, brown surface beneath. "She must have left her shell and then accidentally fallen off the side of the table onto the tile floor," I tell Brandon.

"Why'd she do that?" he asks.

"Hermit crabs' shells are their homes. Sometimes they want a new home so they leave their shell to go look for one."

"But there's no other shells," he says.

"She didn't know that." I give him a hug.

Amias says, "Hermit crabs leave their shells when they're under stress too."

"Really?" I ask.

Amias confirms, "I read about it in the hermit crabs book."

"We need to bury her," Kayla says.

I nod and warn, "Don't touch it." I walk towards the kitchen to get a paper towel and some sort of container. As I go, I see Devon laying on the floor watching the tragedy unfold. From the waist down, he's in the garage, but the top half of him is sprawled on the floor inside the house. Seeing me, he growls. His meltdown escalates from 0 to 100 in 1.9 seconds. He stands and begins slamming the door over and over and, again, shouting that I've locked him in the garage.

I do my best to ignore Devon's antics as I use a paper towel to scoop Shelly into the small plastic container that will now be her coffin and snap on the lid.

"What's that boy showing out about?" Aniya asks when she arrives.

I tip my head toward the garage door. "I'm not keeping him in there. He just wants an excuse to throw a fit."

Aniya tuts. "Listen, you go about your business and let me deal with that boy. He needs to stop controlling this whole family." Heading toward the garage, she calls into the living room, "Y'all have a good day at school?" Kayla and Amias wave hello, and Brandon runs to hug her around the legs. "You know, Ms. Niya needed some love today," she chuckles and pats his back.

"Shelly's dead," Brandon tells her, and holds up the plastic container.

Aniya peers through the clear sides. "Poor little thing. What happened?"

"She wanted a new home. And she died."

Amias calls to Aniya, "She fell off the table. She wanted a new shell or maybe was stressed."

Aniya's face is drawn with sympathy as though Shelly was a beloved family member. "Should we give her a little funeral?"

Brandon nods solemnly.

"Let me take care of your brother and then we'll take care of

Shelly," Aniya tells him. Then, she shuts herself in the garage with Devon.

I listen to the banging and hollering. After about half an hour, I bring Aniya a glass of ice water. She's pulled out a lawn chair to sit on and her skin is glossy with sweat. The air is thick and stifling. I think of opening the garage door to the outside, but then all the neighbors would hear and see.

I hand Devon a cup of water too. He gulps it down before hurling the plastic cup in my direction. "You get out of here you ... you ... stupid girl. Get out now!"

Aniya says, "You take care of those other children. Get some work done. I've got Devon." Putting a shrug in her voice, she adds, "I don't mind staying out here all afternoon, if that's what he wants to do."

Not long after, Devon decides he's done and comes inside for a snack. He eats his peanut butter crackers as if the last few hours never happened.

Aniya sags into a chair, exhausted. She hasn't forgotten about her promise to give Shelly a proper farewell, but needs a few minutes to gather her energy. I feel badly for her, but I'm also relieved she's finally seen "it." Seen the real Devon.

Now, like an unstoppable breach in a dam, Devon begins to throw tantrums every time Aniya comes over. Mr. Josh and Brianna still haven't seen a fit, but they seem more concerned now that someone on the team has seen it for themselves. They also agree that Aniya should teach me how to "do holds."

"You can't go on like this. You can't let him hurt your other kids and destroy your house," Aniya says. I look around the living room. The bookshelf hangs askew, with one side pulled from the wall. The books are in disorderly stacks on the floor. Many of our favorites, the ones that I read over and over with the kids when they were little, are shredded at the bottom of the landfill—*Stinky Face, Hooway for Wodney Wat, Good Night Moon*, and so many others. Since Delano left, the damage has gotten much worse.

Aniya coaches me through Devon's next tantrum. Lowering myself to the floor, I bear hug him from behind with my legs wrapped around his waist to hold down his legs. I grip his wrists, crossing his arms over his chest. He bucks, trying to slam his head back into my face. I arch away.

"We don't want you to hurt yourself," Aniya croons. "Calm down so your mom can let you back up."

At first, I'm not sure Devon can even hear Aniya over his own voice. But, after a few minutes, his livid screams deflate into howls and then into whines. When he's calm, Aniya tells me to let him go. I flop back onto the floor and the cool tile feels good. I struggle to catch my breath.

    I can do this. A five-minute hold curtailed what would likely have been an hours-long tantrum.

    But, after the first few times, Devon warms to the holds. I think he even enjoys them, especially when I'm exhausted, and my attempts at "therapeutic" holds devolve into little more than wrestling matches. Before long, I'm having to do it daily, sometimes more than once a day. They last longer and longer. Ten minutes, then twenty. And then, I can't manage it any longer.

34

There it is. Devon's telltale, "I'm-gonna-throw-a-fit" look. I discreetly tell Amias, Brandon, and Kayla to go next door to Auntie Becky's house. "Run," I tell them.

They do.

When Devon hears our front door open and close, he hurdles after them. He bangs on Becky's door, but one of the kids had the wherewithal to lock it.

Devon picks up small rocks and throws them at the windows of her house. I try to coax him back inside, but he grabs a large rock and snarls at me.

I'm not sure of my next move. Sam spent the night at a friend's house, and Delano is still in Canada. If I chase after Devon, I'll only make a fool of myself. No doubt, he's faster than me. Out of options, I call the Springbrook emergency hotline.

Aniya lives close by and soon pulls into my driveway wearing dark, puffy rings around her eyes and a pink pajama set. She's been in constant crisis mode right alongside me for weeks. "Let's get inside to that nice cool air conditioning," she says, in a barely veiled ploy to lure Devon inside. She winks at me, and I follow her into the house.

Seconds behind us, Devon bursts through the door. "I'll just come in here and make trouble," he jeers. The minutes crawl by like hours as Devon whirls around the house. He throws books and toys. He kicks walls, swings on doors to try to pull them from the hinges, and flings chairs onto their backs. He gets in our faces and makes high pitched howls and yelps, to prevent us from having a conversation.

Aniya tries to talk Devon down and has me restrain him twice. Each time, he calms enough to be released, then he works himself up into a frenzy again.

Aniya reports in to Brianna, who says she's coming by even though it's a Saturday. Aniya warned her, but Brianna is shocked by the juxtaposition of the Devon she's seeing today and the charming, polite young boy who she knows from their therapy sessions. Brianna tries to talk to Devon, but he turns on her like he has on Aniya. All she can do is sit down with us and wait him out. Three adults at the whim of a child who is calling all the shots.

And he knows it. Devon stops the tantrum when he's good and done, like he's flipping off a light switch. I begin to clean up the mess. There's nothing I can do to compel him to pick up after himself. In fact, trying will just set him off again. It's easier to do it myself.

Before Brianna leaves, she tells me the team is going to "staff" the case. At my perplexed look she explains that means they're going to have a meeting to determine the best course of action.

I heat up a Jamaican spicy beef patty for Aniya. They're her favorite. "Listen," she says. "You have to stop telling people that Devon has 'tantrums.' These are no tantrums. These are rages. When you call them tantrums people aren't going to help you."

I gratefully slip that nugget of advice into my back pocket.

35

Devon sprints toward the entrance of the partial hospitalization facility. It's a one-story brick building across the street from Eastside. I trudge through the parking lot to where he waits for me, bouncing on the balls of his feet with his hand on the door knob.

Until Springbrook referred us here, I didn't even know a service like this existed. Brianna had explained that Partial Hospitalization Programs (PHPs) are for mental health patients who don't need to be hospitalized but who also can't manage being at home full-time. Devon will be here during the hours when he would otherwise be at school. He'll be with other children and a certified teacher. He'll receive education, individual therapy, group therapy, and medication management.

The outdated waiting room is clean, and framed student artwork hangs on the walls. We wait only a few moments before a male staff member calls Devon back. I watch as his big hairy hands pass over Devon's youth medium, Yoshi graphic tee, patting him down like he's some sort of pre-pubescent thug. It's surreal.

I'm taken to meet with the psychiatrist, Dr. Alexandria. She's a caricature, only four-foot-something and shaped like a can of chicken noodle soup. Her whole face is screwed tight to hold glasses askew on her nose. She gestures for me to sit as she squeezes behind the desk. "Tell me what's going on with," she pauses, and glances at a paper, "Devon."

I recite Devon's social and medical history as she makes notes. I tell her how he pushed Brandon down the stairs. "When Devon flies into a rage, I can't—"

Her head pops up and she interrupts me. "How often is he having rages?"

After being ignored and dismissed by so many people for so long, her response is gratifying. "Rage" *is* a magic word. "He has rages almost every day," I tell her. "Sometimes more than once a day. And they last for hours."

"Why hasn't Springbrook removed him?"

"Removed him?"

"Put him in foster care?"

I try to speak but the very idea has me speechless. What is she talking about? I'm not sending him away.

"We can get him into a foster home tonight." Dr. Alexandria resumes jotting notes on her pad.

This is moving too fast. I search frantically through the ruins of my mind for a way to backpedal.

"You said you're restraining him?" She continues without looking up, "You shouldn't be restraining him at home."

"They taught me how. Springbrook did," I falter. "Really, we don't need to send him away. I really think having him here during the day will help. Can we give this a try first?"

Dr. Alexandria peers at me over the top of her glasses for several awkward moments. She probably thinks I'm exaggerating about Devon's behavior. Why else would I now be refusing her help? My face and neck flush hot. Finally, she says, "We can see how it goes for a couple weeks, but we need to keep a close watch on this."

That afternoon, Devon proudly shows me his first points sheet from PHP: 100 points. My heart sinks. Tuesday and Wednesday—he earns full points for everything again. Thursday too. The reward for earning these points is being able to walk across the street to Eastside's cafeteria to eat lunch. Kids who don't earn their points have a lunch tray brought back to them by staff.

As Devon does well, day after day, my uncertainty grows. The glint in his eye is a constant reminder that the joke's on me. Aniya calls it, "the honeymoon period," and says sometimes it lasts a few days or even weeks. "Don't you worry. They'll be seeing the real Devon soon," she reassures me. But, by the end of the first week, Devon hasn't had a single behavioral problem.

If he flies through this program, if he doesn't choose to act up, he'll be discharged without getting better. I worry over this while washing dishes.

Sam leans across the counter and asks if he can go to the theater to watch *Dark Knight* with his friends.

"Can I go too?" Devon says, bouncing up and down.

"That's not a movie for little kids," I tell Devon. And to Sam, I say, "It's R-rated. And, I don't think it's safe."

"That freak's in jail," Sam blurts. "And it's PG-13." Sam is like a woodpecker against my temple, a strategy that often works, but not this time.

They're calling him the "Batman shooter" and I can't get the images out of my mind. How could no one have seen the warning signs? The bright orange hair. The crazed eyes. I only have to look at him to know he's mentally ill. The people in the theater didn't even duck or hide—they thought the gun shot sounds were part of the special effects.

My anxiety begins to careen out of control. I call Amias and Kayla from the playroom. They're cheerful, unlike Devon and Sam, who have resentment drawn all over their faces.

"You know the guy who shot up the movie theater in Colorado? The Batman movie?" I ask. I know they've caught bits and pieces of the story from the radio or TV news I'm always listening to. "That will probably never happen to you …"

"Yeah, exactly," Sam mutters.

"If there's ever a shooting where you are, I want you to drop to the floor and play dead. Don't get up … even when the shooting stops. Wait for the police."

Sam rolls his eyes. "Don't you want them to hide?"

"Hide if you can. Otherwise, drop to the ground and play dead."

Amias collapses, limbs splayed out on the tile floor and tongue lolling out of his mouth. He opens one eye. "Like this, Mom?"

"This isn't a joke," I say.

Devon rears back a leg. Kicks Amias in the side. Amias clutches his stomach. Rolls into a ball. Sam grabs Devon. Pulls him away.

36

On Monday at PHP, Devon refuses to write his spelling words. When he doesn't earn the associated points, he knows he won't be going to the cafeteria for lunch. He flips his desk. He dumps the contents of the trash can out on the floor. He runs around the classroom screaming. He kicks his teacher.

The nurse calls to notify me that Devon was restrained. Her words instantly conjure the image of someone bear hugging him from behind like I do—only they're calm, professional, and wearing scrubs. But what the nurse goes on to describe runs like ice water down my spine.

Devon had kicked and bucked as two staff members put him in a place called "the seclusion room." They pinned him down to a gurney and cuffed his ankles and wrists. Spit streamed down his chin as he shrieked and arched against the restraints. They fastened another strap around his stomach. Rearing his head back, he'd spit in one staff person's face.

Despite the nurse's business-like tone, my mouth is dry and my heart is thudding in my chest. In my imagination, I'm there, the one being restrained. I'm panicking. Terrified. Claustrophobic. I gulp for breath.

"He was in the restraint for 17 minutes before he'd calmed enough for us to release him." The nurse adds that they "had eyes on" him the whole time. From her tone I can tell this is meant to be reassuring, but I am far from reassured. I am horrified.

We end the call and I'm sick to my stomach. I try to be calm and rational. Try to reason with myself. At least Devon has a serious deterrent. He'll be good from now on, because there's no way he'll dare risk getting strapped to the restraint bed again.

...

Two days.

That's how long it takes.

37

Kayla is quite proficient at using my debit card to buy Skittles, Sprite, and salt and vinegar potato chips. She can't count cash, though. Or tell time. SCA Grammar has done testing and identified a math learning disability which qualifies her for an Individual Education Plan (IEP).

I'm familiar with IEPs because Devon has one too. His plan includes one-on-one, pull-out instruction, extra time on tests, and modified assignments. One thing I'd asked for was the ability for me, as his parent, to modify his assignments and their due dates. Given our struggles at home, I thought it would be helpful to have the option of reducing his math assignment from 30 problems to 20. Or the flexibility of turning his homework in on Monday instead of Friday to give us the weekend to work on it.

It was a hard-fought battle, but I did eventually get this accommodation added to his IEP. Unfortunately, I quickly found that Devon was more than happy to accept modified assignments from his teacher, but refused to accept any modifications from me. So, in the end, it was a non-starter and a major disappointment. I'm hopeful, though, that Kayla's IEP will be more useful because she wants to do well in school.

The IEP team is led by Mrs. Conner, a middle-aged woman with short spiky hair. The team also includes the assistant principal, Mrs. Larson and Kayla's teacher, Ms. Smith. When I arrive at the conference room, Mrs. Conner is already filling out forms on her laptop while projecting her screen onto the wall. Clutching my paper coffee cup, I place a box of assorted muffins from Panera on the table.

We begin by discussing accommodations for Kayla, including additional time on assignments and tests, and being able to mark in the test booklet instead of using a bubble sheet for her answers. After we agree on these, we watch Mrs. Conner tediously cut and paste information to various parts of the form. Ms. Smith picks out a blueberry muffin.

"How's Devon doing?" Mrs. Larson asks, fingering one of the heavy pearl earrings that is sagging from her earlobes. Nearing retirement age, she's wearing polyester pants, and a lime green sweatshirt embroidered with applique flowers.

"He had to go into partial hospitalization," I say, defensively. "He's not doing very well. They're having to restrain him a lot."

Mrs. Conner stops typing and looks up. "I have to tell you, when you told us Devon was having those awful problems at home, in his IEP meeting, I really didn't believe you."

I force a tight-lipped smile. I *knew* it.

She continues, "He's such a sweet boy. Then, well, when he punched those kids last year. I've never seen anything like it." I let her words hang in the air. In the awkward silence, she coughs, ducks her head, and begins typing again.

Mrs. Larson turns toward me, shielding our conversation from the others. "I have an adopted daughter too, and she has similar problems."

"Really?" I can't keep the surprise out of my voice.

She nods empathetically and tells me her story. It began when Katie was eight. She would scream and destroy things, and she lied about even silly things that didn't matter. Katie hid her behaviors from Mr. Larson, and he brought her candy every afternoon when he came home from work. Residual distress bleeds through Mrs. Larson's voice as she talks and I realize those aren't smile lines aging her face. They're the tracks of exhaustion and frustration.

When Katie reached her pre-teens, she stole, ran away, and became physically violent. Finally, she was admitted to a psychiatric facility. While Katie was there, Mrs. Larson became pregnant. One day, she was at the facility visiting Katie, and a worker pulled her aside. The worker whispered urgently, "Don't let her go back home. She'll end up killing your baby."

I put a hand over my mouth in horror. "What did you do?"

"Eventually she ran away from the facility and went to live with her birth mother in Michigan. She's an adult now. She calls from time to time. She's been in and out of jail. Living on the streets. Doing drugs."

Suddenly aware of the thick silence around us, I glance up. Mrs. Conner and Ms. Smith quickly avert their eyes as if they weren't eavesdropping. Mrs. Larson waves a hand apologetically. "Please, please continue, ladies."

The team focuses back on Kayla's IEP, but questions snap like firecrackers in my mind. What facility did Katie go to? How was she able to go live with her birth mom? Is that even legal? Are there really other kids like Devon?

38

Only a few short months after her breast cancer diagnosis, Mush passes away. Dr. Alexandria doesn't approve of us traveling to attend the funeral. I assure her that I have a plan for the long drive and that Devon will be perfectly fine once we're with Delano. I leave at 8:00 at night. There's cash tucked away in an envelope on the counter for the maid who I've hired to come in and clean while we're away. There was just no way for me to keep up with the housework on my own.

Devon snuggles beneath a yellow Pokémon throw. Sam grudgingly sits next to him, just in case. Amias shares his Red Power Ranger throw with Brandon, and Kayla's blue mermaid blanket drapes onto the floor with the tail fins spread out.

They're all comfy as I hand out the melatonin. It takes Amias and Kayla being told to look out their respective windows and not at each other, two-bathroom breaks, a few squabbles, and a pinching incident—then, finally, the little kids fall asleep.

Sam puts on a DVD and his headphones. I turn on my audiobook to help me stay awake through the night. Brené Brown's, *I Thought It Was Just Me,* washes over me like vinegar. Too much coffee too much adrenaline, too raw, and too vulnerable for self-help, her words quickly become too painful to listen to. I have to turn it off. I flip through the radio stations looking for NPR or some other impersonal talk radio station.

I make good time, but we still have a couple hours to go when the kids blink awake into the bright morning sun. I pop in the first DVD from my Redbox stack. With stops at Dunkin' Donuts and Subway, the last leg of the journey seems endless. We don't arrive in Toronto until mid-afternoon.

As I'd known he would, Delano keeps Devon close by as his special helper. It would be a major faux pas for one of his kids to misbehave in front of extended family. We stay in Mush's rent-controlled apartment. The kids share pull-out trundle beds. Delano and I sleep on blankets on the living room floor.

The funeral is a highly emotional affair. Mush was much

beloved and hundreds attend, dressed in better than their Sunday best and wearing grief like an extravagant accessory. During the ceremony, there's spontaneous singing and wailing. The soloist breaks down weeping for long minutes on stage before, physically supported by two family members, she resumes and finishes *Wind Beneath My Wings*. Several people fall out in the aisles of the church. Some faint. Delano takes our kids to the front to kiss their grandmother's face. He lifts Brandon and levers him into the casket so he can reach. I wince and wish that I'd known this was going to happen. I would have prepared them for it. Clearly, though, I'm an outsider to cultural nuance, and I'll have to pick up the pieces later.

Delano says he can't handle the drive home because it will hurt his back. And, besides, he can't deal with listening to me fussing at the kids. He helps me pack up, and I head home the next morning. After we cross the US border, we exchange our Redbox DVDs at a kiosk. I stop several times to nap in gas station parking lots, while Sam keeps look out so I can feel safe enough to rest. We arrive back in Charlotte in time to pick up Delano from the airport.

Delano complains about the laundry, irritated that I haven't kept up with it. He hasn't found anything to criticize about the cleanliness of the house, though, and I definitely won't be mentioning the maid. Folding a fresh load, he calls Devon over. "What that man called?" he asks.

Devon looks up at him curiously.

"That huge man who come to watch you …"

"Mr. Josh?"

"Uh huh. Mr. Josh. Your mother ever sends you away so her can talk to Mr. Josh alone?"

Outrage pulses through me.

Devon bobs his head.

"Did them go upstairs?" Delano demands, a half-folded towel suspended mid-air in his hands.

Devon nods solemnly. "Mommy told me to stay downstairs."

"How long was them up there?"

Devon looks at the floor, shifting his weight from one foot to the other. "I dunno."

He doesn't know because it's a big, fat lie. But Delano insists that Devon has no reason to lie about this and would not lie to him.

I have no fight left.

I call Springbrook and make up a lame excuse to cancel Josh's two scheduled afternoons for next week. Exhausted by the whirlwind trip to Canada, I lay on my bed to rest.

Kayla comes in with her *Babysitter's Club* book. She sits and reads, leaning against me, using me as her backrest. Her body is warm against my stomach and I drift into a restless sleep.

I startle awake with a pain running through my body. An electrical current pulses up my side.

I scream, but Kayla doesn't notice.

Am I asleep? This must be a dream. I try to relax, a technique that I've found helps me wake up when my body is paralyzed in sleep. That's what this has got to be, right? I will myself to float back into sleep. It's not real. It's not real.

Suddenly, I bolt awake and fling my arm into Kayla.

"Ow!" she cries out.

"Sorry," I pant, brushing my hands frantically over my body. I can feel the current burning on my skin and I have to get it off of me. But I can't find any wires or cords. It's long moments before the stinging across my skin fades away.

This is it. I am finally losing my mind.

As the weeks drag on, I curl into a ball and I watch myself sink into murkily black depression. I send all my calls to voicemail, even my mom and boss. Becky listens to my messages and returns the calls for me. She sorts my mail and makes doctor and dentist appointments for the kids.

She asks me for Brianna's phone number.

39

Springbrook gives up on us. Well, they don't say that, exactly. Just that they aren't making progress on Devon's therapeutic goals and are spending all their time managing crises. Also, Brianna and Becky had a long talk, and Brianna is now convinced I cannot manage Devon at home. PHP isn't going well, either. Devon is being restrained multiple times a week. Brianna has staffed the case with Dr. Alexandria, and both agencies agree that he needs to be in a higher level of care.

"PRTF stands for Psychiatric Residential Treatment Facility," Aniya tells me. We're sitting at my dining room table, and the kids are playing kickball in the backyard. The windows are open so we can watch them from inside while we talk. It's overcast and the thick air oozing through the windows is clammy. I hold myself tightly in my own arms around a shiver.

Aniya says, "They're facilities for kids with emotional, psychological, and behavioral problems. It's a highly structured and secure environment."

"Where do the kids sleep?"

"They have cottages with four or five kids and staff who are like house parents. They make it feel homey."

"What can he get there that he's not getting now?"

"The facilities are highly structured. Kids have to earn privileges and there are high expectations. Everything is earned so they learn quickly." She goes on to tell me how PRTFs are strict like a military camp.

My stomach churns. I run my fingers through my tangled hair, not remembering if I brushed it this morning. "But why does he need to live there?"

"Devon needs 24/7 supervision, and intensive treatment. We can't provide that outpatient." She puts a hand on my arm. "Keri, you know that."

At her touch I feel as brittle as a husk, as though I may break into a million pieces. I blink back tears feeling like a complete failure. "How long will he be there?"

"He should be able to come home after three months. No more than six."

By the time Delano arrives home from work, Aniya is gathering her things, and I'm ready to move forward with this plan. The kids are still playing outside and I've put on a warm sweatshirt. Full of optimism, I tell Delano about the PTRF plan.

"P-R-T-F," Aniya corrects, as I try to unscramble the acronym in my mind.

Delano shakes his head no. "Him not as bad as that."

Aniya turns to face him. "While you were in Canada, I was here almost every day to help your wife. He's not misbehaving when you're here, but I've seen it. I've been here for hours and hours."

Delano scoffs. "Him need parenting."

"Your wife can't control him. Your baby boy, Brandon, he's scared."

"Keri lets him do whatever him wants. Her doesn't want to parent him. That's the problem."

Angry tears streak down my face. "If you're going to quit your job and stay home to take care of him, fine. If not, we're doing this."

Delano shakes his head and mutters as I turn to walk Aniya out to her car. "You're doing the right thing," she says, as we walk down the driveway. "Even at PRTF, he's probably not going to get better."

"You don't think it will work?" I ask.

I watch her pick her words. "I've been doing this for 15 years. Kids like this, they don't get better."

"What should I do then?"

"To be honest, you're going to have your hands full getting him to 18 in one piece. He's still young, but he'll start racking up criminal charges pretty soon. I don't know how you're going to manage him." After a pause and no response from me, she asks, "Have you thought about sending him back?"

"Send him back? We legally adopted him. We ... we can't do that."

"I know they say you can't reverse an adoption, but I've worked with a few families who've done it. It's something you should think about." Aniya climbs in her car, starts it, and unrolls the window. Burger King bags are crumpled across the floor. In the cupholder there's a large soda cup with a straw poking out from the top. "He's not going to get better. Your other babies are suffering. You're suffering."

As I listen to the tick of Aniya's old car back down the driveway, it takes everything in me to summon the will to go back inside.

Part III
ANGER

40

Devon swivels in a padded chair while Amy, our chirpy intake coordinator, describes the PRTF program at New Hope Treatment Center with the breathless enthusiasm of a travel agent pitching an all-inclusive vacation package: hiking, bowling, swimming, gardening, drumming, yoga, crafts, movies. She arches perfectly contoured eyebrows at Devon. "Do you like chocolate cake?"

He bobs his head eagerly.

"We have the *best* chocolate cake here, and you can have as much as you like."

I want to smack the Cheshire cat grin off his face. This is not what I signed up for. "Devon is not here to be rewarded for his horrific behavior."

Amy's perky face freezes. She opens her mouth as if to say something, but then closes it, apparently at a loss for words.

I turn to face Devon, reminding him with my unflinching glare that I know the score, even if Amy doesn't. He stops spinning in the chair and hangs his head theatrically. I add, "He's here to learn to behave himself."

"O-kay ..." says Amy, judgment and condescension jam packed into those two syllables. "Let's see if our clinician is available." Reaching a hand to Devon, she leads us out of the room and down a long corridor with thin brown carpet. The yellow concrete block walls are reminiscent of an old school building with layers of paint caked over decades of mayhem.

Devon and I wait in the hall outside of an office while Amy has a hushed conversation inside. I eye the neon exit sign. Devon leans against a wall, curling his body in on itself and drops his chin. Seeing his melodramatic frown, I consider how he must seem to Amy: small, innocent, and vulnerable.

Amy returns with her colleague, a tall woman with long brown hair and blunt cut bangs. "Ms. Williams, I'm Beth." Her pale hand is chilly as she shakes mine. I follow her into the office and Amy ushers Devon away, probably for a piece of that chocolate cake.

The office is crammed tight with a desk, a tall filing cabinet, and two folding chairs. Coloring sheets and kids' drawings are taped to the walls, and a boxy computer monitor is on the desk. Beth sits and motions me to a chair.

I remain standing.

Beth says, "Amy tells me you have some concerns?"

"Devon is going to see this place as a reward for his bad behavior."

In that patronizing way therapists do, Beth doesn't respond. She fixes me with a patient gaze, which is incredibly awkward since we only met two seconds ago. Provoked by her silence, I finally blurt, "It's going to make him worse."

"Tell me more about that." Condescension drips from every word making me feel foolish. Stupid.

"He's having violent tantrums. Rages," I say.

Nonplussed, Beth lets the silence stretch.

I already don't like this woman. And I can tell she's judging me. "He's bad at home. So, we send him here to swim? To go to the movies? How does that make sense?" Then, like a car out of gas, I splutter, lurch, and stall out.

"Wow. You're *so* mad at him." Beth looks at me in a detached way like I'm a specimen from a science exhibit or something. "I don't understand what a little boy could have done for you to be so mad at him."

Choking on my outrage, I reach for the door knob. "I can't leave him here. I just can't—"

"Wait. Please." Beth motions me back. "Let me explain our philosophy."

With reluctance, I settle into the chair. I don't want to disappoint Brianna and Aniya after they worked so hard to get us in here.

Beth explains how, when a child experiences abuse or neglect at an early age, their brain does not develop normally. She tells me about the specialized therapeutic model they use at New Hope to treat this. "We'll identify underdeveloped areas of Devon's brain. Then, we'll use therapeutic activities and interventions to stimulate development of those areas." As she describes the program in more detail, I pick at the chapped skin on my lower lip and consider her words. "Let's do this," she says. "Leave Devon here, go home, and do some research on our model, then see how you feel."

Before deciding, I need a few minutes to think. Passing under the neon exit sign I pull out my cell phone and call Becky. My words come out around a sob. "He's going to get worse here …"

"You *have* to get him out of your house. Nothing else matters right now."

"But he'll see this as a reward."

"I don't care if it's Disney World." Becky says. "Leave him."

I return to Beth's office and tell her Devon can stay. For now. They've already taken Devon to his cottage and Beth explains that I won't be allowed to see or talk to him until after the 21-day orientation period. I stumble through the parking lot feeling disoriented, confused, and nauseous.

Later that evening, I sit in bed and pull up New Hope's website. I find the name of the therapeutic model they use and Google it. When a child experiences trauma, the areas of the brain that are affected depends on their stage of development at the time when the trauma occurs. Like a domino effect, if lower parts of the brain are underdeveloped, higher levels may not develop properly. Clinicians begin at the lowest level of under-developed function and work in the same sequence as normal brain development happens to try to stimulate the development to occur. Therapies include music, yoga, and drumming to target specific areas of the brain. I'm impressed. It's scientifically based. I like that.

Despite my misgivings, I'm cautiously optimistic. I'm going to give this a chance.

41

My body is rooted in place. I'm not sure that I can go in. Not exploring my culpability or letting down my shield of determination is how I've survived all these years. But I *have* to do this. Devon will be coming home in just three months. Steeling myself, I open the car door and go inside.

Marianne's specialties are anxiety, relationships, addictions, family, and parenting. She is older, with butterscotch hair, soft wrinkles, and blue eyes. I relax as we fill out paperwork. Name, address, emergency contacts, and insurance details. No feelings. I can do this. By the time that is finished, we have only 15 minutes left.

Marianne says, "Tell me about why you're here today."

Shrinking into the corner of the arm chair, I grasp for the right words. After a few false starts, like whitewater rapids, the story rushes out. By the time I've finished, I'm gulping out words. "I don't love him. There's something wrong with me. I don't know how to make myself love him." I take a tissue and jab at my eyes.

Marianne assures me that we can work through these issues together. We schedule a next appointment.

I leave to pick up the kids from school and drop Amias at soccer practice. As I park at the side of the field, my phone rings. It's Devon. "How are you?" I ask, waving Amias out of the car. "I'll be there soon," I mouth to him. Brandon leaps from the car to play on the swing set, but Kayla stays sitting next to me.

Devon's voice is cheerful. "When are you going to visit me?"

"I'll have to ask Ms. Beth about that, but I'm sure soon. How do you like it there? Have you made friends?"

"Can you bring me McDonald's?" As he dictates his order to me like I'm a drive-thru attendant, I'm suddenly overwhelmed by the need to get away from his voice. "My call days are Mondays and Wednesdays," he tells me. We talk until his 10 minutes are up.

"I'll call you tomorrow," I promise.

"Don't forget McDonalds. A number two and a number four. No, a number six." He hangs up without saying goodbye.

I call Devon's cottage the next evening and can hear the worker's muffled voice saying, "It's your mom."

Then Devon: "I don't wanna talk to her."

"You sure? She wants to talk to you."

Devon doesn't come to the phone. My nerves snap and tingle. He's ten. How is this his choice?

...

I'm sitting in Marianne's office listening to her calming voice, "Inhale. One, two, three, four, five. Exhale. Five, four, three, two, one." My eyes are closed as I try to re-learn how to relax. Simple, but I've been so busy surviving that I've forgotten how to breathe. "This is something you can do anywhere," Marianne says. "Riding in your car, sitting at your desk, anytime you are feeling anxious."

Marianne asks about my relationship with Devon and I slip my flip flops off and curl my feet beneath me. Have I ever felt attached to him? Am I attached to my other kids? What's my relationship like with my own mother? What is it like when Devon is living at home? How do I feel now that he's gone?

Great. I feel great, and that's the problem. I hide my new candy pink acrylic nails under my thighs. Since Devon's left, I've had my eyebrows waxed too, into a sophisticated arch. Kayla calls them my "angry eyebrows," but I think they make me look younger. I've started reading a novel and bought tickets to take the kids to the circus.

Even so, I'm not enjoying this "new life." New Hope is a mistake, and it's going to come back to bite me worse than before. Devon has won, and he's going to be impossible for me to manage. He's escaped consequences. In my daydreams, he taunts me as he skips to the pool surrounded by boys and girls in bright swimsuits, chocolate frosting smeared around his mouth. "It doesn't make sense. If he ends up in juvenile detention, he sure won't be playing in a pool or eating chocolate cake."

Marianne patiently listens to my diatribe. Then she asks, "Have you thought of trying some medication for your anxiety?"

I haven't.

She tells me I've developed PTSD, based on my symptoms of irritability, hypervigilance, severe anxiety, social avoidance, and sleep disturbances. I brush this off—PTSD from being a mom?—but Becky makes an appointment for me with my primary care doctor to request an antidepressant.

42

Powder donuts are Devon's favorite.

    Pro: Beth will think I'm a good mom

    Con: I can't reward Devon for his bad behavior

    Pro: I really need Beth to think I'm a good mom

I leave the shop with my usual coffee and a powder donut in a waxy white bag. By the time I reach New Hope, I've changed my mind. I throw the bag in the trash can as I walk into the main building.

Devon is already in Beth's office. "Hi," he says, mopey and hanging his head.

I bristle at the obviously contrived drama, glad I didn't bring him that donut after all. "What's the matter?"

He twiddles his thumbs round and round like roosters chasing each other, but doesn't answer.

Beth prompts: "Devon, why don't you tell Mom about your concern? The one we talked about earlier."

He still doesn't respond or look up.

Beth speaks for him. "Devon has had a few rough days because he's been trying to process his hurt feelings over you not calling him like you promised."

I straighten in my chair. "I called every night." I count it out on my fingers. "Thursday, Friday, Saturday, Sunday, and Monday I called. You refused to come to the phone. Isn't that true, Devon?" I demand.

He doesn't respond.

"Are you sure staff didn't tell you that your mom was on the phone?" Beth's voice is as soothing as aloe vera on a sunburn. "Maybe you didn't hear them or got confused?"

"Yeah. I … I was confused," he mumbles.

Beth nods understandingly, but I snap, "That's not true. There's nothing confusing about it."

"I didn't know they was asking me to come to the phone," he insists.

I let out an uncouth snort and flop back into my chair.

Beth swivels away from me and toward Devon. "Why don't you

tell your mom about how you've been using your coping skills."

"I been taking deep breaths and walks with staff."

"How has that been working for you?" Beth asks.

"Good, 'cept yesterday."

"Let's talk about that," Beth says.

He gnaws on the skin around his thumb nail.

Beth says, "Unfortunately, Devon's negative behaviors disrupted the classroom. He was throwing things and his peers had to be removed for their safety. But, I'm so proud of him." She accentuates the statement as if punctuating it with three exclamation points. "He showed wonderful self-control. He stopped engaging in negative behaviors in time to go with the class to swim and didn't miss the rest of his day."

She can't be serious.

Devon glances at me with obvious trepidation.

I ask, "He went swimming? What was his consequence?"

"We don't consequence kids here, Ms. Williams. We focus on rewarding good behaviors."

Devon has his eyes fixed on the floor, but in the profile of his face I see a smile round his cheeks.

Beth must read the dismay and shock on my face because she motions for Devon to stand. "Say goodbye to Mom now. It's time to go back to class."

A thousand ants race under my skin as I attempt to mentally regroup while Beth is gone. She returns and fixes her gaze on me and waits. "You know he'll just do it again," I splutter, half way to hysteria. I can barely string words together. "Now that he knows he can. All he learned is that he can misbehave when he doesn't want to do something, then stop being bad when he wants to do something else."

"If we consequence kids, it's all we'll be doing and we won't be able to do therapy," she says. "When Devon has an incident, the goal is to move on as quickly as possible. Nothing is gained by giving him a consequence."

"How does he transition home then? I can't ignore the bad behavior and not give him consequences at home. That might work here, but not at home."

"As we address the underlying issues, the negative behaviors will diminish. No child is bad on purpose." Her tone is shaming. And, I am shamed.

I mull over the family therapy session as I drive home. It seems that Beth didn't know who to believe about the phone calls: me or

Devon. Stopping at Walgreens, I pick out a small notebook with a pink polka dot cover and snappy elastic clasp. Waiting in line to check out, I claw at my forearms wanting to peel my skin off. I take out my bottle of antidepressants and swallow a pill. Not remembering if I took one yesterday, I swallow another.

I don't have to wait long to christen my new notebook. That evening the nurse calls and I write the date and time and take notes as she speaks:

> New Hope nurse call—Devon throwing tantrum for over 3 hours in quiet room. Nurse asking permission for PRN.

I don't know what the acronym, PRN, stands for, but Devon has had them before. A nurse at Eastside once explained to me that PRNs are injections of calming medications, like Benadryl.

"What upset him?" I ask.

"The trigger seems to have been his family therapy session this morning," the nurse from New Hope says.

They're blaming *me* for his meltdown? I add to my notes:

> Trigger: Mom

43

I pull onto the long, wooded drive and follow the winding road to the main parking lot of New Hope's campus. Devon has had time to settle in and this is our first family visit. "You need to act like you want to see Devon," I say to a chorus of groans from the kids.

We walk down a sidewalk through the grassy courtyard surrounded by squat brick buildings. It's a sunny Saturday morning, but no one is outside except for us. We pass a gangly metal swing set, benches, and a basketball hoop atop a small concrete pad. The "cottages" are small rectangular buildings each occupied by up to eight kids. Some are co-ed, while others are single sex. Each cottage has two staff members on duty 24/7. They call this level of care "line of sight" supervision because the kids are always in view of staff. At night, when the kids sleep, the staff checks on them every 15 minutes.

The first cottage that we approach is called "The Bee Hive." I laugh and wonder who thought that name was a good idea. Amias runs ahead to read the sign on the next building. He calls, "Mom, this one is 'Camp Carefree.'"

Devon greets us at the door of Camp Carefree wearing a magician's top hat and cape, and I assume they're part of a dress up collection *for preschoolers*. I have zero patience for how this place is coddling his immaturity. Behind Devon stands a young man with a goatee. "I'm Mr. Desmond," he says, holding the door open. He's willowy and wearing low slung jeans and a tee-shirt.

Devon leads us down a narrow hallway, which opens into a common area. The rustic smell reminds me of that timeshare we stayed in when we took the kids on a mountain vacation a couple years ago. There's a soggy 1970's era, avocado sofa, and, along the opposite wall, a galley kitchen flanks a rectangular table and chairs.

"You wanna see a magic trick?" Devon asks Brandon, waving a chintzy plastic wand in the air. Brandon jumps for it.

"Where are the other kids?" I ask, scrunching my eyebrows into a question mark. I quickly smooth my features, remembering how Sam says the wrinkles between my eyes look like a Wi-Fi signal.

"We have to put the other clients in their bedrooms when visitors are here for their privacy," Mr. Desmond says.

Devon leads us to his bedroom, beaming as if it's the Hilton. A tree blocks the window and obscures most of the sunlight. There's a basic twin bed pushed against one wall, built in shelves, and a five-drawer bureau. The floor is painted concrete slab.

Sam says, "Nice. This is real nice, Man."

"Why don't we go outside," I suggest, guiding them out of the room and toward the door. Devon leaves his magician accouterments on the table. Back outside, the boys play basketball while Kayla and I watch from a bench. They whoop and holler. Sam is too competitive to take it easy, even on brothers half his age. He dribbles, easily dodging them and making basket after basket. Brandon hangs on Sam's arm and soars through the air when he shoots.

I look at my cell phone, knowing I have to stay at least an hour for appearances. The boys sweat. Kayla grows antsy. "Is it time to go yet?" she whines every few minutes. We stay for exactly one hour then walk Devon back to his cottage. He jogs to a shelf in the common room and returns with some coloring pages for us: Care Bears and rainbows with pots of gold. What happened to the notion that kids rise to expectations?

As we leave, Devon stands at the door with the top hat back on his head. "Thanks for coming," he calls, waving madly as if we're leaving a tea party, not a psych facility.

...

"The kids didn't want to visit him," I tell Marianne.

She nods thoughtfully and sets down her pad and pen on the low table between us. "How do you think living with Devon has been for your other children?"

I picture Brandon cowering behind my legs as I twist the marble elephant bookend out of Devon's hands: *Afraid*. Amias sobbing because Devon refused to get in the minivan and he's missing his soccer game: *Angry*. Kids at school whispering about their brother breaking a window: *Embarrassed*. "He terrorizes them."

Marianne nods letting me think aloud. She's like a comfortable grandma.

"He keeps them from having a normal life. They miss sports games and birthday parties." I taught Amias to read when he was four, but I haven't had time to teach Brandon. Another parenting failure. Sam is in his last semester of high school, but he may not pass his classes. I take his online math quizzes for him. I'm going to give his teachers gift cards for Christmas, hoping they'll feel too guilty to fail him. Yes, my lofty parenting ideals are long gone.

I rub at my temples as my angst mounts. "I keep thinking how odd Brandon's anxiety is. Amias was never like that. Maybe it's from the stress of living with Devon? He was around all that chaos from the time he was born."

Marianne nudges the tissue box toward me. "If you think about it, he was exposed even in the womb. It makes sense that he'd be anxious and hyper-vigilant."

I've known the last few years have been unpleasant for the kids, but she's right. It's been so much worse than "unpleasant." Guilt wrings my heart like a dishrag. Never again. Whatever it takes. I will never make them live like that again.

Marianne and I spend the rest of the session discussing practical ways I can help Amias, Kayla, and Brandon heal from their trauma: listening to and accepting their feelings, creating a stable and safe environment, and not forcing them to spend time with Devon until they're ready. At the end of our session, Marianne suggests counseling for the kids and jots down the names of three child therapists.

Walking toward my car, I notice a missed call from my mom and several new work emails. Ignoring them, I scroll through the browser on my phone looking up the first therapist on the list.

My phone vibrates. "New Hope" flashes, stealing away the screen and my attention. "I'm calling to inform you about an incident Devon had today," the New Hope nurse says in a clipped voice. "He didn't want to participate in a group activity with his peers. When staff intervened, he kicked and hit them. Then he took a jump rope and wrapped it around his neck."

Her words knock the wind out of me and I have to lean against my car to steady myself.

44

"Did you go to the circus without Devon?" Beth looks at me quizzically.

We did. The kids ate popcorn and face paint smeared around their smiles while they watched the clowns, acrobats, and animals.

"I don't understand why Devon wouldn't have been included in the circus trip," Beth persists. She looks at me, no doubt purposely allowing the silence to grow uncomfortable.

"We haven't had any off-campus visits yet," I hedge. Her office is too warm.

"Yes ..." she draws out the word as if she's trying to draw out awareness in me of what a bad mother I am. "But you could have scheduled the circus trip for when you could take him with you. He is part of the family."

"Honestly, if Devon was there, we wouldn't have gone," I huff out. "I could never have trusted him to behave."

"I don't think that's true and I know he would really have enjoyed the circus." Beth gives me her perfected look of disapproval.

I return a look of complete incredulity.

Stalemate.

Devon comes in for the second half of the session scuffing his sneakers. They're torn. "These aren't even two months old," I say. Taking a closer look, I can see they're not torn at all. The cuts are straight as if they were made with scissors.

Beth shrugs one shoulder. "They play hard. What were you playing yesterday? I saw a bunch of you out there. Was it Capture the Flag?"

I stare into Devon's dark eyes and he stares back. It's a game. He knows it. And I know it. But Beth has moved on, unaware or unconcerned. "So, tell us how your week has been?" she says.

"Pretty good."

"Let's look at your notes." Beth swivels her chair to face the desk and pulls up Devon's electronic record. "It looks like you had an issue on Monday with peers. Then on Thursday you were kicking Ms. Tina?"

I pull a notebook paper with my grocery shopping list from my purse. It's folded in half and I fan myself with it. I glance up at the dusty air conditioning vent as Beth continues. "Looks like over the weekend, you met with Dr. Bradley and you asked him for some medication for enuresis."

"You're wetting your bed again?" I interrupt, looking at Devon wide-eyed. I thought he'd stopped that nonsense a while ago.

Beth confirms, "According to the notes, once or twice a week."

"He does *not* need medication for that. He wets on purpose."

As though she's got the final word, Beth says, "A lot of children have issues with bedwetting. It's not uncommon. This medication will help."

I shake my head no.

"If *he* thinks the medication will help," she tries.

I shape my lips into an emphatic, "No." To make sure there's no misunderstanding, I add, in slow enunciation, "I do not give my consent for Devon to take that medication."

Beth presses her lips together, obviously not pleased with my response.

Several days later, I make a special trip to New Hope to drop off a pair of Timberlands. Luckily Devon is still fitting in the less expensive big kid's size. The receptionist calls Beth to the front desk, and I hand her the boots. "They're expensive, but indestructible," I say.

She nods. "Certainly, these should last."

"When Devon rips them up, and he will, I will *not* buy him new ones. I will duct tape them."

Beth indulges me with a nod.

45

Beth says nothing. What can she say? She can't possibly chalk the flopping Timberland boot sole up to "wear and tear." Even I have no idea how he managed this level of damage. I pull a roll of silver duct tape from my purse and wrap as Devon shoots Beth distressed looks.

We discuss Devon's week, and toward the end of the session, Beth mentions that his enuresis is getting worse. He's now wetting his bed every night.

"I wake up like that," Devon blurts, defensively, glancing from me to Beth.

Beth would like me to reconsider the meds. She all but insists. From her disapproving look, I know that, by refusing, I'm risking her reporting me for being negligent. I plow ahead anyway. If I allow her to usurp my authority like this, I will never be able to manage Devon when he moves back home.

I point to the calendar on the wall and tap on it to draw Devon's attention. "Listen to me. If you wet your bed even one more time between now and December 24th, you will not be spending the night at home on Christmas Eve. I'll pick you up Christmas morning instead. Do you understand? Start behaving yourself, or there will be no overnight home visit."

Beth looks on disapprovingly. "I think that's enough for today."

I narrow my eyes at Devon and reiterate, "That's four weeks. Not once. Not even one more time."

...

December passes uneventfully, and Devon doesn't wet his bed again. Not a single time. He also behaves in class and in the cottage. Beth is so encouraged by this progress that she begins to discuss him moving back home. I start to make preparations too.

My father comes to visit for Christmas. The kids call him "Papa." He has a round belly and big white beard. I take him with me to pick up Devon on Christmas Eve and as we walk through the courtyard,

I plop a Santa's hat on his head. The kids in the cottage, who for some unexplained reason aren't sequestered in their rooms as usual, crowd around him and shout, "It's Santa."

"Ho, Ho, Ho. Merry Christmas," he says, and gives Devon a bear hug.

We walk back towards the car and I shiver in the chilly afternoon air. Devon chatters away, telling Papa all about the fun things that he gets to do at New Hope. He's the best basketball player there, he does pet therapy with dogs, and they've planted a winter garden.

Back home, we go next door to Becky's house, which is where we have celebrated holidays for years. The last time we decorated our own house for Christmas—and really, calling it "decorating" is an overstatement—the kids cut out a paper "tree" and drew ornaments on it with markers. I taped it to the living room wall. The kids were delighted by their handiwork, but seeing it made me feel pathetic.

Decorating for Christmas at Auntie Becky's house has always been part of our holiday tradition. Handmade decorations both our kids have made over the years hang on the tree. Devon hurries over to look for the glitter-covered walnuts, bread dough wreaths, and other ornaments that he's made. They're all marked with his initials. He collects "his" ornaments and hangs them jumbled together off of one branch.

As is our tradition, we watch *VeggieTales: Saint Nicholas: A Story of Joyful Giving!* The cousins line their shoes around the tree, seven pairs in all. The line starts with Brandon's size 4T and ends with Sam's hulking sneakers. Devon proudly straightens his brand-new Jordans along the line. They're a pair that Beth pulled out of the items donated to New Hope and gave to Devon to replace his damaged Timberlands. Three weeks later, they're still in perfect shape. In the spirit of St. Nick, Becky and I will fill the shoes with stocking stuffers and oranges after the kids go to bed.

Jason and I sit at the dining room table working on a Peanuts Christmas puzzle while Becky makes messy, elaborate gingerbread trains with the kids at the other table. By the time we head home for the night, the kids look as if they have been dipped in frosting and showered with sprinkles.

On Christmas morning, we go next door to open "stockings," the St. Nick shoes, and have a yummy pancake breakfast with real maple syrup that Papa brought us from back home in Vermont. Then we open presents. Jacob and Abby huddle around one large box, and my four little kids around another. "Ready. Set. Go," Jason yells, balancing a video camera to capture them tearing through the wrapping paper.

"It's a You," Jacob shouts gleefully.

"It's a Wii." Sam corrects, and rolls out of his chair laughing.

They unwrap games—*Super Mario Bros.*, *Just Dance*, *Wii Sports*—a controller for each of them, and other accessories. Sam gets a new phone. Kayla and Abby open karaoke players. Devon, Amias, and Jacob unwrap remote control cars.

Devon gives me a mason jar snow globe that he made at New Hope. There's a snowman and tree inside. "This is beautiful," I say, lightly shaking it and watching the "snow" swirl. "I love it," I tell him.

I'd reviewed the New Hope "Allowed Personal Items" list and bought a few extra gifts for Devon: socks, tee-shirts, a *Diary of a Wimpy Kid* book set, a football, and a Magic 8 Ball. As he packs them into an oversized gift bag to take back with him to New Hope, I say, "You'll be able to play with the Wii and your remote-control car when you come on home visits." He pastes on a smile, but a shadow settles like a death pallor over his face.

Standing in the kitchen sipping coffee, I nudge Becky's side and gesture toward Devon. We have a whispered conversation about him feeling upset and about me feeling guilty. Even so, I know it's a lesson he needs to learn. There are consequences to bad behavior. He's at New Hope because he refuses to behave himself. If he wants his presents, he needs to make better choices so he can move back home.

It's getting late. I set my mug on the kitchen counter and go in search of my purse so I can get Devon back to New Hope by check-in time. I take a few minutes to pick up some of the torn wrapping paper strewn across the floor. I find my purse which is hanging on the back of one of the chairs that's still circling the Christmas tree.

As I turn the corner into the kitchen, I see Devon, with his head angled oddly over my coffee mug. He jerks upright. A strand of spit strings from my mug to his lips.

46

I stumble to the trash can. Gripping the edges, I vomit violently. My mouth gapes open but the contractions in my throat prevent me from taking in any air. I feel as though I might suffocate before the gasping breaths come. When I'm finally able to stand, I'm alone in the kitchen. My coffee mug sits, seemingly undisturbed, on the countertop. Had I come into the kitchen a few seconds later, I would have never known. I would have … I begin to retch again.

I rush out of the room looking for Sam. He's setting up his new cell phone. "My coffee," I say, fighting to breathe without gagging. He doesn't look up. I can't get the words out, so I tap on his arm. "Please. I need you. to. throw it. away. In the trash. The mug. The mug too."

"What's wrong with it?" Sam asks.

"I can't." My throat twists. "I can't talk about it. Please." I consciously force the image of Devon spitting in my coffee from my mind, and I concentrate to actively refuse to let it surface again.

Once I have regained a meager measure of composure, Papa and I drive Devon back to New Hope. Devon rides in the back seat and caresses his Magic 8 Ball. "Can it really tell the future?"

"Let's see," says Papa. "Is it going to snow?"

Devon shakes the ball. "Doubtful," he reads.

"Well, there you go, Kid," Papa says, chuckling.

Devon asks, "Where are my other Christmas presents?"

"It has to be a yes or no question," Papa explains.

After a pause Devon asks, "Will I get more presents for my Christmas?" He shakes. Shakes again. Smiles and reads, "It is certain."

The next day, when the staff calls, I take notes:

> Fit for 3 hours. Shredded books, slammed 8 ball on the floor until it broke. Stuffed sock down his throat to choke himself. Urinated on himself and his bed

47

At Devon's January Child and Family Team (CFT) meeting, Beth runs through the same questions she asks every month, starting with, "What's going well for you?"

>Devon: I'm usin' my coping skills. I was behavin' most days.
>Beth: What's not going well for you?
>Devon: I get upset. Sometimes.
>Next, we go through Devon's goals:

```
Goal 1: Oppositional
WHAT: Devon will increase compliance
AEB following directions and staying
on task within 2 prompts.
```

Devon's plan has five goals like this. In past CFTs, I've restated them in child-appropriate language, like: "That means an adult shouldn't have to tell you more than two times to do something before you do it." A few months in, I've realized that these CFTs are a formality, a required monthly meeting and paperwork to check the boxes to qualify for Medicaid. So much of the "process" is just that—jumping through hoops. So, I relax back into my chair and let Beth proceed.

Under the "How" this goal will be accomplished section, Devon isn't even listed. This is true to New Hope's philosophy. Circumstances and the people around Devon—mostly me—are to blame for his behaviors. Therefore, he's not responsible for any of the action items to change them:

```
Psychiatrist will provide medication
management; parents will participate
in    family    therapy   and    follow
clinical recommendations; PRTF will
provide    NMT    activities     like
drumming, swimming, and yoga.
```

Devon will do nothing to help himself. He will watch and laugh, making fools of us all.

Beth adds this month's update:

```
Structure of PRTF is working for
Devon. He is learning coping skills
to manage his mood. Mom is actively
participating in Devon's treatment.

What's not working is he continues
to exhibit anger outbursts, threats
to kill, and physical violence. He
must reduce these significantly to
return to the home setting.
```

Beth has updated Devon's diagnoses, as well. I clamp my mouth shut when I see that she's added enuresis. I cannot understand why she is determined to give him a medical "out" for his defiance and stubbornness. She insists that no child purposely wets their bed or would purposely humiliate themselves like that.

It's futile to argue with her.

She's also added Reactive Attachment Disorder (RAD) to his diagnoses, which she explains in more detail after dismissing Devon back to his cottage. The acronym RAD—pronounced like someone would say, "That's a *rad* skateboard"—occurs when a child doesn't bond with their caregiver early in life. They're unable to attach to others. They might stiffly refuse hugs or discourage physical affection with poor hygiene. When I look at Beth without responding, clearly unconvinced, she adds, "You need to understand that no child wants to be bad. Devon isn't doing any of this on purpose. You need to show him you love him and accept him no matter what he does."

"That may all be true," I say carefully, "but he is also being bad. When he came home for Christmas, he ..." my hand flutters to my mouth at the memory. I squeeze my eyes closed and try to make myself disassociate. I forcibly clear all images from my mind so I can say it. I picture a large field of flowers and don't allow myself to think about the words I'm saying as I shudder them out, "He ... spit ... in my coffee."

Beth crosses her legs and inclines her head to one side with a "come-on-now-stop-being-ridiculous" look on her face. "How do you *know* that he did that," she says, very slowly, and it feels like an accusation.

"I saw him do it," I insist.

Beth says, "Well, let's try to look at this from Devon's perspective. You'd just given him nice Christmas presents. I'm sure he felt badly because he didn't have anything to give you. Could this have been his way of giving you a gift?"

I blink rapidly. She can't be serious. I begin shaking my head, but she holds up a hand to stop me from objecting. Ignoring her, I insist, "He knows that's disgusting."

Beth tucks her chin and pinches the bridge of her nose. "Children with attachment issues only want to love and be loved back. Devon is so desperate to please you that he would want to give you any gift he could. He has no money or way to get you a gift. This is all he had. Why don't you do a little research on RAD and we can discuss this more next time."

Reeling, I stand to leave. Beth asks me if I'll be picking Devon up on Saturday morning for this week's home visit and I confirm that I will. Picking my purse up off the floor, I pause. "There is one other thing I wanted to talk to you about. I sent Devon's birth mom, Sarrah, a Christmas card with pictures of the kids."

"That was kind of you."

I awkwardly shrug off her words. "She wrote back and asked if she could write to them. I'm not sure what to think of that."

Beth says, "I'd let her write the letters. You can always save them for when the kids get older. You'll have to decide what's best for your daughter, but with Devon's attachment issues, let's not mention this to him."

I do as Beth asks and don't tell Devon, but, increasingly, I don't think that's the right choice for Kayla.

...

Inspired with energy that I've lacked for years, I bring home stacks of paint swatches and hold them against the walls. I decide on a soft green called "April Showers" for the living room and a deep pink called "Azalea" for the family room. Everyone helps. Soon, the entire downstairs is fresh and bright. There's one hole in the living room wall that is too large to patch. I "borrow" a large metal butterfly from Becky's loft wall and hang it, positioned so its wings hide the damage.

Sam scavenges the attic for discarded picture frames. Using white spray paint, I upcycle them into an eclectic set. I sort through digital pictures, find all my favorite snapshots, and order prints—careful to make sure there's exactly the same number of pictures for each of the kids.

The best photos, the ones where the kids' happy laughter skips and dances from the frames, are from the years right after we moved to Charlotte. They're from our vacation weekends in Myrtle Beach, speed birthdays, of all the cousins biking, swimming, roller skating, and exploring the science museum. Of our vacation in Tennessee. Of all those afternoons at the park.

By the time we've finished, our new picture wall circles the foyer and stretches from the bottom of the stairway up to the top and the transformation of our home is fathoms deeper than paint and picture frames.

48

"How much did you buy me for?" Kayla asks.

"I didn't buy you, Silly." I run a small section of her springy curls through the flat iron. Steam floats off the metal, leaving her hair too hot to touch. I use the comb to separate the next thin section. The trick is to use protectant serum and straighten painstakingly small sections of hair.

"But you had to buy me."

I smile, thinking she must be kidding, but she's not.

"For real. How much did you buy me for?"

"People don't buy children. Why would you think that?"

"Yes. You can pick them out online like at the puppy pound."

I think of a website like AdoptUS. Seeing it through her eyes, I guess it might seem crass like "adopting" a pet. I grope for a way to explain. "Well, if parents have a little boy, they might want another boy close in age. Or they might want to adopt a girl. But the kids aren't for sale."

As I pin another section of her hair up, Kayla peels the top off a strawberry yogurt. "It's true. They are for sale," she says knowingly. "I read about it in my book." She spoons a scoop of yogurt into her mouth.

"What book is that?"

"*Caging Animals* ...? Something like that." She shrugs. "We're reading it in class."

"What's it about?"

"This kid is in an orphanage. He goes to foster homes. They don't feed him and lock him in closets."

"What does that have to do with buying kids?" I ask.

"Parents who can't have kids of their own go to the orphanage and pay money to buy one."

"Hmmm. I'll have to get a copy of that book and read it," I say. Steam hisses as I flat iron the short curly hairs around her face. Kayla sits perfectly still, no doubt remembering the handful of times when I've accidentally nicked her skin on these tricky edges. I lean back to inspect my work. "All done," I tell her. "And, I didn't buy you, Silly."

My phone rings and I answer, putting it on speaker as I begin to clean up all the hair styling paraphernalia. "I got me a lawyer," Devon says.

"You what?" I ask, not sure what he could mean.

"I met with her today."

"You met with a lawyer?"

"Yup," he says, confidence brimming through the phone line. "We're gonna talk to the judge and he'll let me come home."

...

Beth heaves a sigh as I pull out my notebook and read my notes from a casual conversation that I had with Mr. Desmond when I picked up Devon for his weekend visit.

> Devon didn't want to participate in activity / jump rope / tried to strangle himself. Staff intervened / kicked and hit them / tried to strangle himself. Also: bit a kid's neck in a fight earlier this month!!! He has screaming outbursts whenever he's told no

I look up. "Why hasn't anyone called me about any of this?" I ask. Staff is required to report any incident, all PRNs, and restraints to parents.

"Well, let's see." Beth scrolls through the daily logs on her computer, but she doesn't find corresponding incident reports. "Sometimes staff get busy and forget to fill out the paperwork," she says. "I'll follow-up with them."

I tuck my pink notebook away, trying to ignore how her eyes follow my movements. "Devon called me earlier this week and said something about going to a judge and having a lawyer?"

Beth nods. "All the residents see a judge every three months. That's their legal right to contest being committed. The judge comes here on a Saturday, so we don't need to transport anyone to the courthouse."

"I don't understand. What do you mean it's his legal right? I'm his mother."

Beth says, "Well, in Devon's case it is a technicality. The process is meant for adults who are involuntarily committed. It allows them to explain to a judge why they feel they should be discharged. In the case of minors like Devon, the judge will follow the recommendations of our psychiatrist."

"So, why does he have a lawyer then?"

"Again, that's just part of the process. It's his legal right."

I shift in my seat and narrow my eyes. "Okay, but that doesn't make sense. If Devon thinks there's a chance the judge will discharge him, he won't cooperate with his treatment."

Beth gives a half shrug. "There's nothing we can do about it. It's his legal right."

I sit back in my chair, stunned at how counterproductive this is. "He's also gaining a lot of weight," I say. "I spoke to the nursing staff over the weekend, and they say he eats three or four servings at meals and sometimes ends up throwing up."

"We don't make an issue of food here," Beth says, dismissively.

"Even if it's not healthy? He has an issue with gorging and throwing up. He's been doing it for years."

"That's just not something we're willing to make an issue out of here."

"It's not just about gaining weight. Throwing up like that can damage his throat and teeth."

Beth deftly pivots. "Have you had a chance to research RAD since we last met?"

I nod slowly, shifting gears. "Yes, I did and it does seem to fit Devon," I tell her. In fact, my own research on RAD uncovered far more than what Beth had explained to me. Kids with RAD can have extreme behavioral issues. They fly into rages, destroy property, hoard food, manipulate adults, have violent outbursts, and weaponize their feces, urine and spit. Some of the stories that I read were frightening.

This reminds me of something else that's been on my mind. "Have you been following the news about the Sandy Hook school shooting?" I ask.

Beth's eyes wince. "I can't imagine how hard it is for the families. The children were young. First graders, weren't they?"

I nod. Just before Christmas, a young guy killed 20 children and six adults at an elementary school. I've been unable to tear myself away from the news coverage. My mind is an echo chamber for the questions of the news commentators. How did this happen? Why didn't his mother get him help?

I ask Beth, "Did you see the blog post, *'I am Adam Lanza's Mother?'*

She shakes her head.

"It was written by a woman who has a kid who is violent. She's afraid her son might grow up to do the same thing." I pause. "It's gone viral." I take a deep breath. "I can't help but wonder the same thing about Devon."

"Devon is nothing like that," she says, firmly reprimanding me. "Right now, we need to focus on the relationship between you and him. That's what is causing him to act out. Your love and acceptance are what he needs. Then he won't need to exhibit these negative behaviors."

My face flames. "I can't force feelings I don't have. I don't think it's all me either. I'm attached to my other kids." I know that I sound too defensive, but I can't stop myself. "I'm one of those parents who didn't use strollers and always had my babies in my arms. Brandon *still* sleeps in my bed. I'm as attached to Kayla as if she is my birth child. If I'm the problem, how would that be possible?"

Beth holds up her palms. "I don't know of any other parent who's here for every meeting, every appointment, every therapy session. You do love Devon. You just don't *feel* it."

If only that was true. I have a deep sense of responsibility for him, absolutely, but that's not love. I know exactly what mother-love feels like because I have it for my other kids. I've tried so hard to force those feelings for Devon, but they just won't come.

When I don't respond, Beth says, "A couple weeks ago, you told me a story about eating cereal after Devon because you were concerned about his feelings. Do you remember that?" She arches her eyebrows, and I nod. "That was a big deal for someone like you, who gets grossed out easily. That told me how much you do love him."

I'm unable to form words around the guilt and shame.

She continues, "What I'd like to do is begin some therapy to work on your attachment. Devon is missing key bonding experiences. One session we'll have you sit in a rocking chair and rock him like a baby. Another session we'll have you spoon feed him like a toddler."

I barely manage the words, "I'm willing to try anything that might work." In truth, I feel incredibly conflicted because I can't imagine ever spoon feeding and rocking an 11-year-old.

…

"Beth makes it sound as simple as slotting memories into folders to fill gaps that are missing in the filing system in Devon's mind. That just doesn't make sense to me…" Marianne sips herbal tea and regards me pensively as I tell her about Devon's new RAD diagnosis and the proposed attachment therapy. "I've tried so hard with Devon, but I just don't have those feelings." I say. "With Kayla, it wasn't instant love—it took time, but I feel that way about her now. I don't know what to do to fix myself with Devon."

"Could this be a little like the chicken and the egg?" Marianne asks. "You're assuming something is wrong with you. What if it's because of his inability to attach to you and his behaviors? It's not realistic to expect instant love. Adopted kids come to their families as strangers, and it can take time to build a bond."

Unsure of how to respond I let my hair fall like curtains around my face.

"You've been under tremendous pressure, for years, and with a child who behaves in a very unlikeable way. Do you think it's realistic or natural for you to love him?"

"But I'm his mother," I say, in a whisper.

"In many ways, Devon is like a domestic abuser. He torments and abuses your other children. And you."

"I'm not sure I'd call it abuse," I interrupt.

Marianne stays me with a lifted hand. "As a society, we don't like to think about this in the context of children, but kids can be abusive to their parents." She goes on to explain how unhealthy and unnatural it is to love our abusers, and how our feelings about this get even more complicated when our children are the abusers. She says, "I know that's hard to hear. It's a lot easier to acknowledge when we think of an abusive spouse or partner instead of a child."

I nod and try to look attentive, but she's already lost me. I absently run a jagged fingernail across the inside of my wrist. I know this will be my last session with Marianne. I'm tethered to this nightmare life already. If I indulge in self-pity or excuses, I'll never get through this.

49

On my way to family therapy, I recognize a wiry woman just outside the entrance to the main New Hope building. She's one of the regular staff in Devon's cottage, but I haven't seen her recently. "How are you?"

She cocks her head. "They didn't tell you?" She holds up her arm to show me a cast covering her thumb and wrist. "Devon was upset ... you know how he gets."

I gasp in genuine shock. This poor woman. Surely, she isn't paid enough for this. Not knowing how else to make this right, I offer weakly, "I'm so sorry. I'll understand if you decide to press charges."

"No, Ma'am. I'd lose my job. We're not allowed to file charges on the kids. But that ain't nothing ..." Taking my arm she leads me out of sight of the windows that are leering at us like dark, spying eyes. "Did they tell you what he did to Desmond?" she asks in a hushed voice.

I shake my head.

"He got a root canal done. His face was all swollen, and he'd told the kids to be careful."

I wince, sensing where this story is going.

She pops a fist through the air. "Devon punched him right in the mouth."

My hand flies to my own cheek.

She leans in close. "Don't let that boy back to live with you. He's dangerous. Very dangerous."

Moments later, I'm sitting in Beth's office. "He broke her thumb! And punching Mr. Desmond is a major escalation," I insist. "Devon's never attacked a man before."

"It is a bit concerning," Beth says, looking markedly unconcerned.

Fear stumbles over the mangled edges of my mind. Is Devon no longer intimidated by men? When he moves home, will he behave for Delano?

"That's why Devon is here." Beth holds a hand up in a what-do-you-expect gesture. "He needs treatment."

That's true, he does need treatment. But I'm not at all convinced that the treatment here is doing him any good. Beth never wants to talk about that, though. Instead, she constantly redirects me to look beyond Devon's behaviors. She wants me to praise his good behavior and ignore the bad. Even if I accept this as part of his "therapy," how will he transition back home to consequences, homework, and chores? How will he transition back to the real world? I ask some variation of this question in every session.

Each time, Beth dismisses me like I'm some sort of Munchausen mommy. "Let's not worry about that right now. He won't be going home until he's ready."

Devon senses the disconnect too, and today's session is no different. As usual, he's had incidents every day for the last week. Yet, he still thinks that Beth will be sending him home. Of course, he does, because he's had no consequence for any of these behaviors. It's all in my notes.

> Upset in class b/c told to stop talking. Threats to suffocate himself with a plastic bag. Asked to go to the quiet room. Screaming, choking supervisor, tried to slam her hand in the door. Said he was going to piss everywhere and did. Tried to strangle himself with his shirt. Restraint.

Beth asks Devon, "What coping skills did you find helpful this week?"

"Umm, take deep breaths. Take a walk with staff. A self-five."

Absurd. Their answer, to get Devon to stop choking a supervisor and trying to strangle himself is to tell him to take deep breaths. Unable to tolerate the farce any longer, I say, "*Or,* you can *choose* to stop."

There's an uncomfortable silence.

I continue, "I realize everyone thinks you can't control yourself but you and I both know you can." And that is the crux of the problem. Devon has to choose to do the right things. And, he won't.

My pink notebook has pages and pages of examples.

> 9:25 pm Mr. Desmond—Earlier today Devon was upset and exposed himself to two girls

> 9:30am Last night Devon had a tantrum for 3 hours because he didn't want to go to bed. This morning he won't let anyone in the cottage eat breakfast

What I'm the most concerned about is that Devon isn't reacting to some major injustice. Everyday life is triggering him—not getting his way, being told no, having to go to bed at bedtime. At New Hope he's developed a habit of responding violently to small, insignificant triggers.

"Treatment" is making things worse.

50

There are hair products scattered across the double sinks in my bathroom and discarded clothes on the floor. The scent of the flat iron singes the air. I hurry past Kayla and into my walk-in closet. "You're not going to be able to use my bathroom if you keep making such a huge mess." I slip on yoga pants and pull my nightgown off. I fumble with my bra, pull on a black tee-shirt, and run my fingers through my hair. Unplugging the flat iron, I tell her, "Don't use this while I'm gone."

Hurrying down the stairs, I call to Amias, "I want your room cleaned before I get home." He's sitting at the table playing on his school iPad and ignoring me. I snatch the iPad from his hands. "I'm checking your room before you get this back," I warn. As I reverse my car down the driveway, Amias stands in the doorway watching me. His mouth is moving. I can't hear what he's saying, but I don't need to.

Driving toward New Hope, I begin to mentally replay Devon's latest incident. By the time I walk into family therapy, I'm confident that this time it will be the eye-opener Beth needs. Devon is telling staff, explicitly, that he's misbehaving to force them to take him to the hospital. Can he be any more obvious? I read to her from my notes:

> Suzanne: Devon has been screaming for hours. Says he's going to strangle himself. Wants to go to the hospital and says he knows what to do to get us to take him there. He's "being so horrible" the nurse wants permission to give him a shot of Seroquel

I look at Beth expectantly.

Beth sighs and leans forward. "Devon is discouraged. He's done so much hard work, but he's still here. He's lost all hope."

My face sours. What hard work has he done? How can she not see how calculating his actions are? He *chooses not to* participate in school work, but he *chooses to* participate in rec time and swimming. I take a deep breath, letting Beth's naïveté roll off me like big, fat rain drops off an umbrella. I tell her, "This isn't about being discouraged. He's not getting better because there are no consequences or rules here. He has no incentive to behave."

Beth clears her throat, and I look up from my clenched hands. "At this point, we're going to need to step him down and see how he does."

"Step him down?" Anxiety seizes me with its sinewy fingers and wrings the breath out of my lungs. I finger my notebook like a talisman. I flip through and read Beth an incident from last week:

> Violent. Removed from peers. Threatening to kill staff and others, suffocate self with sock. Says he's going to get a gun and shoot his mom in the face. Threatens to tell supervisor Ms. Samantha "touched" him

"He's not safe to be at home," I say in conclusion.

"With appropriate supports ..."

"He's threatening to get a gun and shoot me in the face! You said he wouldn't be discharged until he's ready. He's clearly not ready."

Beth clucks her tongue. "He's showing improvement. He's using his coping skills more often."

"He's definitely worse than when he first came here," I insist. "Maybe he's improved since last week, or last month, but he's way worse than when he got here." Shrill panic mounts in my voice.

"Let's look at this in a more positive way. Devon wants to be at home. This is an opportunity for you to focus on your relationship. He's trying so hard to show you how much he loves you."

"But he *spit* in my coffee," I splutter. "That is not him trying so hard."

"We talked about this." Beth shakes her head as though disappointed that I'm still bringing this up. "Now, if you're not comfortable with him coming home, we can look at putting him in one of our foster homes and in our day treatment program."

I hold up my palms in protest. "We adopted him *out* of foster care. He needs to get better and come *home*. That's why he's here. And doesn't he need stability? Why would you want to move him?"

Beth leans back in her chair and admits, "Medicaid isn't going to approve a longer stay. He's been here for almost a year, and our average stay is six to nine months."

My whole world tips beneath me. Now I understand. This is

about money.

I drive home utterly discouraged and beaten down. I stumble through the front door like a zombie and Amias rushes over. "Come look at my room. I cleaned it." I pull his iPad out of my purse and hand it to him, no longer caring either way.

I trudge upstairs and flop onto my bed. How has it come to this? I hear a sniffle and pry my eyes open. Kayla stands next to the bed. Tears leak in long drips down her face. Alarmed, I ask, "What's wrong?" I can count on one hand how many times I've seen her cry.

Her whole face seems to droop. She wipes at her cheeks and mumbles, "You said I can't use your bathroom."

Realization slams through me, and I sit and pull her into a hug. "I'm sorry. Mommy was frustrated and rushed."

"I don't want to be kicked out of your bathroom." Her voice quivers, revealing emotions leagues deeper than our interaction this afternoon. "I thought we're supposed to share everything."

"We do. I'm sorry." I smooth her hair back from her face and pressing my lips to the side of her head, I whisper, "Girls stick together."

51

To avoid small talk, I scroll through news headlines on my cell phone. Emma, the New Hope foster care coordinator, sits at one end of the long conference table. She's petite with a blonde bob and glossed lips. Her cute sweater set and capris make me feel middle aged and frumpy.

Beth strides in. "Devon's new clinical assessment," she says, handing me a manila folder.

After an awkward wait, Devon's New Hope foster parents arrive, and Emma makes quick introductions. Srujana is about my age, with a soft glow, warm honey-colored eyes, and black hair. She and her husband, Naman, look as though they fit as perfectly together as salt and pepper shakers. He's got greyish-white hair and is short and stout like Srujana. All I know about them is that this is their first foster care placement and they have children of their own.

Once we are all seated around the table, the meeting begins. Shoving my hands beneath my thighs to stop them from trembling, I say, "I was a foster parent myself for years, so I know how this works. You probably haven't been told the truth. I won't let Devon come home because he's not safe. He's not safe to be in your home either."

Gratified by the flicker of surprise in Srujana and Naman's faces, I rush off script. "Have you been told how violent he is? He throws rages for hours and destroys property. He punched a man in the face and broke a woman's hand." A blend of confusion and pity cloud Srujana's eyes. "I know you have kids too. You need to be thinking about their safety," I say every word with absolute certainty.

Naman turns to Emma, with his eyebrows raised.

Emma responds in a cool, professional tone, highlighting that I'm a raving lunatic. "Devon needs to practice his coping skills in a family like yours so he can return home. As therapeutic foster parents you've been trained to work with these types of children. We're here to support you all along the way." She smiles warmly at them.

Srujana leans forward and rests her elbows on the table. Her eyes radiate sincerity towards me. "We've heard what you said. We're going to take good care of your son. This time apart is for you to learn how to be a better mother for him."

Fury pulses at my temples. What have they told her about me? My child is not in foster care because I have lost custody of him. He isn't here because I need parenting help. He's here because *he* needs treatment. I open my mouth to respond, but by the time I do, Emma has already taken advantage of my stunned silence to move on.

As soon as the meeting adjourns, I rush to my car, looking straight ahead. I will not let them see me cry. Once hidden behind the tinted windows, I pull out Devon's new clinical assessment. Resting the packet against the steering wheel, I flip through the pages.

Beth reports that Devon's peer interactions have improved and that he's making progress on his therapeutic goals.

Not true.

She says he's reduced his number of incidents and has not needed to be restrained in the last month.

Not true.

To my shock, she's also written that I'm supportive of his stepping down to foster care.

Not true.

Then Devon's prognosis pops from the page like a punch in the face:

```
Fair.
```

My tears slosh onto the paper as I read why:

```
Devon's mother is an active
participant in therapy and is open
to new concepts, but demonstrates an
authoritarian style of parenting and
a strong belief Devon is consciously
choosing to engage in behaviors that
disrupt the family.
```

Where is Devon's responsibility? Where is his agency? Where is the acknowledgement that he's a damaged child? According to Beth, this is all my fault. Devon's prognosis is only "fair," *not* because his brain is underdeveloped, *not* because he experienced early childhood trauma, and *not* because he refuses to comply with treatment. Devon has only a *fair* likelihood of getting better because of me.

52

Newly paroled, Sarrah joins Facebook, and her privacy settings are wide open. I discover this during my weeks upon weeks of insomnia boredom. I scroll through her pictures and status updates. She has a penchant for duck-face selfies and over-the-shoulder poses to show off her Kardashian-esque bottom. She calls her boyfriend, a handsome black man with an ankle monitor, her king. She is his queen. According to her "About" page on Facebook, they're in an open relationship.

Many of Sarrah's pictures showcase the word "Coogie" tattooed across her chest. I find the term in the online Urban Dictionary: "A cool-ass mutha fucker. A cool gangsta."

Sarrah and I couldn't be more different, but I've had a soft spot for her since I read about her in the Blue Books. I set up an anonymous Facebook account and upload several recent pictures of Devon and Kayla. I send Sarrah a friend request. Moments later she accepts. I send her a message explaining who I am and she's ecstatic. She tells me that she has a job assembling furniture and lives with her boyfriend at his mother's house. She's especially proud to have earned her GED and cosmetology license while in prison.

Over the next weeks, I upload more pictures, a photographic timeline of the years Sarrah missed. In my favorite picture of Devon, he's wearing a yellow bicycle helmet and peering at the camera shyly. In another, from one of his birthday parties, he holds Chuck E. Cheese tickets up for the camera with a huge smile on his face. In my favorite picture of Kayla, she's perching high up on a tree branch, as nonchalant as a cat.

Sarrah shares the pics with her Facebook friends. They comment that the kids look like her. I notice the resemblance too.

Sarrah uploads a picture of her tattoo of Devon's and Kayla's initials, and I can't resist showing Kayla. "Look, she loves you so much she tattooed your initials on her ankle." Kayla stares at it in awe. I show her more pictures, and we giggle together at one of Sarrah wearing a gold grill and fanning out twenty-dollar bills while squatting to show off her bottom in tight white pants.

"I wonder what her voice sounds like," Kayla says.

"Do you want to message her?" Kayla nods and slides in closer to me. After they type messages back and forth a bit, Sarrah asks, "May I please speak to Devon too?"

Trying to find the right answer, my fingers hover over the keyboard. I can't tell her, of all people, the truth. The truth that I can't take care of him either. The truth is that Devon is doing great living with his new foster family. I settle on telling Sarrah that Devon's therapist doesn't think it's a good idea for them to have contact yet.

...

"I'm strict." To emphasize her point, Srujana chops one hand against her palm during our CFT meeting. "It's like the military at my house, and that's what he's responding to." Devon sits next to her, head down looking at his hands which are folded in his lap.

To Devon's other side is a day treatment worker. At one end of the conference table is Emma who facilitates these meetings and at the other, Wanda, who has replaced Beth as Devon's therapist. I'm sitting alone on one side of the table like the subject of an interrogation. I stare out the window, watching some scrappy birds pecking around in the few stalks of grass that have been able to make their way up through the hard ground.

I don't bother responding to what's being said. What's the point? I'm also strict and structured. Why, in my case, is that a problem, but they applaud Srujana? Devon is only at her house, awake, for about three hours per weekday. She doesn't have him during the day, doesn't even drive him to school. She doesn't have him on the weekends. I do.

Once Srujana is done bragging about her "success" with my son, Emma turns to the day treatment worker for an update. It's always someone different, seemingly anyone who happens to be available. And these workers aren't mental health professionals. This is an entry-level position that requires only a GED. They're little more than babysitters. Today's worker says, "I personally got no problems with him."

"How often is he being restrained?" Emma asks, pen poised for the answer.

The worker looks at the ceiling thoughtfully. "I'd say at least a couple a week. A few days ago, he was upset waiting for his turn on the computers." He looks at me and adds, apologetically, "We only have three computers so they have to take turns." Returning his focus back to the entire group he says, "He punched a female peer in the back of her head 'cause he wanted her computer."

"I got the note home about that," Srujana interrupts. "I had him write 1,000 sentences as his punishment. It took him three days, but he wrote them. Isn't that right, Devon?" She asks, as she reaches into her bag.

Devon nods, without looking up.

Srujana slaps a spiral notebook onto the table. "I brought them to show you." It's folded open to a page crammed with penciled lines of numbered sentences. The sentences on that page start with 351.

I say, "When he was living at home, I would give him 100 sentences as a consequence. His brother and sister, *who are a year younger than him*, would do them. But he would refuse to do even ten." Devon shifts uncomfortably in his chair, and I'm glad. He should feel embarrassed by his behavior. I continue, "He wouldn't even do one. If he did 1,000 sentences for her, that shows he just doesn't *want* to do what I say."

Srujana nods in agreement. "He can do it."

Wanda, who has yet to schedule a family therapy session with me, clears her throat. She's elegant, with red acrylic nails and a confident poise that I envy. "Srujana, you do not need to worry about consequences for Devon's behavior at day treatment," she says. "We need you to focus on encouraging his good behavior in your home."

Devon presses his lips tightly together, but can't stop the smile turning up the corners of his eyes. Yes, I'm probably the only one who notices, but that doesn't mean it's not there.

Wanda turns toward me. "Writing sentences does not work for Devon. That is not an appropriate consequence for him."

Devon looks up, wide-eyed at hearing her admonish me, his mother, in this authoritative tone.

I throw my hands into the air. "Well, did day treatment consequence him? What consequence should he get for punching a girl in the back of the head?"

"You keep referring to Devon's behaviors as if he's choosing them. You need to understand this is not a choice for him."

"*Of course,* he's choosing these behaviors." I vibrate with outrage. "A sneeze is involuntary. Punching a girl in the back of the head is not." Wanda holds up her hands to calm me, but I truck on. "Devon's behavior is completely unacceptable. He's able to control himself if he wants to. He's not punching her kids in the head," I say, with a nod toward Srujana. "He *chooses* to do it at day treatment because he knows he can do whatever he wants here."

ANGER

195

Srujana nods her agreement.

"Ms. Williams," Wanda says, and her haughty tone creeps under my skin. "It is *our* responsibility to create an environment where Devon will be successful and consequences do not work for him."

"What does work for him then?" I snap.

"Well, for example, we have recently moved Devon to a group with older kids, where he is the youngest. His physical aggression toward his peers is already beginning to diminish. He is doing great."

Devon straightens up as though proud of this accomplishment. But I'm not having it. "You mean because they're bigger than him, and he's scared of them? What happens when he comes home to his little brothers and sister? He needs to learn to be around younger children without bullying them."

Wanda gives me a disdainful look, but no response.

There's a clunky silence before Emma moves on to discharge planning. The system is set up in levels, and Medicaid likes to move kids up and down the steps in order. Devon moved from PRTF down to Foster Care and the plan is to now move him down to living at home with services. No date has been set, but they're talking about early summer.

I look back out through the window at the birds, as the team discusses the calendar and schedules next month's CFT meeting. Don't those birds know there is nothing for them here? Why do they keep pecking the ground anyway? Why don't they fly away?

When the meeting ends, Devon is taken back to the day treatment program and Srujana and I walk in awkward silence to the parking lot. As I turn towards my vehicle, Srujana places a hand on my arm. "You're too strong," she says. "You need to cry and beg them for help. That's what they want."

I nod uncertainly, surprised and confused by her words and not knowing what to make of this.

She goes on, "I hear how they talk about you when you aren't there. They think there's nothing wrong with Devon. They think it's that you don't want him. When I first met you, I didn't know who to believe or what to believe. Now, I understand exactly what's going on. I want you to know, I'm with you."

My heart kicks. I finally have an ally.

...

I pull into the Red Robin restaurant parking lot at 7:30 am on Saturday to pick up Devon for his weekend home visit and see Srujana's Lexus idling in wait for me. It's our regular meeting place to exchange Devon for his home visits. He's with me from Saturday morning until Sunday evening. Srujana and I now chat during these exchanges, but neither of us has let on to New Hope that we are friendly.

Devon hops out of Srujana's SUV and walks toward me. His hair is bushy. I slide open the minivan door as he bounds over. "Hey, Devon. Hop in," I say, then walk toward Srujana's vehicle. She unrolls her window and rests her arm in the open sill. Her youngest son, a little older than Brandon, sits next to her on the leather seat, wearing headphones, and playing on an iPad.

"I'll have his dad take him to the barber this weekend," I tell her. "How have things been going?"

"That boy won't shower." She wrinkles her nose. "He smells so bad. I was picking up my sons from school yesterday, and I made him stand outside the car during carpool. He says he's scared of the shower." She tilts her head cynically.

"He's not scared of the shower. He's always showered fine at my house."

Srujana sips from her can of Diet Coke. She drinks Diet Coke constantly, like I drink coffee. "When he was standing outside my car that day talking to me, his eyes were empty. No emotion. Empty. It's like he's evil."

I know the look that she's talking about: cold and detached. I'm not sure I'd call it evil though. He loves animals. Isn't harming animals a classic sign of any psychopath? No, he's not evil. He's just unbelievably oppositional.

Srujana squints in the brightness of the rising sun. "You're right to keep fighting them about letting him come home."

"I feel like giving up. They're so unreasonable."

"I hate to say this, but what about his birth mom?" she asks. "Have you thought of giving him back to her?"

The idea has been a lurking traitor in a back alley of my mind for a while, but I can't bring myself to say it out loud. I ask, "Did you see that story about those parents who tried to give their son back? It's been in the news. Ohio, I think."

Srujana shakes her head.

"They adopted the kid out of foster care. They dropped him off to child services and were arrested. I bet he's just like Devon."

"Wow …" she shakes her head.

"Anyway, Devon is adopted. I can't send him back even if I

wanted to."

Back home, Delano trims Devon's hair and takes him upstairs to shower and brush his teeth. All the while I hear Delano lecturing, "teaching," Devon how to shower, as though that's the problem. So gullible.

The next day, after church, the kids play in the backyard. Jason keeps an eye on them as he repairs our communal fence. I walk by Devon's bedroom and notice his red comforter askew. As I straighten it, I catch the acrid stench of urine. I pull down his bedding and pat gingerly expecting my hand to sink into spongy pee. It's dry. Then I notice a wet patch on the carpet in one corner of the room.

At first, Devon denies it. But he wilts beneath my glower. "I … I didn't mean to. I couldn't make it to the bathroom."

"*This* bathroom?" I say, sarcastically, pointing to the door that's kitty-corner to his in the hallway.

He looks at me. Blinks rapidly.

"You could stand-up and make it to the corner to pee, but not to the bathroom?" I begin to pack his clothes into his backpack. "It's time to go back to Ms. Srujana's house. I'll be talking to New Hope about this tomorrow. We'll have to go back to day visits if you're going to pee on the carpet when you spend the night." It's an empty threat. New Hope will never back me up. I know it. He knows it.

We pull into the Red Robin, and I tell Devon to wait in the car. Srujana rolls down her window, and I walk over. "Devon peed on his carpet," I say.

"He's never done that at my house."

"He's going to tonight, for sure," I predict. She rears her head back, but I continue. "That's how he'll try to prove he can't control it and how he'll try to prove he didn't do it at my house on purpose."

Srujana vehemently shakes her head. "Not at *my* house. His bathroom is right outside his bedroom door."

I press my lips into a firm line. I guess she'll have to learn for herself.

The next morning, I'm driving to drop the kids off at school when the caller ID for "Srujana" flashes across the screen of my cell. She doesn't bother saying hello. She blurts, "That boy. I'm so mad."

53

Wanda finally schedules our first family therapy session. According to her, she and Devon have been "building rapport." I seethe over this for the thirty-minute drive to New Hope. How could a therapist treat anyone's kid for months without even talking to the parents?

Wanda's office has a desk in one corner. In the center of the spacious room, two armchairs and a couch form a seating area complete with a coffee table and a cozy rug. I take a seat on the couch.

Wanda settles into one of the chairs, her royal blue suit skirt creasing as she crosses her legs. "Your son is such a sweet, smart boy. He and I have gotten to know each other quite well."

"Is Devon not coming?" I ask.

"I thought we could do a few sessions with the two of us first so we can get on the same page."

I purse my lips and my eyes are already flashing. I'd like to get on the same page too. Wanda gives Devon electronics even though they are against the rules. Devon is the only kid at day treatment allowed to roam campus to find and see her without an appointment. He eats contraband candy in her office and plays on her computer. None of this is appropriate. So, yeah, I'd like to get on the same page.

Wanda clears her throat. "You are going to need to learn how to parent Devon in a way that works for him."

Ambushed, and completely unprepared for her words, I fumble. "What … what do you mean?"

"Devon is a sensitive child. Your authoritative parenting style is not a match for him. In our sessions, he and I have been exploring other ways you can parent him."

I watch her red, lip-sticked lips moving over bright, white teeth no longer hearing a word she's saying. I bite out: "I'm willing to listen to your suggestions, but we need to talk about Devon's behavior too. After being here, he thinks it's normal to not receive consequences no matter how horrific his behavior is."

"I am not sure Devon needs any consequences."

I nearly choke on my coffee. "What?"

"Explain it to me," she says, spreading her hands magnanimously. "Why would you feel the need to give Devon a consequence?"

"When he hits his brothers or sister, breaks toys, throws a screaming fit. What do you mean, why would I give Devon a consequence? His behavior is terrible."

Wanda looks at me for long moments, as though considering how best to respond. Then she says, "If you do consequence Devon, it should not feel like a consequence at all. You can send him to watch a cartoon or play with toys."

And with that, I know for sure—I have fallen headlong down a rabbit hole.

…

Wanda and I may not be on the same page after our first session, but I make sure Devon and I are on the same page. During our next home visit, I narrow my eyes at him and say, "You listen to me, this game of yours is not going to work. You may have tricked Ms. Wanda but I'm the boss, not her."

Devon stares back at me, his dark eyes unreadable.

Feverishly, I continue. "You need to stop this because as long as you're being bad, you will not be coming home. If Ms. Wanda tells you anything different, she's lying to you."

After that, our weekly family therapy sessions are contentious at best. Devon smiles and ducks his head as Wanda showers him with praise. He looks at her with puppy dog eyes when she mentions his "attention seeking behaviors."

I try to frame my concerns in various ways, but I seem unable to communicate with Wanda effectively:

"He bit one of the boys in the cottage and kicked him in the face? And he gets no consequence? That's ridiculous!"—too pissed off.

"He refuses to participate in class? Of course, he can do third grade work. He's in sixth grade. He just doesn't want to."—too judgmental.

"He needs to see you for therapy every single day? He's manipulating you."—too angry.

Devon tells Wanda that he hates puzzles and I force him to do them when he's home. She says that I need to stop. Devon's father treats him like Cinderella and that also needs to stop. Devon is very hurt because I have only a couple pictures of him on my photo wall and many more of his siblings. Wanda suggests that I let Devon pick out some pictures of himself to frame and hang to make it fair. I quickly discover that it doesn't matter what I say about any of this. It's quite obvious that Wanda believes Devon over me.

Wanda tells me that I need to take Devon to Golden Corral during his home visits. He's identified that as what will make him feel loved. It's Wanda's mouth moving, but I hear only Devon's voice when she speaks. He's literally trying to use Wanda to control me. I've explained this to her, but she scoffs at the idea that a professional such as herself could ever be manipulated by a child in the way I'm suggesting. But, I *know* he's pulling the strings.

And, so, each family therapy session, week after week, month after month is nothing more than an unproductive, verbal sparring event. Devon doesn't seem to mind. He sits back and watches the show.

It's been ten months of foster care and day treatment when New Hope announces that Devon is ready to move home. Wanda, as his clinician, is the decision maker. I argue that his violent behavior is escalating so he can't possibly be ready. But, Devon has said he wants to move home and, so, Wanda is hell-bent on sending him home—ready or not. New Hope sets a discharge date for the second week in June.

54

26 days until discharge

"Why don't you tell Mom about the hallucinations you've been experiencing?" Wanda prompts Devon as we sit in her office.

Devon curls into the corner of the couch opposite to me and wrings his hands. He mumbles, "Her won't believe me."

"I'm sure that's not true," Wanda coaxes, although she knows perfectly well that I don't believe a word that he says, and why. When Devon doesn't respond, she tells me, "Devon has been experiencing hallucinations. He describes seeing a man holding a knife ..."

"Covered with blood," Devon interrupts. "Dripping blood." He gesticulates animatedly. "He's tall and skinny. Wearing a black suit and tie. His face is white and he tells me to do bad stuff."

My skin crawls with anxiety like an itchy wool sweater.

Wanda holds up a hand for him to let her speak. "Sometimes the figure tells him to hurt his family."

"To strangle you and stab Brandon," Devon whispers as though petrified.

I narrow my eyes at him, calling out his obvious lie. These "hallucinations" are way too similar to Slender Man, a popular horror meme. He's tall and skinny with a white face and wears a black suit. I only know about Slender Man because he's been on the news. Two twelve-year-old girls stabbed their friend 20 times and claimed to have been acting on the bidding of Slender Man. 12-years-old. About Devon's age.

Wanda says, "We're keeping open communication. Whenever Devon has hallucinations, he comes to see me, and we talk about it." After praising Devon for having the courage to share this with me, and reassuring him that she's always available to talk, Wanda leads him from the room back to his class. She returns and closes the door behind her.

"You don't really believe he's having hallucinations, do you?" I ask, incredulity threading my voice.

Settling back into a chair, Wanda regards me calmly. "Staff

caught Devon and one of his peers looking up the side effects of their medications online. First, he was flopping around, saying he was dizzy." She chuckles as though reminiscing over a nostalgic memory. "Then he acted like he had stiff limbs. He worked his way through the side effects, all the way to hallucinations. He's settled on that one."

"Why don't you tell him you know he's lying and to stop?" I demand.

"That would not be therapeutically appropriate. In fact, it would harm our relationship. Devon needs to know I believe him and he can talk to me about anything."

"Letting him think you believe his lies is enabling him."

Wanda dismisses my concern with a wave of her elegant hand. "He will get bored soon. There is no harm in it."

My fingernails bite into my palm. Through gritted teeth I say, "That will make him lie more. Devon has completely manipulated you."

Wanda's only response to that is a deep, patronizing sigh. She says, "Let's talk about why you're concerned about him moving home."

"He's violent," I say, in an "are-you-serious" tone.

She looks down her nose at me. "That's not true."

"Yes, he *is* violent and he scares my other kids. If he moves back home, I'll have to put an alarm on his bedroom door."

"That would be totally inappropriate and hurt his feelings." Wanda shakes her head as though I'm proposing tarring and feathering a kitten.

"There are three or four staff here watching him at a time, and they can't manage him. How can I? I am one person with three other kids. My oldest son used to help me but he's in the Army now, so I won't even have his help. And my husband works most of the time, so I'll be alone with him."

Wanda gives me a long, appraising look. "This is not about Devon. There's nothing wrong with Devon. This is about you."

Her words spear through my hollow chest and I wrap my arms protectively around my middle. In an angry whisper, I say, "He's not ready to come home. He's throwing fits every day."

"At day treatment, but he is doing well in his foster home."

"It's not the same thing," I insist. "He's only at Srujana's house to sleep."

"He has not had any problems during home visits either," Wanda says.

"Of course not!" I snap, out of patience. Out of my mind. "He has no chores or homework. And visits are on the weekends when my husband is there. Just because he can hold it together for a visit doesn't mean he'll be okay living at home full time."

"You need to accept that he is coming home. The discharge date is still a month away, so we have time to work on your parenting."

No, not a month away.

26 days. I'm keeping count.

My pulse thrums in growing panic.

"June is the worst time for him to come home." No matter how hard I try, I can't keep the pleading out of my voice. "He won't even have school during the day to keep him busy. He'll go from not living at home to being home 24/7."

"How about a summer camp? Devon would love that."

"What summer camp is going to take a kid with his behaviors? He'd get kicked out," I snort.

Wanda looks thoughtful for a moment then snaps her fingers. "Here is an idea. You can buy a summer camp curriculum and snacks. Let him run a summer camp for your other children. He could even invite the neighborhood kids."

Run a summer camp? Devon? *Run* a summer camp? Without a word, I stand and walk out.

Later that evening, still struggling with insomnia, I scroll through the online articles about that Ohio couple. They tried to "return" their adopted son to social services because he was violent and threatened to stab them. The journalists don't even consider how those parents may have been in an impossible situation. They insist there is nothing a child could do to warrant this. The mother was forced to plead guilty to avoid jail time.

I read:

```
The prosecutor said he hoped the
case would stand as a message and a
deterrent to parents who seek to
abandon their children in a similar
fashion and would focus attention on
issues raised by the case.
```

A thick ball forms in my stomach. Using online property records, I find what I hope is their mailing address. I pull out a piece of lined paper and begin to write.

55

22 days until discharge

Holding the curtain back, I watch Delano back his car out of the driveway. He's going to see a movie, a pretense that I've come up with to get him out of the house for a while. Kayla is at a friend's house.

As the garage door grinds closed, I steel myself for what I must do. Devon has only been behaving during home visits because they're short, fun, and Delano is home. He goes back to New Hope and takes out his pent-up aggression on the younger kids. If he had to do homework, chores, and go to bed at eight o'clock on school nights during these visits, they would not be going so well. How long would it be before he started stabbing Brandon and Amias with pencils and punching Kayla in the back of the head?

In a forced, cheerful voice, I say to the boys, "Why don't you go out back and play basketball?" They scramble to their feet. As they head for the back door, I call, "Devon, you need to stay inside."

He turns. "But, why?'

"You know you need to be supervised, and I'm too busy to go outside with you right now."

His hand rests on the door knob. I hear the basketball slap against the court. Amias and Brandon's shouts spill through the open door. I waiver in my resolve, but I have to prove to Wanda that if I take even one little thing away from Devon, he will flip into a rage. That's the only way she'll understand that he *is* too dangerous to move back home.

"I'll be good …"

"Sorry."

Devon slams the backdoor closed.

Feigning disinterest, I flip on the news and begin to tidy up. Devon fists his hands at his side and stares daggers at me. Saying nothing, I let him stew. He walks to the bookshelf and flings a book across the floor. Toys begin to clatter and slap against the tile.

That's my cue.

I retrieve colored pencils and a sketch pad from the hall closet.

"Come to the table and do some drawing."

He ignores me.

I hate myself for doing this, but I'm already holding rehearsal in my mind: "Devon wanted to go outside, but I couldn't supervise him. When I told him no, he started to throw a tantrum. I followed your advice, Wanda. I didn't use the word 'consequence' or 'punishment.' I let him draw, because he loves art."

Out loud I say to Devon, "Come on over here. You can draw while the boys play outside."

Devon spins on his heel and disappears down the hallway. I hear the tear of papers and of something hitting the floor. The door whooshes open. "I'm leavin' this bastard fuckin' house," he screams.

I've proven my point. The second that Devon doesn't get his way, he'll flip out. Walking through the hall toward the front of the house I pick up Brandon's crumpled watercolor flower and the pieces of Kayla's pottery fish. Devon's green, clay frog squats safely on the shelf next to his drawing of a spaceship with aliens, both unharmed.

The front door is open. I peer out. Devon is picking up stones and hurling them at the house. "Come on in. I'll have the boys come in and watch a video with you," I say in a conciliatory tone.

Two neighborhood girls skip up the sidewalk and he screeches at them, "You get away, you niggers."

With a sharp intake of breath, I rush toward the girls and help them pass safely. Devon holds up a large rock menacingly. "I'm gonna kill Brandon." He lurches toward the backyard.

I rush through the house to the back door. I hear Devon struggling with the gate and trying to climb over the fence as I call frantically for Amias and Brandon to come inside.

I slam the door closed as Devon boomerangs around the back corner of the house.

He beats his palms on the glass.

My heart slams in my chest.

Devon leers at me through the window. He mimes a gun with his fingers and shoots me.

...

Wanda doesn't wait for family therapy to address our disastrous home visit. She calls me. "Why would Devon have different rules than the other children?"

"I have to supervise him. He can't be outside without an adult."

"I am not sure why you think that," she says.

"At New Hope, the kids are under constant supervision, aren't they? Why would he need to be supervised there, but not at my house?"

Wanda doesn't answer my question and, instead, says, "I am trying to understand why all the children could not stay inside until Devon was able to go outside."

My conscience twists my insides until it sends words flaring out in defiance. "As a parent, it's my prerogative to tell Devon when he's not allowed to go outside. That's no excuse for him to go berserk. If I'd told Amias or Kayla no, they might have stomped up the stairs and slammed a door. They would not have thrown rocks or threatened to kill me."

There's a silence between us then Wanda says, "And you forced him to draw instead?"

"I did exactly what you said to do. I gave him a consequence that doesn't feel like a consequence. He loves to draw."

"That is not what I said." Her voice is sharp and slices through me despite the miles between us.

56

11 days until discharge

I juggle my phone on my shoulder as I grab a gallon of skim milk out of the grocery store cooler. The phone crackles with bad reception, but I can hear recognizable wailing in the background.

"What's he doing now," I say, on the tail of a deep sigh.

Mr. Tommy proceeds to tell me the story. Devon and Andy were talking and laughing as they waited for their afternoon cabs. Devon has told me about Andy. He's in the older group that Devon is now a part of. He lives with his grandmother, smokes pot, and sneaks his iPhone into day treatment. He's quite popular. Andy told Devon that he was going to see a movie on Saturday.

"I'm goin' to see a movie this weekend too," Devon said.

Andy's cab pulled up, and Andy hopped in.

Devon walked to the garden and kicked at the flowers. He dug in the dirt with the toe of his sneaker. He stomped on a flower then looked around to see if anyone noticed. No one told him to stop.

Then Devon's cab driver pulled up and honked the horn, ready to take him to Naman and Srujana's house. Devon grabbed his backpack and opened the door. It was his usual driver. "Hey, Man, jump in."

Devon paused.

"Let's go," the cab driver said.

Devon threw himself backward onto the ground. Stabbing a finger toward the open door of the cab, he shrieked, "It's a dead man. He's in there. He has a knife."

Mr. Tommy peered inside the vehicle then drawled, "No one's in there."

"You can't see him. No one but me can." Devon thrashed on the ground. Saliva dribbled down his chin, mixing with dirt and leaving muddy smears across his face. He refused to get in the cab. Refused to stop screaming. Refused to talk to anyone.

"I'm gonna call your mom," Mr. Tommy said, holding a

cordless phone in his hand.

Devon shrieked, "It's her fault. Hers the one making the dead man try to kill me. Her wants me dead."

"Ma'am, our shift is over and we're not sure what to do with him," Mr. Tommy tells me over the phone. "Can you come pick him up?"

I offer to talk to Devon, but doubt that it will help.

"Hey, Devon, your mom wants to talk to you," Mr. Tommy calls.

Devon screams, "Hers trying to kill me. Her sent the dead man to kill me."

"I think you should call his foster mom. He's supposed to be going to her house tonight," I say. "Maybe she can come get him."

"This kid is something else," Srujana huffs into the phone later that evening. "I had to rush over to New Hope. It took forever with traffic. My husband had to pick our boys up from school. Devon was laying on the ground on his back, kicking, and screaming."

"Totally crazy," I say, mirroring her exasperation. I balance the phone to my ear as I pull the flat iron through the last section of Kayla's hair. She's going to her first middle school dance tonight. To my chagrin, she's wearing a pair of black, ripped jeans, a white button-down shirt untucked, and a sleek black suit jacket.

"You know his old therapist?"

"The one he had at PRTF?"

"Yes. I can't remember her name …"

"Beth," I say.

"Yes, Beth. Beth was watching. I heard her say, 'Poor boy, it's all the mother's fault.'" I take her words like a kick in the stomach, but Srujana doesn't notice and keeps relating to me what happened. "He kept saying there was a dead man in the cab, but I looked in there, and it was empty."

"Of course, it was empty. He was making it up."

"I had to get home, so I told him we could stop for ice cream. He got into my car and chatted with me as if nothing was wrong." Fury rises in Srujana's voice. "I got him the ice cream, but I didn't want to. I know he'd tell them if I didn't."

"Oh yes, he definitely would have told them."

"Listen, they're saying you set him up."

"Who's saying that?" I ask.

"The staff at New Hope. They're saying at the last home visit you got him upset on purpose."

I laugh lightly and shrug it off. "I didn't set *him up*. I set a *situation up* where he'd actually have to follow directions he didn't like, and he threw a tantrum. I mean, really. Am I not allowed to say no to him?"

"I'm glad you did. The minute you say no to that boy, he flips out, and New Hope's answer is just to never say no to him. I don't know what you're going to do with him," she says resignedly.

"Me either," I say, and we end the call.

I slide Delano's wallet out from under the recliner cushion. Kayla is nervous and wants exact change. I pull out a five-dollar bill for admission then several ones for pizza and soda. I drive her to the school, and she nervously climbs out of my car to walk toward the cafeteria where the dance is being held. I see some girls in fancy dresses join her. I watch them enter the school all smiles and giggles before I pull away and head for home.

Later in the evening, my cell rings. It's Eastside calling for consent to treat. Apparently, after Srujana and I'd hung up, Devon ran into their garage. "Take me to the hospital you bitch dummy girl," he'd demanded of Srujana. He scrambled up onto a workbench and found a jagged piece of plastic. He scraped it along his wrists, but it wasn't sharp enough to break the skin. Then he licked the bottoms of his shoes and banged his head against the wall. All the while he demanded to be taken to the hospital.

Devon said he would have Srujana arrested for child abuse—*she* was the one trying to cut him, *she* was the one making him lick his shoes, *she* was the one slamming his head into the wall.

Srujana called New Hope's emergency line, and they instructed her to take him to Eastside. Remembering me telling her how Devon used to try to climb out of my car window and kick my head while I was driving, she refused to be the one to take him. Half an hour later, Wanda pulled into Srujana's driveway. Devon skipped to her Escalade gleefully calling, "I'm going to the hospital. I'm going to the hospital."

I give the nurse at Eastside consent to treat and agree to go by there first thing in the morning.

57

7 days until discharge

Nancy, the Eastside social worker, has silver hair and kind eyes. She leads me to a hospital conference room. Wanda is already there, as well as a man in scrubs. The room is narrow and tightly packed.

"Devon is very frightened by his hallucinations and doesn't want to hurt anyone. He's afraid the hallucinations he's seeing will force him to. Poor thing," Nancy says.

Based on the looks of concern all around the table, I'm the only one who thinks Devon's "hallucinations" are an all too convenient cover for threats he's been itching to verbalize for months. Struggling to compose my face into an appropriately maternal expression, I gaze out the window. A potted plant obstructs my view. Its wilted leaves droop over the sides and trail along the window sill. Beyond, I glimpse vibrant grass and shrubs flanking lush grassed areas with walking paths leading away from the hospital.

When I reengage, Nancy is saying, "At this point, we can't release Devon, because he hasn't contracted for safety."

And by refusing to "contract for safety"—refusing to agree to not harm himself or others—he's able to stay in his favorite place, the hospital psych ward, a little longer. I squeeze my eyes shut against the frustration throbbing through my brain. It's either that, or roll my eyes, which won't reflect well on me.

"Devon became upset once yesterday," Nancy tells us, "and attempted to kick staff, so we put him in the seclusion room." I'm already aware of this incident because the nursing staff called me for permission to give him a PRN. Devon was kicking staff, urinated on the walls, and made himself throw up. Then he licked his vomit. Nancy doesn't mention any of those details. She only says, "Don't worry, Mom, he calmed down by dinner time."

Of course, he did.

"He's had," she runs a finger down her page searching, "a total of seven restraints since he's been with us. He's so frightened to be here." In quick words she adds, "... which is normal. Kids often find the hospital to be a scary place."

"He's not scared. He loves the hospital," I say.

Nancy looks a little taken aback. "I don't think so. He's quite scared. To help him sleep, the nurses have been pulling his mattress out by their station."

More special treatment. I shake my head but know it's pointless to continue this thread of the conversation.

Wanda says, "Before this incident, Devon was preparing to be discharged from foster care and move back home with his family. The discharge plan will not change."

I surge up out of my chair. "He's threatening to stab his little brother and strangle me. How can you *still* think he's safe to come home?"

"Devon is *not* a threat to anyone," Wanda says. "Prior to being admitted to the hospital, he has not had any incidents of self-harm or aggression in over a month." Panic curls its fingers around my throat as her patronizing voice crawls up my spine.

I slap my notebook onto the table. Despite the humiliating flush spreading down my neck, fury oozes from my every pore. "*No* incidents in the last month? Really?"

I read:

> May 3: Antagonizing peers, throwing books and objects, struggled to process.
> May 4: Threatening to kill his mother. Claims to see hallucinations on TV. Screaming fit for hours.
> May 4 afternoon: Stabbed a peer with pencil, kicking, hitting, threw desks, broke computer monitors. Wasn't restrained.

I glance up and am bolstered by the gaping look on Wanda's face. Apparently, she didn't know that I keep my own documentation. I continue to read.

> May 13: Attacked staff, screaming in quiet room, biting nurse, was given injection PRN.

> May 15th. Using n-word/b-word, threats to kill mom and Brandon. Put a shirt around neck to strangle himself.

I look around the table. "Should I continue?"

Wanda skewers me with her eyes. "You need to be supportive of what's in Devon's best interest."

58

5 days until discharge

As I nurse a frozen strawberry margarita, a shiver runs through me. "I can't imagine going back to living like that."

"They're not going to send him home," Becky says, for at least the tenth time. Our conversation has been going in circles for two margaritas and a shared order of pulled pork tacos.

Even after the showdown at Eastside, Wanda is holding firm. She sees no reason why Devon is not safe to return home. Srujana and Naman, however, refuse to take Devon back. It's a violation of their contract, and they'll lose their fostering license. They don't care. They're done. Devon is their first and last foster child. New Hope has nowhere to put Devon, so they've asked the hospital to keep him until the date when he is going to be discharged to home.

I tell Becky, "Srujana says I need to cry and beg for help. She says I'm too strong."

Becky nods to concede the point. We've talked before about how, in her own experience as a teacher, she's found this sort of thing to be true. "You're a Yankee. Southern women aren't so direct. It could be off-putting. It wouldn't hurt for you to show some emotion. And not your anger. You need to let them see your sadness and fear and desperation."

My phone vibrates. "Mom keeps calling and texting. I can't handle it right now."

"I'll talk to her and tell her what's going on," Becky says. "Srujana is probably right. You don't get emotional in front of people, and they're reading that as you not caring. All they are seeing is how angry you are."

"But he's got Wanda wrapped around his little finger," I say, furiously. "It's like she's decided to force me to take him back home no matter what."

"We're going to keep fighting, and you'll leave him at Eastside if you have to."

"It's risky."

"I know, but we don't have a choice."

"Maybe the adoption woman will help me."

"Well, you need to cry and tell her how scared you are for Devon and for the other kids. Beg her for help."

"I'll try," I mutter, not knowing if I can allow myself to be any more vulnerable than I already am. Anger is the only defense I have left.

"I'll do it," Becky says, emphatically. "Call me when she's there, and I'll come over and cry if that's what they want."

Panic cork screws its way through me. They're going to send him home. I just know it, and I need a plan. "I'm going to buy him a video game system. I'll get him cable for his bedroom. A mini refrigerator too."

Becky tucks her hair behind her ear. "What about when he has to go to school?"

"I don't know," I mumble.

Becky peers at me. "When's the last time you brushed your hair?"

I shrug and sip my margherita. It's been a long time—months. I haven't gotten it cut either because I can't bear the thought of making small talk. Now, the broken ends tangle together in an unruly mess.

After a thoughtful pause, Becky says, "Here's what we can do. Next time he's throwing a fit, I'll take all the kids to my house. Then you'll let him hurt you, seriously enough that you can call the police and file assault charges."

My eyes snap up.

Becky nods, agreeing with herself. "That's what we have to do."

"It's so extreme." We stop talking as the waitress clears away our plates and places the bill on the table. I say, "The other kids are doing so much better with him gone."

"I know. That's why we have to do whatever it takes to keep them safe. You can't destroy their childhood. It's not fair to them."

I finger the bill folio. "Maybe if he came home I could ..."

"No," Becky says, emphatically. "It would be different if you could help him. You cannot help him. You cannot fix him."

59

4 days until discharge

Skimming through my scribbled notes, I draw a dark box around "siblings are scared." The words swim in front of me and I startle at the doorbell.

Hannah's casual air of ordinary sets me at ease. We sit at the table and she hands me her business card. She's a post-adoption social worker. She pulls a legal pad and pen from her quilted satchel. "I'm glad you called. I'm going to do everything I can to help you."

There's a pile of documents on the table between us. I have everything, but I start with the call from the adoption worker about two adorable, practically "perfect" foster kids.

"We fell in love with them during our first visit. They had some concerning behaviors, but nothing out of the ordinary for foster kids. We believed they only needed a forever family." I explain to Hannah how things gradually got worse over the years. "I didn't want to send him away, but I had no other options. Now Medicaid is refusing to authorize him and New Hope is lying on the paperwork and saying he's gotten better so they can send him home."

The door bursts open and Amias, Kayla, and Brandon clomp down the hallway leaving their backpacks in a heap by the front door. I introduce them to Hannah.

"How old are you," Hannah asks Brandon.

He proudly holds up six fingers.

"And you all go to the same school?" she asks.

They tell her about school and the sports that they are playing. After a few minutes of chit chat, I send them outside to eat their snacks at the picnic table. Hannah says, "They're so cute. And well mannered," as they bustle out through the back door.

I'm glad she's seen them and understands what's at stake as I continue my story. "Devon is claiming to hallucinate, but everyone knows it's a lie. It's his way of …"

"His therapist doesn't believe he's having actual hallucinations either?" Hannah clarifies.

"Oh, no. She knows he's not." I tell her about Devon searching for his medication's side effects online, then acting them out. And how his supposed hallucination is the image of Slenderman. "This is his way of threatening me without getting into trouble. I'm afraid he'll think he can act on the threats too and get away with it."

Hannah taps her pen on her chin. "What reason are they giving for saying he's safe to move home?"

"That Devon is being good at the foster home. But that's comparing apples to oranges. He's only there about three hours a day Monday through Friday. Awake, I mean. He does sleep there." I clear my throat. "My son, Sam, used to help me. He's 19 and in the Army now. And it's not just the other kids. He's doing things like wrapping his shirt around his neck and trying to choke himself. He's just doing it for attention, but he could still accidentally hurt himself. I can't watch him every minute like they can at New Hope."

Hannah writes a few notes on her pad. "He's still at the hospital?"

I nod. "I need to know what my options are. If he's dangerous to my other kids, can they still force me to bring him home?"

Hannah sets down her pen. "Well, yes. And no. As his legal guardian, he's your responsibility. In these situations, parents sometimes have no choice but to refuse to pick their child up from the hospital."

"What would happen to him if we did that?"

"He'd go into foster care."

"Is it true that my other kids could get taken away and put in foster care too?"

"Technically, it's possible. The hospital would report you to CPS for abandonment, and they'd open up an investigation. You'd have a hearing, but you have a lot of documentation." She waves at the stack of papers between us on the table. "You've gotten him so much treatment. The judge will almost definitely take that into account."

Hannah asks for Wanda's phone number and the security code to use to call the hospital. She promises to make some calls and begins to pack up her things to leave.

I text Becky: Come now.

60

1 day until discharge

I've made up my mind and I'm so disgusted with myself that I can't work, can't sleep, can't help the kids with their homework. They're asleep in their beds, for a second day skipping school, and I'm still in my pajamas. I spend the morning sitting at my desk, but my computer monitor remains black. I stare at it, looking for some solution to materialize, but I can only see my own reflection.

The phone rings. Twice. Three times. I force myself to answer before it goes to voicemail.

At the sound of Nancy's voice, I'm already choking on a sob. "As you know, we're going to be discharging Devon tomorrow morning," she says. "Hannah Carter, I believe you know her, she's a post-adoption specialist for the County, contacted us about the situation."

"Uh-huh …"

There's a long pause, then she says, "The doctor can't understand why New Hope is trying to send Devon home. We all want to make sure he's in an appropriate setting where he can get the help he needs. The doctor is recommending a higher level of care for Devon. I just faxed New Hope."

Clinging to her words like a life preserver, I ask, "Does that mean they can't send him home?"

"They'll need to either admit him back into their program or find a new placement."

Air whooshes out of my lungs. This impossible choice, a choice that no parent should face, has been lifted off of my shoulders.

Part IV
BARGAINING

61

I start with the foamy waves because they look tricky. That's where I like to begin, with the most challenging section. Devon would like this puzzle, and, at this rate, they'll be plenty left when he comes for his next home visit. It's my favorite brand, Ravensburger. The pieces snap together exactly as they should. I've been at it for a few weeks, fitting in a handful of pieces each day while I help the kids with their homework.

"What's Papa's name?" Amias asks. He and Kayla are hunched over their school iPads across the table from me. As they use my answers to build their family trees, I try to tamp down my misgivings. When I'd asked the teacher for a modified assignment for Kayla, she offered two alternatives: she can use her adoptive family or create a family tree for someone famous like Barack Obama. "It doesn't matter what she uses," the teacher had said.

But it does matter. Both diminish who Kayla is and her unique life story. Having her bring in a random chart of a famous person would be like branding her with a Scarlet A: Adopted. Different. Kayla said that she was okay with using her adopted family tree, but disquiet worms through me.

This isn't the first time we've faced adoption insensitivity. Once, when I was filling out waivers at an indoor trampoline park, the attendant had asked, "Are you sure these are the correct birthdates?"

I'd glanced at the forms. They were for Amias and Kayla. "Those are right," I said, turning away to secure a wristband on Devon, while keeping an eye on Brandon, who was putting his shoes in the cubbies.

"These birthdates are only three months apart," she'd pressed.

Stunned by her intrusiveness, I swung around. "One of them is adopted, but that's none of your business." I'd walked away, fuming at her rudeness and imagining how damaging that could be for a family who isn't as open about adoption as we are.

The sound of Kayla and Amias squabbling draws my focus back to the present. "I'm black like Sam," Amias says, emphatically.

Brandon looks up from his coloring page. "What am I?"

"You're mixed," Amias tells him, adding, "Devon is too."

Kayla nods her agreement without looking up from her iPad. "But I'm white."

"You're not white," Amias insists. "Isn't that right, Mom? She's mixed."

"Well, Sarrah is white and as far as we know, Kayla, your dad was black."

Kayla holds up her arm and her complexion is similar to mine. "I'm white," she insists.

Amias starts to speak, but I hush him. It's always seemed best to let the kids make their own choices about how they'll identify. I find the puzzle piece I was searching for and slot it into place. "What's Daddy's dad's name?" Amias asks

"Selvin Williams."

"Wait …" Amias squints at his screen. "You're both Williams? Daddy was a Williams and you were a Williams too?"

"Pretty unusual, isn't it?" I say.

"You were related before you got married?" Kayla asks.

"No. There are thousands and thousands of people with the last name Williams. Lucky me. I didn't have to go through the work to change my name."

"Your mother did change her name," Delano calls to us from the living room. Knowing what's coming, I shake my head and make a silly face. "She changed it from *her* Williams to *my* Williams," he says.

I roll my eyes dramatically at the kids, and they giggle.

It takes most of the evening for Kayla and Amias' to complete what turn out to be identical family trees. Kayla, Devon, and Sam hang alongside Amias and Brandon, like apples from my branch of the tree. It marginalizes their birth mothers, contrary to everything that I believe in. Contrary to everything that I've done to help them see adoption as normal and beautiful.

On impulse, I ask, "Kayla, would you like to include Sarrah too?"

She looks up with eager eyes. "Can I?"

I take her iPad, determined to fix this for her. She chews a fingernail as she watches me. They're bit down to the quick. I click on Kayla's name, hit enter, and, below it, type, "Sarrah, birth mom."

It's not perfect, but it seems that nothing with adoption is. It's the best I can do.

...

New Hope arranges a temporary foster home for Devon when he's discharged from Eastside while they go through the admissions process with a new agency. The two weeks that he spends with foster parents Kevin and Sara Spearmon are uneventful, and they report that his behavior is "excellent." That is, other than him inexplicably claiming to be a vegetarian.

Devon tells me the story as I drive him from the Spearmon home to his new placement with Bridgeton Group Homes. On the first night, Mrs. Spearmon had placed a plate of chicken, rice and veggies in front of him for dinner and he blurted out: "I'm a vegetarian." Apologetically, Ms. Spearmon had replaced his dinner with eggs and toast. After that, she went out of her way to make him nutritious, meat-free meals.

The only problem was that Devon is not a vegetarian. For the following two-weeks he enviously watched as they ate hamburgers and chicken but didn't know how to, or wouldn't, back down. It's one of the few times he's suffered the natural consequences of his actions. I can't help but laugh. Devon grins, seeming pleased that I'm amused, instead of annoyed, by the story.

I meet Devon's new therapist at our first family therapy session. Wearing tight fitting clothes styled for a few decades ago, Kira has an Eastern European accent. "So nice to meet you, Ms. Williams," she says, the words rolling pleasantly off her tongue. I sit on the loveseat in her office, and Kira turns her desk chair to face me.

"Please, call me Keri," I say, and notice that her warm smile reaches all the way to her eyes.

"I spoke with the group home staff a few minutes ago, and Devon is on his way here. As you know, I have been meeting with him for the last three weeks while he's been in orientation."

Dread squats heavy on my chest. I sip my coffee and try to hide my nervousness.

"So, tell me what your goals are for Devon while he is here," she says.

"New Hope wanted to send him home. Kayla and Amias are at least close to his size. They can defend themselves. Brandon is much smaller." As I continue to talk, Kira squints her eyes, and I realize my rambling is out of order and incoherent. I stop and go back to the beginning. This new placement is a blank slate, and I'm determined that, this time, the *real* issues will take center stage. "If I didn't have other kids, things would be different. But I can't handle him."

"So, what I am hearing is you are fearful about Devon being sent home before he is ready." Kira sweeps a lock of pumpkin spice colored hair back from her face. "I can assure you, I will not recommend Devon to come home if his behaviors are as they are today. I have read his file, and he is certainly not safe to live at home."

The exhausted mother in me sags with relief. "Devon got so much worse at New Hope. They weren't documenting it. They kept saying he was improving and trying to send him home."

"Facilities like those have to show positive outcomes to keep funding. Bridgeton does, as well. But, I am an independent contractor. This can be helpful."

"I really thought he would get better when we started at New Hope, but he is much worse now than when he was living at home."

Kira nods regretfully. "In treatment facilities, kids learn how to work the system. They become institutionalized. They pick up negative behaviors. It is a double-edged sword."

"What happens if they're never well enough to go home."

"Unfortunately, they bounce from facility to facility until they turn 18."

"And then what?"

"He might qualify for disability. It is something for you to consider. That would give him a way to get transitional services. I understand he'll be starting at Crossroads Academy but hasn't been in school for a couple years?"

I lean forward, glad that she brought this up. Crossroads Academy is an alternative public school. I'm personally unfamiliar with it, but I have been told that they're able to manage kids with behavioral problems. "He's basically missed the last two years of school. At New Hope he had the choice of doing only the school work he wanted to. He has all As, but that's because they only graded the work he chose to do. I don't know how he's going to catch up."

"It's one of the challenges when kids are in these facilities," Kira says. "It is something we will work on."

"I also think it's a huge problem that Devon is in the CFT meetings," I say. "He's hearing all the conflict between the adults, and he uses that information to triangulate between us. It's really inappropriate too, when we need to say things that might hurt his feelings."

"In North Carolina, Devon has the legal right to be a part of his treatment team. I hear what you are saying though, and I will talk to our director, Ms. Jesi, about having a time for the adults to talk, then having him come in."

There's a sharp knock. Devon has arrived. Kira opens the door, and I stand. I wrap my arms around his stiff body in a hug. He sits with me on the loveseat.

"I was talking to Mom about your treatment goals. How do you think you have been doing?" Kira asks.

Devon smiles broadly. "I'm gonna make Level."

"Why don't you explain that to Mom."

"Everyone starts at Level 1."

"Since you are telling Mom, why don't you turn and look at her," Kira prompts, and Devon turns towards me. "For Level 2, you have to earn 200 points and be here for one month."

"When can you level up?" I ask, using the same video game vernacular.

"Wednesday. Durin' the group home meeting."

Kira says, "He is doing well. He is following rules and participating. We are looking forward to getting started with family therapy."

I am too.

62

Devon's first home visit is scheduled after his orientation period is complete, and, by then, we've had several family therapy sessions. I step into the boxy living room of the group home and wish that I hadn't brought Kayla, and Brandon with me. The small, single-story house is far too cramped for all of us. Mr. Ryan introduces himself and shakes my hand. He's petite with dark skin, a spattering of reddish freckles, and a goatee. "Devon, your family is here," he hollers down the narrow hallway.

Devon emerges, rubbing his eyes. "Sorry. I was sleeping." He yawns and stretches.

"Sleeping? It's nine o'clock," I tease, in an equally exaggerated tone.

"They let us sleep late." Devon leads us down the hallway to show us his bedroom. Dark-paneling covers the walls and makes the space feel even smaller and more outdated. He points out a small shared bathroom on the way. His bedroom has a twin bed, dresser, and a single window. It's plain and clean.

"I'll have him back by six. Does that work?" I ask Mr. Ryan.

"Yes, Ma'am," he drawls, feet crossed on an oversized desk that occupies more than its fair share of the living room.

Turning to Devon I stage whisper, "Should I let Mr. Ryan know that you're a vegetarian?"

He grins back and shakes his head.

Flicking glances through the rearview mirror as I drive, I see how far we've come. Brandon giggles at something that Devon says, and I smile at them. It seems a little time has scabbed over old wounds. We head for the local elementary school to watch Amias' basketball game. Delano and Amias are already there. By the start of the second quarter, Brandon, Devon, and Delano are loudly cheering and even more loudly ref'ing from the sidelines.

Kayla and I sneak away and head to the playground. We sit at a worn, graying picnic table. Before calling Sarrah, I remind Kayla of the rules we have for Facebook messaging. They're the same for phone calls: We don't talk about the city we live in, what our address is, or the name of the school Kayla attends. "Remember, we don't really know Sarrah. We can be friends with her, but we need to stay safe too."

I dial Sarrah's number. She picks up on the first ring. "I'm so excited," she titters.

"Kayla is too. I'm going to put you on speakerphone, okay?"

Sarrah says shyly, "I'm so nervous. What if she doesn't like me?"

In that moment, the vulnerability in her heart connects with the vulnerability in mine—birth mom to adoptive mom. Moving a few steps away from Kayla and turning toward the wooded edge of the playground, I tell her, "Of course she's going to like you. You've been talking on Messenger, and she already likes you."

At first, the conversation is stilted. Kayla gives yes or no answers. Sarrah tries to coax her out with questions. "Do you like school?"

"Yea."

"What's your favorite subject?"

Kayla shrugs, and I try to help them along. "Sarrah, why don't you tell Kayla what your favorite subject was?"

"I loved reading. Do you like to read?"

"Yes," Kayla mumbles and digs her sneaker into the dirt.

"Do you like Harry Potter? That's one of my favorites. What's your favorite book?"

"*Three Times Lucky.*"

"I've never heard of that one. I bet it's real good if you like it. I'm gonna go right out and buy myself that book."

As a smile breaks across Kayla's face, the ice breaks too.

Kayla and I return to the bleachers in time for the last quarter of the game. Devon is happy to be back in school, and he tells me all about it while we watch. I'm relieved and encourage him to work hard and behave. He'll need a high school diploma to be an independent adult.

"I can't do my work with a crayon," he says.

For the first couple of weeks at Crossroads Academy, he was doing exceptionally well. In fact, the staff were puzzled as to why he was at the alternative school instead of in a "real" school. They reported to Kira and myself that Devon wasn't having any behavioral problems at all.

Then he stabbed a classmate with his pencil. Because he's in this alternative school, and because he has an IEP, he was not suspended. After a second stabbing incident, Devon is no longer allowed to use pencils. I plug one ear to block out the sounds of the cheering fans on the bleachers around me and tilt my head and uncovered ear toward Devon to hear him better. "Are any other kids not allowed to use pencils?" I ask.

"Some of 'em."

"Did you ask the teacher when you can use pencils again?"

He nods.

After a long pause I prompt, "And what did she say?"

"I dunno."

"When you do get them back, you need to remember you'll lose them again if you stab someone." With a light laugh, I add, "If you feel like having a fit, maybe throw your math book."

"Okay," he says, a bit too cheerfully.

I cringe, but since medications and therapy don't seem to be working, maybe I can at least teach him to survive. I tell him, "You realize the parents of the kids you stabbed could press charges? It's very serious."

"I'm not scared of 'juvey,'" Devon says with swagger.

I don't know what to say to that. Any reprimand from me will push him toward the bad behaviors. So, I switch the subject, and we talk about his new friends at the group home. I want to tell him about Sarrah. I have a feeling that he would love the opportunity to talk to her. But I remember Beth's words of warning and don't.

...

After Sarrah and Kayla's first phone call, they begin to talk on the phone regularly, and I listen in less and less as time goes by. Sarrah is like a teenager, and I remind Kayla of this often because I want her to have realistic expectations. Still, Sarrah is remarkably appropriate and respectful. It makes me think she must be getting guidance from her court-mandated therapist.

Kayla and Sarrah swap "emoji stories"—multi-line strings of emojis that the other person must interpret as a story—and pictures of their hairstyles and outfits. When Delano upgrades his cell phone, I mail his old iPhone to Sarrah. Now, some afternoons, she and Kayla dance to the radio together courtesy of FaceTime.

In one private phone call, I explain to Sarrah a little bit about the situation with Devon. She says that he reminds her of herself when she was a teenager in group and foster homes. She'd been rebellious and had screaming fits, although she was never violent. She says, "I want the absolute best for him. I've waited a long time to hear his voice, and I'll wait longer if it means he can get the help he needs."

Meanwhile, on the other side of town, Devon tips desks. He throws books at other students. When the teacher asks if he'd like to take a "self-five," he runs down the hallway. He kicks a teacher in the face. I can't quite visualize the particulars of that, but that's what the guidance counselor tells me. She asks me to come to the school right away.

63

Crossroads Academy is a twenty-minute drive from our house. It looks like any ordinary public school, with a sprawling rectangular footprint and brick facade. I sign in, and the kindly office lady walks me upstairs to the seclusion room. As we turn the corner halfway up the stairwell, she stops and points to the rail running across the landing at the top. "Last week Devon was up there."

"On top of the rail?" I gasp.

She nods grimly. "He was running through the halls and came in here. He said he was going to jump."

I suck in a sharp breath. "Oh my God."

"I don't think he really wanted to." She begins the trudge up the remaining stairs ahead of me. "When we did a suicide assessment, he said he did it because he was bored."

In the silence of the second-floor hallway, I'm self-conscious as my flip flops slap on the floor like some sort of contorted Morse code distress signal. "Even if he wasn't trying to, he still could have slipped and fallen," I say.

"That's why he's lost his shoes." At my perplexed look, she explains, "They're less likely to run in their socks."

I hear the thumping and yelling long before we enter a classroom with several jumbled rows of desks. Devon's head pops in and out of view through the small square window of what I assume is the seclusion room as he hurls himself against the door. With each thrust a wiry man, a teacher-turned-jailer, pitches backwards. He resets his feet to maintain balance and hold the door closed.

This is the first time I'm seeing a seclusion room for myself. It's like a walk-in closet built into one corner of the larger classroom. The door closes, but, apparently, it doesn't lock. It's frightening. I get that the staff have to keep him from hurting himself, attacking other people, and damaging property, but surely there's a better way?

"Mr. Jones, this is Devon's mother, Mrs. Williams." My escort makes the introduction and heads back to the office.

"Something has to be done about this." Spit sprays from Mr.

Jones' mouth. "This has got to stop. We can't be doing this every day."

I'm embarrassed to be putting him out, but I'm also a bit indignant. Isn't this his job?

"Devon," I coax. "I'm here. Calm down so we can open the door, okay?"

"Back away," Mr. Jones hollers at Devon in an angry staccato. "Back! Away!" His body jolts with another impact. To me he says, "This has gotta stop. Every day. He does this every day." To Devon: "Back! Away!"

I peep through the window so Devon can see my face. I call to him, soothingly, "Did you hear that? Back up. Calm down, and he'll open the door."

The thumping stops. I peer through the small window. Devon stands, panting near the back wall. "He's calmed down," I say. "Let me go in."

With a disapproving grimace, Mr. Jones reluctantly steps back, and I swing open the door. It's heavy, like the door to an industrial walk-in refrigerator. I step in, fighting my own claustrophobia by reminding myself that there's no lock. The room is dim. The air is stale.

"Let's try to relax," I tell Devon, finding it nearly impossible to keep my tone calm. Taking measured breaths, I sink to the floor and press my back against the thickly padded walls. I'm surprised at how hard the floor is beneath me. I motion to Devon to sit beside me. "What happened?" I ask.

He flops down and bounces the back of his head on the padded wall behind him. "They was bein' mean to me. They locked me in here for no reason. No reason," he bites out.

I take deep breaths as I listen to him. Inhale. One, two, three, four, five. Exhale. Five, four, three, two, one. "If you calm down, we can go sit at a desk to talk instead of in here. Wouldn't that be so much better?" Five seconds in ... five seconds out.

Devon's head bounces softly back against the padded walls and he thinks about it.

Five seconds in ... five seconds out.

The door peels open and Mr. Jones sticks his head in. He barks, "You stop banging your head. Right! Now!"

Devon glares at him. He slams his forehead, hard, off of the floor.

64

With each family therapy session, the angry knot inside me unravels a little more. Kira isn't trying to create some sort of phony attachment between Devon and me. She's not trying to thrust him back into our house before he's ready. She's gently picking out the tangle that is our relationship, and it's working. I don't get that sick feeling in my stomach anymore when I'm driving to family therapy. I'm genuinely happy to see Devon. Our sessions feel productive.

I usually meet with Kira for about ten minutes before she brings Devon in. Today, I tell her about Sarrah. "I have a good feeling about her, and I've started letting her talk to Kayla on the phone."

She leans forward in her chair. "That is fascinating. It may be a window of opportunity. She may struggle to stay clean after she is released from supervision."

Kira is confirming my own thoughts. Because Sarrah is on parole, she's taking her prescribed bipolar medication, seeing a therapist, and is regularly tested for drugs and alcohol. It may be literally a once in a lifetime moment for Devon and Kayla to connect with her in a healthy way. "What do you think about her having contact with Devon?" I ask.

Kira doesn't respond immediately. She leans back and looks thoughtful. "Do you think she is supportive of the adoption?"

"She's not trying to compete with me. It's more like she wants the role of a friend or older sister."

Kira's stacked cosmetic jewelry rings flash as she gesticulates. "It could be for Devon very positive. How would you do it?"

"When he's home for a visit, we could call her on speaker phone. That's how it started off with Kayla."

Kira nods as she stands and reaches for the door knob. "I am excited about this. It could be for Devon a wonderful connection. Let me see if he is here yet and we'll bring him back."

Devon slouches and shuffles his sneakers against the carpet. I hand him the wax paper Dunkin' Donuts bag that I've brought and sweep the hood off of his head. He peers into the bag. Seeing his favorite treat, he grins. "Can I eat it now?"

Kira reaches for a napkin in her drawer. Devon settles next to me on the loveseat and bites into the donut. "Let us start off with what is going well for you," Kira prompts.

Devon holds a finger to his lips. "Mom don't like when people talk with food in their mouths. Her thinks it's gross."

"Mom *doesn't* like it … and you're so right." I give his knee a pat.

Finished chewing, he says, "I'm keepin' my room clean."

Kira shifts in her chair. "You are very neat and clean. I have heard that about you. What else?"

He devours the remaining donut in one huge bite. "I'm good during rec time."

"Recreational time is fun? You have to work on behaving during not so fun times as well."

"Did you make it to Level 2 yet?" I ask.

Licking his fingers, Devon shakes his head. "Them didn't want to give it to me."

Kira clucks her tongue. "How did it really happen?" When he doesn't respond, she says, "For what reason was it that you did not make level?"

His eyes loll to the floor and his head droops. "I gotted upset and ripped up my room."

"You broke the TV? Now none of you boys has a TV. You need to try again to make level. What do you think, Mom? Do you think Devon can do it?"

"He absolutely can," I say, with complete confidence. I've never doubted that Devon *can* do it. Will he *choose* to do it? That's another story.

He grins sheepishly.

"How was your last home visit?" Kira asks me.

"It was good. We went to the bike path," I say.

"Was that nice, Devon?" Kira asks.

"We went to Golden Corral," he says with a big smile.

Kira leans forward in her chair. "This weekend will be your first overnight in a while. Your first since coming to Bridgeton. How do you feel about that?"

"Good." Devon says, wearing a smile and a white powder mustache.

…

Devon presses his hands to his ears as the alarm screams.

"You need to earn trust back," I explain, soberly but not unkindly. I test the alarm on his bedroom door one more time. "For now, this will let me know when you leave your bedroom at night."

Devon keeps his face expressionless. Are his feelings hurt? Is he upset by the alarm? I hope not. But what else can I do?

It's Devon's first overnight since threatening to kill Brandon and me. I'd asked Delano to sleep upstairs, instead of in his recliner, so we wouldn't need the alarm. "Him not do nothing," Delano said, hissing his teeth. Delano has still never seen the frightening side of Devon. In fact, Devon is eager to please when Delano is around. He's always volunteering to vacuum or sweep. He seems to enjoy flaunting his relationship with Delano as if to show what he's withholding from me.

That night, I lay in bed wondering if Devon will figure a way around the alarm. Amias asked me to hide the knives. I did, but anything could be a weapon if we're asleep. Brandon snuggles on my right side and Kayla snores on my left. Amias stretches across the bottom of the bed, and I have my legs folded uncomfortably to make room for him. The kids are way too old and big to be in my bed. It's a long, restless night.

My eyes burn in the bright morning sunlight as I walk to the mailbox. The shadow of a migraine lurks behind my eyes from not sleeping. The box is packed full with several days' worth of mail. Sorting through, I find what I was hoping for, two hand-addressed envelopes, one for Devon and the other for Kayla—both from Sarrah.

A few weeks ago, at Kira's encouragement, Devon had his first conversation with Sarrah. I'd placed the phone on speaker and Sarrah's eager voice greeted him. Devon's responses were limited to, "Uh huh," "No," and nodding his head, which I reminded him she couldn't see. I didn't sense a lack of desire to talk to her, it was more that she's a stranger to him. I created a small collage for Devon with a picture of Sarrah forming a heart with her fingers. Next to that, I put a picture of her tattoo with his initials. I laminated it and gave it to him during a session with Kira. I heard from the staff that he keeps the laminated collage under his pillow.

Last time we spoke, Sarrah told me she was saving money to buy video games for Devon and Kayla, but I'd said not to worry about expensive gifts. "They'll love anything you give them because it's from you. It can be as simple as a lucky penny or one of your bracelets." She'd seemed relieved and said she'd put something in the mail for them right away.

I walk up the driveway carrying the envelopes. They're

decorated with doodled hearts and flowers. Sarrah's name and address are written in curly letters on the top left. I carefully tuck my fingernail under one envelope's seal and pry it open, trying not to tear the flap. Devon's card is a folded sheet of copy paper with a hand drawn puppy dog on the front. Inside it says,

> Devon,
> I've never forgotten you. I went through a lot when I was younger. I was living on the streets. I'm so sorry I couldn't take care of you. Please forgive me. I know you might be angry with me, and that's OK, but can we be friends? I thought you might need some luck so here's a lucky penny. Carry it with you everywhere you go.
> Love,
> Mommy Sarrah

There's a shiny penny from the year Devon was born, wedged into one corner of the envelope. Kayla's card has a pencil-sketched kitten and mentions a guardian angel necklace. She's going to be disappointed, though, because there is a tear in the corner of the envelope and no necklace.

Using a little glue, I reseal the envelopes. I find Devon and Kayla and hand them the cards. They tear them open. As Devon reads, his eyes grow wide. He searches the envelope for the penny. He grasps it in his fingers. "I never had me a lucky penny before," he says.

I smile, happy for him, but turn to console Kayla, who is searching the corners of her envelope.

65

"What's he doing now?" I say, recognizing Janice's voice on the other end of the phone. These calls mean only one thing: Devon is in trouble.

"You sure know your son," Janice says. She's one of the regular staff assigned to Devon's Bridgeton group home. "He's started his ballerina thing again."

"Ballerina?" I ask, pushing in my keyboard drawer and standing.

"Has no one told you about that? He has a couple different personalities. One is a ballerina, another is a thug." She tells me how the boys were playing football, and Devon didn't want to go inside for shower time. Left alone in the backyard with Janice, he'd skulked around the edges of the fence looking for sticks and threw them in her general direction. "You're not my boss you nigger," he spat.

I wince, hoping she doesn't think he learned that word from me.

Janice had leaned against the porch door and scrolled through her phone while discreetly tracking his movements. After a few minutes, Devon shook himself like a wet dog. He hooped his arms over his head and did his best imitation of a plié. When Janice didn't respond, he skipped across the lawn, arms haloed over his head, and twirled like a ballerina in a tutu.

I can't help but laugh out loud, picturing him, body like a husky football player, prancing across the lawn.

Janice chuckles. "He's been twirling and walking on his tiptoes for, oh, over an hour now. And he's talking in a high-pitched girl voice. I'm waiting him out, but thought I should let you know."

"I'm sorry," I say.

"Oh, don't be. That's my job." She clears her throat. "Some staff are wondering if he has multiple personality disorder. Have you ever had him checked for that?"

Of course not. How absurd. I can't believe that anyone is taking this "ballerina personality" seriously. But, squelching any sarcasm, I answer, "No. He's never acted that way before."

"Lately he's been blacking out also. He can't remember a thing after his fits are over."

How convenient. "Uh huh," I say, noncommittally.

"When he's in a mood, he throws his shoes away and then says he has no memory of doing it. You might could get him evaluated for multiple personality disorder and the blackouts to be sure."

I wonder if multiple personality disorder is even a real thing or if it's just a diagnosis for melodramatic TV shows. I ask Kira about it in our next session.

She hasn't heard about Devon's personalities and blackouts before either. "Multiple personality disorder has been reclassified as dissociative identity disorder," she explains. "It is rare, and I do not see where Devon meets diagnostic criteria."

I don't know anything about that, but one thing I know for sure is that Devon is faking these symptoms and getting a huge payout for doing so.

With a thoughtful look, Kira goes on. "After working with Devon for several months, I am at a bit of a loss. In sessions he seems to clearly understand what he needs to do, but he doesn't do it. Let us get him scheduled for a psych eval and a neurological and see if it gives some clues."

...

"A ballerina personality? I wish I could see that!" Becky laughs when I tell her about Devon's latest scheme. Then she asks, "Can you come over? My friends who have a kid like Devon are here. Remember, I told you about them?" When she adds a sing-song bribe, "I'll make you coffee," I head over.

I open Becky's front door and am hit with a tsunami of noise. Kids are everywhere, mine included. Running up and down the stairs. Playing ping-pong. I hear shouts of video gaming from upstairs. Becky introduces me to Ted and Carol, who are sitting at her kitchen table eating Tostitos and salsa. I join them.

"Coffee ..." I remind Becky, and she goes to make a fresh pot.

Ted laughs easily as we chat and passes me the salsa with well-worn hands sporting knobby knuckles. Carol is stoic with the look of someone trying to smile for appearances, but not really engaged. Her mind is elsewhere.

Ted tells me how they have one biological daughter, Bella, who's ten, and they adopted three boys out of foster care. The youngest, Ethan, is five. The oldest, Mat—he points through the sliding glass window at a boy with floppy curls—is jumping on the trampoline with

Brandon and Jacob. I can hear his laughter through the glass. There's a middle son too, Jake, and he's upstairs playing video games.

"Keri has two kids adopted out of foster care. I wanted you to talk because her son Devon is a lot like your son Mat," Becky says, directing the conversation.

She stops speaking abruptly as Kayla comes into the room with a petite, little girl who I assume is Bella. "We're going to take Ben for a walk," Kayla says.

"You know Ben is too old to go for walks," Becky tells her.

Kayla shrugs. "I'm gonna carry him." She disappears under the kitchen table and emerges cradling the dog in her arms.

Once the girls have gone out through the front door, Becky looks at me. "Mat has some serious behavioral problems. They sound a lot like Devon."

Carol fixes me with intense dark brown eyes. "He refuses to clean his room, do homework, do *anything* I tell him to. He won't do it just because I told him to. He's the most stubborn kid I've ever—"

Ted interrupts, "He's not that bad. You get frustrated too easily."

"He throws fits like a two-year-old," Carol spits out at Ted and her fury is palpable.

"It has a lot to do with parenting," Ted scoffs.

I hold up my hands. I don't know many details, but these are Becky's close friends and she's heard enough to feel their son has very similar issues to Devon. "Your son may have reactive attachment disorder like mine does. There's a book about it," I pause trying to recall the name, but only images of the cover come to me—purple with a teddy bear. I explain what I know of the disorder and say, "These kids see their mom as the enemy because of the abuse or neglect they experienced. Instead of trying to bond with her, they push her away. And," I say with emphasis and a hard look in Ted's direction, "they hide their behaviors from their dads as a way to control their mom."

Carol is nodding her head emphatically while Ted shakes his.

Becky leans across the table. "Ted, we've been dealing with this for years. Just because you don't see it doesn't mean it's not happening."

By the look on Ted's face, he doesn't agree.

Becky brings over a box of tissues, and Carol takes one. Her voice cracks, "I don't know what to do anymore. I feel like I'm going crazy. And when he broke Bella's iPod and threatened her, I lost it. I want to be loving, but I can't. I can't ..."

"I understand," I say, to reassure her. "You need to get a copy of that book. I think it's called something about love isn't enough."

"What do they do for kids with … what did you call it?"

"Reactive attachment disorder, RAD."

"How do they treat RAD?"

I wish that I had a better answer, but give her the truth instead. "What I've found is that there really aren't treatments to fix this." I tell her a little of our story and how Devon has been getting out of home treatment now for over three years and only getting worse.

Carol presses her hand to her throat. "What can I do?"

"I know I can't give Devon the help he needs at home. I've tried. So, I've had to pick what's best for my other kids and keep them safe. And that's why I leave him in those facilities."

Becky says, "You may need to start thinking like that too."

Ted pushes back his chair, walks to the sliding glass door and lets himself out. The three of us watch him in silence as he walks to the trampoline and begins talking and laughing with the boys.

Carol draws my attention back inside as she says, "I get so angry sometimes. I scare myself. Once, I picked him up by his neck." She extends her arm with her thumb and forefinger forming a C and I can practically see the kid dangling there. Her voice shakes. "I carried him straight up the stairs like that. Ted had to come and pull me away. I lost it."

There's no hesitation in my response now. "You need to get him out of your house. Everyone has a breaking point. You've got to get him out before something bad happens. It's easy to think if you spank them a little harder, or one more time, they'll get it. They won't."

Carol doesn't say the words, but I read the desperation in her eyes and the hopelessness in the slump of her shoulders. I know the unspoken root of this type of guilt. I lower my voice, "I don't tell many people this, but the truth is that I have a strong sense of responsibility for Devon, but that's it. I've tried to love him but I don't know how to."

Carol's rock-hard exterior crumbles. "That's exactly how I feel," she sobs out. "It's been eating me up inside. I don't love Mat, but I haven't ever been able to say it out loud."

66

We settle into a routine at Bridgeton. At our monthly CFT meetings, we review Devon's progress—or, more accurately, lack of progress—on his therapeutic goals. It's been months, and he has yet to get off of Level 1. He knows all of the rules and he knows his discharge plan. He can rattle it off from memory, but he simply won't comply with it. This perplexes the staff and Kira.

But not me.

Devon plans to discharge all right, but on his own terms. This is about him being oppositional. At New Hope, he learned that he can get a special set of rules and rewards. It probably started in kindergarten when Ms. Lizzie took him for walks. That's when he learned that he doesn't have to follow the rules. He's stubbornly holding out for special treatment here too.

We have family therapy every other week, and Devon comes home on the weekends. The kids look forward to his visits. He's a much fought over player for their backyard kickball and soccer teams. He plays Candy Land with Brandon. As night settles over the house, the kids become nervous and fearful. They pile into my bed, despite the alarm on Devon's bedroom door. Devon hates the alarm, and I don't blame him. But, I don't remove it either.

Kira suggests a family therapy session with Devon, Amias, and Kayla to work on healing the relationship. While they meet, I sit in the lobby. I respond to work emails on my phone and scroll through my Facebook feed. I upload a couple pictures—one of Kayla getting ready to clean the bathroom with rubber gloves on her feet like flippers, and one of Brandon asleep, hugging his football like a teddy bear. I tag Papa, my mom, and Becky. I tag Sarrah too.

An hour later, the kids emerge from Kira's office. "Ms. Williams, let me speak with you for a moment." Kira nods toward the receptionist, an unspoken instruction to keep an eye on the kids. Amias pulls his school iPad out of his backpack, probably to show Devon some inane video on YouTube.

I follow Kira into the office and sink into my usual spot on the loveseat. "How did it go?" I ask.

"Devon talked about feeling left out and not living at home. Amias and Kayla discussed some of their fears." She pauses for a long moment as though choosing her words.

I brace for the worst.

She says, "I am glad we did this because I was able to see the family dynamic. Amias and Kayla are very well-spoken for their age. They are mature and have excellent vocabularies. Especially Amias. He thinks and communicates like an adult." She shakes her head as though she was taken off guard.

Did she think that our whole family is a mess? I'm heartened that someone is finally seeing that I'm not actually a terrible mother.

Kira continues, "I am going to have to think about how to help Devon bridge that gap. They are on a whole different level than he is. He's never going to fit in with them."

Before leaving, I snap a few pics of the three kids together. Devon, now twelve, stands in the middle with his arms over Kayla and Amias' shoulders. They make faces, and it's impossible to get a shot with all three of them smiling. I settle for a goofy pose.

I hug Devon goodbye and tell him that I'll see him in a couple of days at his doctor's appointment.

"Am I gettin' shots?" he asks.

"No, nothing like that. It'll just be talking." I give his arm an encouraging squeeze and head for the car with Kayla and Amias.

...

"I don't remember nothin' when I wake up," Devon says, with his trademark, wide-eyed look.

"What do you mean, wake up?" the neurologist asks.

"I wake up and don't remember nothin'. It's all black."

"What about before you go to bed? Do you remember then?"

Devon's eyes slant toward the ceiling. "Yeeeessss," he draws out the word like a string of silly putty.

"You remember what's happened until you go to sleep but wake up with no memory of the incident? That's what you're calling 'blacking out?'"

Devon bobs his head. "I remember what I'm doing before I go to sleep. I wake up and forgot."

The doctor places a stethoscope to Devon's chest and back. Janice and I sit on chairs pushed against one wall of the exam room. As the doctor performs a basic physical exam, he continues asking questions. "Is there anything specific that seems to cause the blackouts?"

"Bein' mad. I saw monsters on my eyelids tellin' me what to do too."

I struggle to school my features. Devon's always thought the best way to sell a lie is to over sell it. At least that makes it easy to know when he's lying. The doctor begins to type notes into the computer.

After a pause, Devon continues, unbidden. "Nobody believes me. But I don't remember nothin' when I'm havin' a fit. Nothing. 'cept sometimes voices telling me to do things. Like throwin' my shoes away or hittin' the window with rocks."

"Do they ever tell you to do other things?"

"What kind of things?"

The doctor shrugs. "Ordinary things? Like, go watch TV? Or look out the window?"

"No. Just bad stuff."

The doctor writes an order for a brain scan, but he tells Janice and me that it's not necessary to have one performed, unless we want to. Devon shows no sign of a neurological disturbance or injury.

Due to liability, I assume, Bridgeton schedules the scan anyway. The results of the neurological exam and the scan are, as expected, both clear. Bridgeton provides this information as well as other documentation, to a third-party clinician who does a new psychological evaluation of Devon. A few weeks later, the results are in.

The report begins with a summary of Devon's social and early childhood history. This time, for the Kinetic Family Drawing test, Devon drew a detailed and colorful setting with stick figure people. When the clinician asked him what the family was doing in the drawing he responded:

```
Dad is about to teach us how to
swim. Mom is watching. She doesn't
do much.
```

I bat away my annoyance and continue reading. The evaluation reaffirms the RAD diagnosis but, this time, explains how it impacts Devon's behaviors in a way that makes a whole lot more sense than what Beth had explained to me:

```
He seems impulsive and resentful.
```

> These oppositional behaviors are a defensive stance to combat past and currently felt humiliations. Deep resentments toward authority figures are projected outward causing frequent social and family difficulties.
>
> Punishments probably only reinforce his rebelliousness, defiance, and suspicious attitude. The desire to provoke fear and to intimidate others likely stems from a need to overcome his own sense of weakness and to vindicate past perceived injustices.

As I read, I hold my breath, daring to feel hopeful. Is this the key I've been searching for?

> In treatment, Devon will likely challenge and seek to outwit therapists by setting up situations that test the therapist's skills, catch inconsistencies, arouse anger, and belittle and humiliate him/her. He may further actively impede progress and rob himself of what steps he has made toward treatment goals. He will likely resist exploring motives and feelings and will likely often blame others for problems and externalize responsibility for his actions. It is unlikely that he will experience guilt or accept blame for the turmoil he causes.

I scramble for my cell phone. As soon as the call connects, I blurt, "You're not going to believe it. I got Devon's new psych eval—"

"Hang on. I can't talk," Becky says. "I'm at the grocery store."

I ignore her. This can't wait. "Listen to this. 'He seems impulsive and resentful …'" I read the paragraphs to her.

"Wow."

"I know. She even realized how he manipulates therapists like he did with Wanda and Beth. I can't believe it." My eyes race ahead. I zero in on a paragraph further down on the page. "Okay listen to this," I say and read:

```
Devon seems to have a difficult-to-
modify character and will likely be
resistant to treatment.
```

"Sounds like she really figured out what's going on," Becky says. "So, what does she recommend?"

"She diagnosed him with RAD and oppositional defiant disorder, like New Hope did, but this woman actually understands how it is affecting him. I can't believe someone finally understands what's going on." I scan ahead, looking for recommendations. I hear Becky talking to the cashier and wait until she's finished. "They recommend he continue in treatment programs long-term. Medication management. And she says we need to get juvenile justice involved early."

"It sounds like this psychologist actually knows what she's talking about," Becky says.

Relieved and optimistic, I agree, "Now that we know what's going on, we can get real treatment."

67

Laughing a little too loudly, Sarrah runs her fingers through her long, fluorescent blue and pink hair. The only flaw on her heart-shaped face is a pale scar, like chipped porcelain, on one side of her mouth. We sit across from each other in a booth at Chili's, and I can see that Devon has her smile. Kayla fidgets, pulling at the strings of her ripped jeans.

This is the first time Sarrah is seeing her children in a decade. "Let me tell you what my boyfriend and I do. We pick each other's noses." She mimes the motion. "Then we make the other person eat it. Isn't that funny?" She hoots with laughter, and the kids think she is hilarious.

Devon is chirpy, eager to capture and hold Sarrah's full attention. He tells her that he likes bowling, video games, soccer, Legos, and dogs. His favorite color is green and his best friend is Bobby. There is no "best friend Bobby," but I say nothing.

He nibbles on a chip, and Sarrah exclaims, "You need more cheese. You're not worried about double dipping, are you? Don't be silly." Dunking her half-eaten chip into the queso, Sarrah levers the whole thing into her mouth. She looks around the table, chomping enthusiastically. As if in slow motion, she lifts a hand to cover her mouth. "Oh," she mumbles. "You don't double dip, do you?" Her face blushes. "I'm so embarrassed. I'm so different than y'all."

It's true. We are very different, but not in a bad way.

We spend the next day bowling, seeing a movie, and painting pottery. Back home, I ask Sarrah to tell us Devon and Kayla's birth stories. With Kayla curled up next to her on the couch, Sarrah pulls Devon onto her lap. "You were my Valentine's Day baby." She kisses the tip of his nose. "All I wanted to do was hold you."

"What was my real last name?" Devon asks.

"It was Hollis. But I like Williams much better. Devon Williams—what a great name." She tickles Kayla's side until they both giggle and roll onto the floor. "All the nurses said you were the prettiest baby girl they'd ever seen." In whispers, and between kisses, she tells them both how much she loves them and apologizes for not being able to take care of them.

Later I assemble shampoo, conditioner, and towel as I watch the end of Sarrah's cigarette float like a firefly in the darkness of the backyard. Once on Facebook, she told me that she has "growing hands." In prison the women would ask her to braid their hair because she would make it grow. I'm pretty sure she has healing lips too.

I call Kayla over to the kitchen and have her climb up on the counter. She lays on her back with her head over the sink. Sarrah rushes over and asks if she can wash Kayla's hair instead of me. Kayla's lips twitch shyly and she nods. Sarrah cradles Kayla's head in the sink. She massages in shampoo and conditioner, stopping several times to kiss Kayla's forehead. I'm overwhelmed at the tenderness of the moment.

They watch *Full House* and Sarrah braids Kayla's hair. Kayla falls asleep with her head in Sarrah's lap, and I put Devon to bed.

"I never abandoned Devon," Sarrah tells me. "I went to the parking lot for a few minutes to meet a guy friend who was going to give me some money. This girl who stayed in the motel was upset because he was her ex-boyfriend. That's why she called the cops on me."

"At least Devon went back to Phyllis," I say.

Sarrah rears her head back. "I hated that bitch." Glancing down at Kayla she covers her mouth. "Sorry. All she wanted was the money. When I came home with Devon, she didn't want me to pick him up and hold him at all. She said holding babies spoils them. She'd leave him to cry and make me leave him too. That's one of the reasons I left."

I feel ill. I've always thought Devon's foster placement with Phyllis was good—more than good, loving and nurturing. After a long silence, I ask, "What happened with Kayla?"

"The social worker took her right after she was born. I'm not gonna lie to you," Sarrah says, her fingertips feathering across Kayla's sleeping face. "I sat on the curb outside the hospital. I had nowhere to go. No one to call for a ride. I gave up right then. I knew I'd never be able to get them back." She was arrested for passing a bad check and told the only way to stay out of prison was to agree to terminate her parental rights. Knowing she could never get her kids back anyway, she signed. Her eyes well with tears.

The next morning, Sarrah and I drop Amias, Kayla, and Brandon off at school. After hugs, kisses, and cheek pinching, we wave goodbye. Before dropping Devon at school, he and I take Sarrah to the airport. She hugs him tight, seemingly unaware of his stiff body, and kisses his cheeks with loud smooching sounds. On a final wave goodbye, she calls, "I love you. Promise me you'll be good."

68

We assemble for the monthly CFT meeting at the Bridgeton offices. "Ms. Kira, how is family and individual therapy going?" Jesi, the director, asks. She's coiffed in a white pants suit and smart red heels. Everyone else, like me, is dressed casually.

"Therapy is fine," Kira's voice squawks from the speakerphone on the middle of the conference room table. "We are not going deep, though. For example, Devon's birth mother came to visit. He was able to tell me what they did—bowling, movies, painting pottery, and so forth—but he didn't discuss any feelings."

"I see he's still on Level 1 and hasn't made any progress. What do you recommend?" Jesi asks.

Kira says, "Honestly, at this point, I'm not sure we can safely manage him in the group home setting given his behaviors. We need to be considering if for him group home is an appropriate level of care."

Jesi asks Janice about Devon's incidents over the past month. Bridgeton keeps me well informed, so I already know about everything she reports: multiple altercations at school, incidents of suicidal ideation, and assaulting staff and other group home residents. There's been a lot of property damage too. The most serious was when he turned on the hose then fed it through a window into the house. I'm waiting on a bill for that. On and on the list goes. Then Janice says, "I'm concerned about his aggression toward his family. He's been saying he's going to fuck and kill his sister and mom."

In uncertain handwriting, I scribble this into my notebook.

Janice goes on, "He also bullies the younger children at the group home. We may need to think about moving him to a house with kids who are older than him."

I try to focus on what she's saying, but I'm trying to make sense of what I've written in my notes. He's 12 and watches *Sponge Bob*. "Fuck and kill his sister?" I can't understand where this is coming from.

Jesi asks, "Why do we think he's continuing to engage in these behaviors?"

Janice shrugs. "Most times, there doesn't seem to be a trigger.

Everything will be going fine for him and then for no reason he starts acting up. And, he can turn it on and off."

Kira's voice calls out from the speaker phone. "It is true. It is one of the more difficult things about Devon to understand. We have not been able to identify specific triggers. And, as Ms. Jesi says, he does have the ability to start and stop the behaviors."

"We're called to Crossroads Academy at least a couple times a week," Janice says. "Some mornings he'll get up and say 'I think I'll cause some trouble today,' like he's warning us. Then, sure enough, he'll start acting up." Turn-it-up-Tuesdays flashes through my mind.

"Is there anyone on staff who he connects with?" Jesi asks.

Janice answers. "He gets along well with Mr. Ryan, but he's on administrative leave."

No one mentions why, because we all know. Two weeks ago, Devon went to school and reported to the assistant principal that Mr. Ryan had punched him in the face. Devon had no marks and when Mr. Ryan, the staff, and the other kids were interviewed, their stories were consistent.

Devon had become upset when Mr. Ryan told him they were out of bagels. Devon wanted a bagel for breakfast and told Mr. Ryan that he'd be getting him fired. At school, he told the assistant principal he was being abused at the group home. CPS had Bridgeton put Mr. Ryan on leave during the investigation. Unpaid leave. We all know the allegations will eventually come back unsubstantiated, and Mr. Ryan will be reinstated. But there will be no consequences for Devon, practically guaranteeing that this will happen again. And again.

We discuss and decide on a new discharge plan. Up until now, it has been for Devon to "step down" to home. Given his continued violent outbursts and the safety concerns, the CFT team changes it to be a "step up," back to PRTF.

Devon comes into the CFT meeting for the last few minutes, and Ms. Jesi reviews the new discharge plan with him.

"But I thought I was goin' home." Devon says, his eyes flickering toward me.

Under the table, I reach out and place a hand on his knee to comfort him.

"You're in control, Devon," Ms. Jesi tells him. "This plan isn't written in stone. It can still change. Show us with your good behavior, so we can help you get home. It takes 30 days, at least, to get you moved. Use that time to prove to us you can be safe."

69

That night, Devon won't shower or brush his teeth. He kicks holes in the living room wall and darts into his bedroom.

He loops a belt around the closet rod.
Laughs wildly.
The on-duty worker rounds the corner.
Devon snaps off his hysteria.
Positions his throat on the belt.
Lets his knees buckle.

70

My car idles in the school car line. I scroll through my phone, reading news headlines while I wait for the afternoon bell to ring. A whistle shrills, and students flood the lanes to find their parents' cars. Kayla and Brandon race toward me to see who will get to sit in front. Today, it's Kayla, and I wince as she slams the door. Brandon climbs into the backseat, thankfully with all his fingers still intact.

"I'm starving." It's Brandon's opening line pretty much every afternoon. Kayla sorts through the Chick-fil-A bag that I've brought and passes him a box of chicken nuggets and a barbeque sauce. Amias saunters toward the car and climbs into the back seat next to Brandon.

The whistle shrills again, and I inch forward. "How was school?" I ask.

"We got our EOG scores today," Amias says.

"Brandon," Kayla snaps. "Chew with your mouth closed."

"You can't tell me what to do," he garbles out.

"Oh, yes I can," she says, and tugs her sweatshirt up over her ears.

Amias tears open his envelope and announces his scores. Kayla hands me hers. At a red light I slip my index finger under the flap and open it. My heart skips a beat, and I swell with pride. "You did great! You got a four in reading!"

Kayla's dimples wink at me and she asks, "I can be a criminologist now?"

"You sure can," I tell her. Kayla loves watching *Forensic Files* and *Unsolved Mysteries* with me. She's fascinated by the techniques that detectives use and has become pretty good at predicting who the culprit is. "Look how far you've come. Last year you got a two. And remember in kindergarten, when you didn't even know your letter sounds?"

"That's 'cause Ms. Laird was so mean to me."

I crinkle my face in surprise. "What do you mean?"

"She didn't like me. She was always yelling at me."

"Why didn't you tell me?" I ask in dismay. "I would have helped you."

Before she can answer, my cell phone rings. It's Eastside. They tell me Devon was brought in late last night for trying to hang himself with a belt and they need consent to treat and some background information.

...

"Buckle up," I remind Devon when I pick him up from Eastside a few days later. I already went by the group home for his things which they'd packed into two black trash bags.

"I'm hungry. Can we get McDonalds?" he asks.

I pull out a Ziplock bag with a peanut butter sandwich. "I brought you this," I say, passing it to him. They'll be no rewards of fast food.

"I'm allergic to peanut butter," he mutters.

He's not.

I navigate onto the highway to begin the long trek to Treehouse Village Family Care in Black Mountain, the new placement that Bridgeton arranged. They focus on Cognitive Behavioral Therapy (CBT), which is behavior modification. That's what I've always thought Devon needs.

Before long, he begins to nibble at his sandwich. I flip through the radio stations and settle in for the ride. Devon watches out the window and nods off for a good portion of the trip.

Two hours later, as our feet crunch across the gravel parking lot, I take in the beautiful mountain view and fresh smell of nature. The sprawling campus has rolling fields flanked by woods and a pasture for horses used for equine therapy. Everything is new and modern and clean. "It's beautiful here, isn't it?" I say.

Devon shrugs.

During check-in, the intake coordinator explains their point system. It's much the same as Bridgeton, but Devon's eyes light up when he hears that he can earn the privilege of riding dirt bikes. As we continue with the paperwork, the counselor explains their two-week orientation period. Devon will be restricted to the locked unit to ensure his safety. Once he's shown that he can handle being in less restrictive settings, usually after ten days, they'll allow him to start taking part in campus activities and begin to earn privileges like riding dirt bikes.

I head for home feeling optimistic. The only downside of the facility is the location. I'll have to take off two days from work every month to travel there for family therapy and CFT meetings. Other than that, it's a promising placement.

Disappointingly, Devon's "honeymoon period" at Treehouse is over before I pull into my driveway two hours later. He insists that he should start at Level 4 and see if he can "keep it." Day after day, I get calls. He grabs female staff's genitals, threatens to rape them, and calls them "bitch" and "whore." He puts socks in his mouth to choke himself and runs around naked. He demands to be taken to the hospital.

Treehouse staff give him restricted time in his bedroom and worksheets to complete as consequences. He attacks the staff, tears up the worksheets, and urinates on his mattress and walls. The workers are surprised by Devon's dogged persistence, but they assure me that they can handle him. Day-after-day, he ups the ante in what becomes a dangerous game of chicken.

One afternoon, he strips naked and runs around the unit. He squats in the corner of his room and defecates. He takes his feces and smears it on the wall.

Then he pops a chunk in his mouth.

A supervisor calls me with the news. "We almost never take kids to the hospital, but eating feces is dangerous." I cover the mouthpiece of my phone and retch. Unaware of my distress, the worker continues, "It's probably good he's there. They'll stabilize him, and, when he comes back, he might be on some new medications that will help."

Running around naked? Eating feces? I never believed that Devon was actually psychotic, until now.

71

Speeding toward Black Mountain, the green trees blur past me. I've been in touch with the hospital social worker and our clinician at Treehouse every couple of days since they admitted Devon. Little did I know, Treehouse was stringing me along, while secretly counting down the days to a deadline I wasn't even aware of.

After 14 consecutive days of Devon not being at the facility, they have the contractual right to discharge him, and that's exactly what they did. I had no way to know about this loophole or any reason to assume that they'd use it.

When they emailed me the discharge documents, I learned that Treehouse had been providing Devon with a one-on-one—they'd been paying for a full-time dedicated staff person just for him because he was unable to go more than a few minutes without escalating to crisis. I understand now that this was a significant financial reason they wanted to get rid of him as soon as possible.

Though they tricked me in order to discharge Devon, I'm thankful the clinician wrote an honest evaluation of his condition to help in finding a new placement:

> It is very clear that client requires constant 1:1 attention which is very difficult for any family to do, especially with other children. Client's mother is very invested in treatment and is concerned that he's been out of the home for so long.
>
> Due to the ongoing behaviors and unsafe symptoms, it would not be in the client or family's best interest for him to be returned home at this time.

In conclusion, the clinician recommends that Devon be "stepped up" to long-term hospitalization.

However, the hospital where Devon is now marooned disagrees. He's had no behavioral or psychiatric issues since they admitted him. As far as they're concerned, he doesn't even qualify for his current admission, much less long-term hospitalization.

Treehouse doesn't have to take Devon back, but they are responsible for securing a new placement for him. Every PRTF we sent an application to rejected him. Finally, the director at Treehouse called-in a favor, and that's how we got a new placement. Now I'm tasked with picking Devon up from the hospital and taking him to the new facility.

As I wait for a nurse to unlock the door, I peer into Devon's small, private room. He's wearing child-sized, tan scrubs and brown hospital socks with slip guards striped across the bottoms. There's a bed and guest chair bolted to the floor and a television mounted high on one wall with a metal grill around it. It might as well be a jail cell.

I walk in, and Devon moves to kneeling on the bed and bounces up and down. "Did you bring me anything?" he chirps.

"How are you doing?" I ask

"Are you takin' me home?"

I sit on the chair. "We talked about this. You're going to a new PRTF."

"I wanna go back to Treehouse. Did you ask if I can?"

It's hard to know how to answer. If I admit that he was too much for them to handle, he'll be more likely to act up in future placements. I settle for a partial truth. "You've been here so long they gave your bed away."

His face drops and he stops bouncing. "But I like it there. Can't they give me one more chance?"

Shaking my head, I say. "They already have a new kid who has taken your spot."

Devon sits back against his pillow, clearly disappointed. He goes back to watching the TV.

I meet briefly with the doctor. He exudes the sincerity and naivete fitting of his baby face and floppy hair. "When I tell you Devon's had no issues, I mean *no* issues. He's been polite and well behaved for his entire stay."

"Wouldn't you say that means he has a lot of control over his behavior?" I ask. "I mean, I'm an adult, and I couldn't handle being locked in a room for 21 days …"

"I know the facility, Treehouse Village Family Care, was it?" He looks at me quizzically and I nod. "They reported some serious concerns, but, like I said, we haven't seen anything like that while he's been here with us."

"So would you agree this is behavioral?" I press.

He hems and haws and doesn't give me a direct answer.

I return to Devon's "cell" to wait for the staff to process his discharge. There's something disturbing about watching him giggle at cartoons. He doesn't seem to have any idea of how serious his behaviors are.

"Devon, turn the TV off. I want to talk to you."

He fingers the remote and reluctantly presses the off button.

"We can't keep doing this. You've been good while you've been here, so, I know you *can* control your behavior, if you want to. Why weren't you controlling yourself at Treehouse?"

His eyes dart around the room belying his numb demeanor. "It's my medicines. Them don't work."

That's an answer I didn't expect. I falter before inspiration hits. "I take medications too. Did you know that? When I don't take my medication, my skin feels like ants are running across it."

Now he looks interested.

"Thousands of ants. Can you imagine? Don't you think that would make it harder for me to be patient? It's harder. But I can do it." I pause, then help him connect the dots. "Your medications work the same way. They aren't magic pills. They make it easier for you, but you still have to make good choices." Of course, I know that the medication is just an excuse. The medications Devon is on now, while behaving in the hospital, are exactly the same as the ones he was taking at Treehouse.

I had to leave my purse in a locker, so I don't have anything—not my cell phone, keys, or a pen. I ask Devon if he has a paper and pen.

"Them won't let me have that stuff."

Seems like overkill. This is a hospital. Devon is a kid. I rap on the window, my gut somersaulting at the reminder that I, too, am locked in here right along with Devon. A nurse approaches, and I ask for a paper and pen. How does being in here not bother Devon? She gives me two pieces of white copy paper and one purple and one blue crayon.

"Let me show you something." I motion to Devon, and he scoots to the bottom of the bed. I draw a purple line and add the outline of a house. "Your life is like a journey along a path. That's our house." I draw another house along the path. I label it "group home." A bit further down the path I draw a box and label it PRTF.

I hand him the blue crayon and the paper. "Imagine you're at a PRTF, like Treehouse, and you want to get home. How do you get there?"

He furrows his brow as if it's a trick question but traces the path I've drawn from PRTF through the group home to home.

"Exactly. That's the path home. But look where you are. You're in the hospital." Off to the side I draw a giant letter H. "And here's what you're doing." I draw loops from PRTF to the hospital and back to PRTF. "You're going in circles. Do you see? Is there a path from the hospital to home?"

"No," he admits slowly.

I continue drawing the circles to emphasize my point. "You can go to the hospital. You know what to do to get here if that's what you want. But it will always take you back to PRTF. Anytime you go to the hospital, it's a detour that keeps you from coming home." Devon scoots back to the top of the bed, clutching the drawing like it's a treasure map.

After a wait of several more hours, Devon is discharged. We drive east from Black Mountain, passing only a few miles away from home, but I don't stop. I'm afraid that, if I do, Devon will refuse to get back in the car to go to his new placement, a PRTF called Archway House. We settle in for another two and a half hours west to rural Hoke County.

On the way, I buy Devon his favorite fast food, a McDonald's number two with a Diet Coke. "I have to make a call for work. I need you to be quiet, okay?"

He nods, his mouth stuffed too full to speak.

Scrolling through my cell, I find the phone number. My client is upset about the delay in their software implementation. I listen to the irate woman detail her grievances. I roll my eyes dramatically at Devon through the rearview mirror when her voice becomes particularly shrill through the Bluetooth. He grins back.

"I understand your concerns," I say, in a conciliatory tone. "Our highest priority is for you to be successful." I go on to explain the steps in our process and how completing each one in order minimizes risks and maximizes the chances of a successful go-live with the software. Then I lay out a detailed plan to move their project forward. By the time our call ends, she's calm, reassured, and satisfied. Devon is asleep.

I flip through AM radio stations. Everyone's talking about the guy who shot up a church in Charleston. So close to home. I listen for a little while, hoping to hear information about his motive or mental health, but it's all speculation at this point. I hit the FM button and scan for a country music station.

My GPS can't find Archway House and I have to call for directions. It's a set of modular homes in the middle of a field, in the middle of nowhere. Mr. Jay, a slow-moving man who is literally wider than the door, lets us into the main building. His shirt strains over his belly. I remark, "Hard to find this place. It's really rural."

He appraises Devon from head to toe and drawls, "We find kids are a lot less likely to go AWOL when they got nowhere to run but the woods."

I raise my eyebrows at Devon with a knowing tilt of my head. He's scared of bears. And the dark. And bugs.

Mr. Jay takes us to the conference room to complete the intake paperwork. These facilities are old hat for Devon and me now. We know all about the locked doors and stripped-down bedrooms. There's always a point system and an orientation period. We'll have family therapy every other week and CFT meetings are once a month. I sign the stack of intake papers without reading them. It's not like I have a choice.

72

After several months at Archway House, Medicaid's length of stay guidelines dictates another move for Devon even though he has not made any progress on his treatment goals and has only become more non-compliant and physically aggressive. This will be his third "lateral move" to another PRTF. Our case worker is concerned that Devon is becoming resistant to treatment, that he's become "institutionalized." She pulls some strings and calls in favors to get him into Spring Harbor, the best facility for attachment work in the county. It's local, which means we can also go back to regular home visits and in-person family therapy too. I'm optimistic that one good placement can reverse our negative momentum.

As I arrive on campus with Devon, I begin to understand why Spring Harbor has such a daunting waiting list. It looks like a college campus, with stately buildings nestled into picturesque woods and set on manicured lawns. Devon's new "cottage" is a modern building with a full kitchen and sunny living room. He'll have his own private bedroom and bathroom.

After we complete the intake paperwork, I briefly meet with Devon's petite new therapist, Molly. She has an adorable bubble of a pregnant belly. I sure hope Devon never turns on her.

Within days, "Spring Harbor" is regularly flashing across my cell phone. Devon antagonizes his peers, damages property, disrupts the classroom, and is physically aggressive. He runs away, and staff, following Spring Harbor's baffling protocol, trails him through the woods for hours. Another time, he climbs over the security fence and takes off down the road. Staff follows him on a bicycle. He gets road rash when they restrain him on the asphalt. When they go for outings, he tries to open the van door and to climb out the windows while the vehicle is still moving.

He breaks a plastic cup and uses the shards as shanks. He throws DVDs, bites, kicks, and punches. He refuses to do any classwork.

What bothers me most are the continued reports that he strips down naked during some outbursts. This behavior started at Treehouse and is still happening with concerning regularity two placements later. What teenaged boy does that? I try to imagine a scenario, any scenario, where Amias would become so upset that he'd strip naked like that. I can't. To me, this behavior may signal true psychosis. And, if so, perhaps we need to relook at his medications.

I have asked Molly about doing a med wash—taking Devon off of all of his medications and starting fresh. Obviously, the medications he's on aren't helping, and who knows how much of his behavior could be affected by side effects and interactions of the medications that have been layered one on top of the other. She said the Spring Harbor psychiatrist refused. No reason given.

Molly discourages me from discussing "incidents" at Spring Harbor with Devon, but I need to understand why he's running around naked. During our next home visit he eagerly watches as I prepare a late Sunday lunch. I'm making his favorite, salmon filets, and they're roasting in the oven. I ask, "They said you got upset about having to go inside the other day?"

"Can I help?" he asks peering across the counter top at the salad I'm making.

I still the knife. I watch as Devon's eyes fixate on the shiny metal. I shake my head. I'm being ridiculous. He's looking at the vegetables. He loves salad. I say, "Thanks, but I'm almost done. So, tell me what happened."

"Them said we could stay out and play. Another kid gotted into trouble. So we all had to go in."

"Everyone gets punished for what one kid does?"

He nods. "Them say there's not enough staff. It's not fair."

I chop a tomato into rough chunks, knowing how many times Devon has been the kid who cost everyone rec time. I agree with him though, it's not fair. "What I don't understand is why you would run around naked."

Devon nibbles on a fingernail and fidgets. If he's embarrassed discussing it, why isn't he embarrassed doing it? After a few beats of silence, he says, "Them won't restrain me if I don't have no clothes on."

A sharp heat slices across my finger. My eyes jerk down to the blood gushing from the wound.

"You okay?" Devon hurries around the counter to help.

I grab a paper towel and wince as I press it to the cut. My finger throbs and blood seeps through the paper towel as I let the full ramifications of Devon's words sink in. Devon gets a Band-Aid out of the junk drawer. I try to put it on myself, but can't do it one handed. "Thank you," I tell Devon as he helps me.

Going back to our conversation, I say, "I don't understand. You take your clothes off so they won't restrain you?"

Reanimated by the topic, Devon throws out his arms. "They don't need to be doin' that. They shouldn't be touching me. They got no right …"

"I wouldn't want to be restrained either." An involuntary shudder courses through me at just the thought of being trapped like that. "But you do understand that they can't let you hurt yourself or someone else?"

"But I'm not gonna really hurt anyone."

Devon clears his throat, then says, in a conspiratorial tone, "I go into the bathroom and bedroom too, when I'm doin' that."

"Why? What do you mean?"

"There are no cameras in there."

And it all clicks. It's a way to avoid being restrained and to avoid the tattle tale cameras. It's egregious, yes, but I still feel better. I've always known his fits of rage are behavioral. Now I know his naked fits of rage are behavioral too. They're just a clever thwarting of the system, not part of some psychosis.

Later, on the drive back to Spring Harbor, I tell Devon, "You know, the staff won't be as nice to you if you keep making things hard for them. They'll find little ways to get back at you."

Devon looks at me through the rearview mirror, uncharacteristically focused.

I continue, "They might not pick you for an activity or let you have extra chances. Or maybe they'll give you the smallest cookie." Do you know what I mean?

He nods that he understands. For his sake, I hope that he does.

The next day, I get a call from Molly. She tells me that Devon is acting up because he had such a bad home visit. He's told them he was made to watch everyone else in the family eat his favorite dinner, while he was given only a bowl of cereal.

73

Devon is agitated. "Mr. Andy punched me in the face. And he kicked me in the ribs." His face looks completely normal with no marks or visible bruises or swelling.

"How could a grown man punch you and not leave a mark?" I ask.

Devon shrugs. "I promise. Him did."

Molly keeps her tone neutral. "Can you tell us what happened?"

Devon mumbles, "I don't remember. I blacked out."

"Let me bring up the incident report," Molly says as she taps keys on her laptop. "Let's see here. You were spraying Axe cologne in your peers' faces. Says here—"

"It wasn't hurting' nobody," Devon interrupts. "It stinked in that room. The kids was farting. That's why I was doin' it with the Axe."

"You threatened Mr. Andy and said, 'I'm going to tell them you punched me in the face so you get fired.'" Molly looks up from her screen. "Did you say that?"

Devon picks at a scab on one of his knuckles and doesn't respond or make eye contact.

"Says here you punched yourself in the face. Then you vomited on staffs' legs, and attempted to bite them?" Molly's face doesn't betray what she thinks. She simply fixes Devon with a long gaze but he doesn't respond.

Molly tells both of us that she's watched the video and the footage shows the entire incident. Mr. Andy did not punch Devon. Devon did punch himself. Despite this, Mr. Andy is now on unpaid administrative leave until the investigation is complete.

Devon ducks his head on a smirk.

"When you were feeling upset about the smell, did you try to use any of your coping skills?" Molly asks.

As they talk, panic punches behind my ribs. What would happen if Devon made an accusation against me? Witnesses, even a video, hasn't saved Mr. Andy from a CPS investigation. At the house there are no cameras and no staff.

Shifting in my seat, I say, "I'm really concerned about the false allegations that Devon is making. For now, I think we should have our family visits on the campus where there are cameras and staff."

Devon's head flies up. "I wouldn't do that to you. I only do that to staff."

"Actually, you have done it to me."

Devon shakes his head.

"Yes, you did just this past week. You told Ms. Molly that I didn't feed you and made you watch everyone else eat."

"I was kiddin'." His eyes glass into teary pools.

"I made that dinner special for you, Devon, because I knew it was your favorite," I say, venturing the tiniest bit of vulnerability.

He begs, "Give me one more chance. Please. I was kiddin'."

In moments like this he's a little boy again with chocolate brown eyes, a spattering of freckles, and a hopeful future. "Sometimes things are too serious and dangerous for chances," I say, softly. I ask Molly, "Do you have staff who could escort Devon on home visits?"

"We don't offer a service like that."

"I'd be willing to private pay …"

But Molly says that it's not possible.

After Devon and I say our goodbyes, she escorts him back to the unit while I wait. When she returns, she says, "There's one thing I did want to ask you about, but not in front of Devon."

"Okay …" I say, apprehensively.

"I know this can be a sensitive topic for adoptive parents, but I think it's important for Devon. He has some basic questions about his birth mom. He'd like to know her name and why he was put up for adoption. We explored this a little, and I feel his behaviors could be due to anxiety over not knowing anything about her."

I give a mirthless laugh, marveling that after all these years, Devon can still surprise me.

Misunderstanding my laugh, Molly quickly says, "Try to not take this personally. This isn't about you. It's about Devon's desire to understand who he is and his own history—"

I hold up a hand to stop her. "It's not that. I chose to contact their birth mom years ago even though it's a closed adoption. I don't know why Devon told you that. He's been in contact with his birth mother for over a year."

Molly's mouth falls open.

"She even came to visit and stayed at our house."

Molly stumbles, "He said … he doesn't know anything about

her … not even her name."

...

Molly calls me to let me know that we don't need to start having our visits with Devon on campus in the visitation room after all. "I explained to him exactly why you're so concerned about false allegations, she tells me. "You could be arrested. You could lose your other kids. False allegations could ruin your life," Molly recounts her words to Devon. She continues, "When I explained this to Devon, he was very upset. Now that he knows how serious this is, you have nothing to worry about."

I'm dumbfounded. Molly has handed Devon the proverbial user's manual to a weapon that can destroy our family. In an earnest voice she asks, "Can I let Devon know you'll be picking him up on Saturday morning as usual for his visit?"

I squeeze my eyes tightly shut knowing I have to refuse, but also knowing Molly doesn't understand, and this is only going to make me look like a bad mom.

74

Devon strips naked and masturbates in front of staff and his peers. Molly says there was no trigger that set him off. Wearily, I end the call and jot down the details in my notebook and put the incident out of my mind and go on with my day.

When Devon calls later that evening, I brace myself for tiresome excuses and blame shifting. "What's up?" I say.

"Ummm, I had a hard time today. The kids was annoyin' me."

"And that's a reason to run around naked? That's not an excuse."

"Staff was makin' me do it."

I've heard enough. "That's unacceptable. When you're ready to take responsibility for your actions you can call me back."

I hang up, and he doesn't call back.

The next morning, I'm driving home after dropping the kids off at school, sipping coffee, and listening to local talk radio. Spring Harbor's nurse calls. "I'm calling to notify you of a second incident Devon had yesterday. This one was at about 10 pm." I shake my head, exasperated, as she continues. "He hit a worker in the eye with a plastic toy then became agitated and had to be restrained. He accidentally hit his head. We took him to the ER last night, and he got 11 stitches, but the CT scan was clear."

I make a U-turn.

Molly meets me at the door of the facility. As we walk down the hall, she tells me the worker that Devon injured, Mr. Jamal, has a scratched retina but is expected to make a full recovery. Since Devon was hurt too, they're investigating and have placed Mr. Jamal on administrative leave. Before leading me into the conference room, Molly pauses. "I want to warn you, Devon's had a rough night."

He doesn't raise his head when we enter. I pull a chair next to his, reach for his chin, and lift his face. I gape. His face is lumpy like a boxer after a match. His lips are swollen. Red bruises streak his throat, and blood is caked inside his nose. Garish black stitches track their way across his hairline. He mumbles something about Mr. Jamal beating him up.

My stomach churns not knowing what's true, what's exaggeration, and what's an outright lie. It's hard to imagine a worker beating Devon. But him accidentally hitting his head during a restraint like what Molly and the nurse have described to me, that I can easily imagine.

Wait.

Are those fingermarks on his neck?

How can *that* be an accident?

Several days later, after reviewing the video footage for herself, Molly confirms there was "staff misconduct." I file a police report and have Devon transferred to another facility.

The new PRTF is four hours away. They have an acute unit onsite, which means that Devon's scheme of upping the ante sky high to get to the hospital doesn't work. He's simply taken across the building to the acute ward, stabilized, then returned to his normal unit.

Life goes on at home. I study for my PMP certification exam, a project management credential. Delano begins working as an armored truck driver and enjoys the job. We plant a garden with snap peas and cherry tomatoes, which the kids pop off and eat as snacks. Devon's empty bedroom seems like a waste of space, so I convert it into a playroom with an Xbox and pullout couch for sleepovers. I can easily put the room back together for Devon when he comes home. The kids' lives are busy with school, sports, and friends.

Most importantly, everyone is as safe as possible. I've learned the way to keep Devon in treatment facilities is by being laser-focused on the danger he poses to himself and his siblings. When it comes right down to it, the therapists don't really care about attachment, food issues, lying, refusal to participate in school, running away, cursing, or any other behavioral issues. They definitely don't care if he's causing me any physical or psychological harm. They only care if he's a danger to himself or other children. If there's a bottom line, that's it.

Unfortunately, by the time Devon has been in any one place for a few months, staff become frightened of false allegations. They promise him puppies and iPads—anything to keep him happy and under control. One worker even hints to Devon that he may be able to get a new adoptive family. This type of false hope doesn't help Devon, but frustrated staff and baffled therapists become more pragmatic and shortsighted as his discharge date from their facility approaches. Devon never stays in any one place for long.

Family therapy, monthly CFT meetings, and near-daily calls

about Devon's "incidents" are my normal. I continue to insist that all of our visits are on-campus and with staff supervision. Sometimes Becky and her kids go with me to the visits. Devon calls home three or four times per week.

Facility after facility, therapist after therapist, I work to keep Devon safely in care. Whenever I wonder if I'm doing the right thing and toy with the idea of bringing him home, Becky is the booming voice of reason. And she's right. I can't supervise him 24/7. If he wrapped a shirt around his neck or tried to hang himself with a belt, I might not even find him until too late. And if I did, I worry that I wouldn't have the physical strength to save him. If staff—big, strong, trained, adult men—can't manage Devon, how can I?

...

Three placements later, I finally receive the Department of Health and Human Services investigation report from the Spring Harbor incident with Mr. Jamal. I print the 47 pages of witness statements, media transcripts, and the official findings and settle in to read.

It all started because Devon was bored. He stripped to his underwear, always good for a laugh, and trotted into the common area. The boys hooted as he flapped his arms like bird wings. The fun didn't last long. The workers called for backup to take the other boys off of the unit.

Sauntering to a window, Devon pulled down his underwear. He shook his naked bottom at the boys outside. Barking a laugh, Mr. Jamal imitated Devon, shaking his own clothed bottom out another window. The other on-duty staff, a woman who I've never met and Devon calls Miss Piggy, laughed.

"You stop it!" Devon shrieked.

In an effeminate voice, Mr. Jamal mimicked, "You stop it!"

When Mr. Jamal didn't stop, Devon began masturbating. Mr. Jamal took the unspoken dare—dangling his lanyard between his legs, gyrating his hips, and moaning.

Several staff members watched via live video feed in a nearby office. They didn't step in. Instead, they discussed updating Devon's goals to include reducing sexual acting out.

With Mr. Jamal egging him on, Devon mimed pushing a pencil up his rectum. Would Mr. Jamal take this dare? Grinning, Devon gingerly lowered his bottom flat onto the bench.

Mr. Mark strode in and told Devon in a firm voice to get

dressed. Devon immediately complied. Mr. Mark took Devon outside for a walk to "burn off some energy."

After that, the evening was peaceful. Devon had dinner, called home, and watched X-Men. Later, in his bed and unable to sleep, Devon caught his name in a few snatches of conversation. Enraged, he rushed out of his room. "You. You stop talkin' about me!" He pointed a shaky finger at Mr. Jamal, who grinned.

"Let. Me. Call. My. Mom." Devon punched out.

"Nope." Mr. Jamal's eyes narrowed into a grin. "Phone-time is ov-ah."

"I'm gonna fuck you up, bitch," Devon screamed, throwing a laundry basket and a trash can. "Stop makin' fun of me," he screeched. Grabbing a plastic art stencil, he flung it toward Mr. Jamal who was now advancing on him.

Yelping and clutching at his eye Mr. Jamal fell to his knees. Blood seeped between his fingers and he growled, "I'm gonna kill that little boy."

"Chill. Chill ..." Mr. Mark intervened, leading Mr. Jamal away.

Devon called after them, "And don't you come back neither or I'll hurt you worse."

Mr. Jamal spun and bolted after Devon, who raced for his bedroom. He threw Devon onto the bed and slammed his fist into Devon's face. Again. Then again.

Mr. Mark dragged him off and away. While calling for backup, Mr. Mark urged Mr. Jamal, "He's not worth it. Think about your family."

Mr. Jamal calmed. "Okay. I'm okay." Standing, he turned toward the door as if to leave. When Mr. Mark relaxed his hold, Mr. Jamal twisted away and hurtled after Devon again. Screaming, Devon ran, but tripped.

Mr. Jamal shoved him into the bathroom, slamming him into the bathtub. Grabbing a fistful of hair, he cracked Devon's head against the faucet and blood gushed from the wound. Mr. Jamal's strong hands squeezed around Devon's throat. Panic stricken, Devon kicked his legs, but Mr. Jamal was bigger and heavier. Devon couldn't breathe. Couldn't escape.

Finally, Mr. Jamal was pulled away and locked out of the unit. Someone helped Devon change out of his blood-soaked tee-shirt. Laying on a bench, he held an ice pack to his head and cried, "I need the police. Call the police."

"Hush now." The nurse patted his arm. "We're going to take

you to the ER, Honey. That cut needs sutures, and we'll get you checked for a concussion."

"I wanna call my mom first," Devon croaked, and someone gave him a cordless phone. Holding it for several long seconds, he'd stared at the glowing numbers before handing it back. "Her won't believe me anyways."

The report shakes in my hands. I set the pages down on my desk and cover my face with my hands. Devon was right, I hadn't believed him. Feeling nauseous, I wonder how many other times I've failed him. Bile rises to my throat as I realize I don't have any good options. Devon isn't safe in these places, but how else can I keep the other kids safe?

Part V
Acceptance

75

12 years after becoming a forever family

Devon is one of the most expensive kids in the county, at my estimation, costing Medicaid hundreds of thousands of dollars. James Jamison has been assigned to help plan Devon's care. The light turns green, and I switch James to my Bluetooth. "I'm sorry I can't be at the Agape Homes intake meeting. I try to attend meetings for all of my kids. Even though I can't make it, I wanted to catch up with you."

In my mind, James is another person to get up to speed. Another person to convince this isn't all about me being a bad mom. Another person who's not going to believe Devon's behaviors are on purpose. And, of course, his real motivation isn't going to be to get Devon the services he needs. It's going to be to save Medicaid money.

James continues, "I've read Devon's file. And it's one big file," he says, with a guffaw. James is the first person who I've ever heard guffawing. "How about you tell me what you think needs to happen?"

Well, this is unexpected. I clear my throat. "He's gotten a lot worse in the system. He's become desensitized to violence. It's like he's got no upper limit. He might lash out and punch someone because he doesn't like lunch or if a kid looks at him sideways." James listens attentively to my long, complicated story about how we got to where we are today.

I shift my car into park in front of Walgreens and try to wrap up, "He needs treatment specifically for violence. I understand therapists want to work on the underlying issues, but Devon will be 18 in a couple years. There's got to be a way to help kids be less violent."

After a foreboding pause, James says, "I used to work in juvenile justice. Unfortunately, that's where violent kids end up. The system doesn't have any good solutions for these kids. I don't mean to scare you, but that's the reality."

I'm not scared. I'm relieved that someone else recognizes this terrible path we are on. James says he doesn't know of any programs specifically designed to address violence in youth, but he'll look into it and get back to me.

When we end the call, I head into Walgreens. My phone rings. It's my mom. "You didn't have to pick Devon up to move him to the new place?" she asks.

"No, the PRTF staff is transporting him. I told you, I don't feel safe spending time alone with him."

"I feel so badly for him. It must be terrible living in those awful places. I'm sure the people there are not very nice to him."

"You know, he's not very nice to them, either," I say wryly.

"He's still just a kid ..."

"Yeah, well people would be nicer to him if he acted better. That's just how the world works and he better figure that out."

"Mmmm. I still wonder if it might be a good idea for me to let him come stay with me for the summer. I can give him the one-on-one attention he's always craved."

I put my phone on mute. She still thinks Devon's behavior is all my fault, even though he's had the same problems at every single facility he's been in. I sort through the Axe products, finding shampoo, deodorant, and cologne—all Sandalwood—and put them in my basket. I'm not sure Devon likes that scent, but I am sure he likes matching sets.

"... anyway, Honey, I guess you can think about if that might work next summer," Mom is saying when I focus back on our conversation.

I unmute my phone. "I'd have to discharge him, and then I probably couldn't get him back into care. Remember how long it took me the first time?" In the snack aisle, my eyes roam over shelves. It's been so long since Devon lived at home that I'm not sure what he likes. "Mom, you do realize he's almost 16 ..."

"I can't believe how grown up all the kids are."

"No. I mean that when Devon turns 16, there's a good chance of him getting arrested." Mom sucks in a shocked breath as I continue. "You do realize that he's committing actual crimes? He's assaulting people and vandalizing property. The only reason he doesn't have charges is that he's in these facilities. If he'd been living at home, he probably would have been arrested a long time ago."

"Dear, God. I certainly hope not," Mom says. "That wouldn't help him at all." When I don't respond she says, wistfully, "I hope they'll be nice to him at this new place."

"I hope they'll focus on getting him ready for adulthood. He's been living in a bubble, where he's had no consequences for far too long." Grabbing a can of Pepsi and a bag of Doritos, I head for the registers.

"What are you going to do with him when he turns 18?" Mom asks.

"I want to help him get an occupational diploma before then. That way, he can get a job. My backup plan is to send him to Sarrah when he turns 18. She'd be happy to let him live with her, and I could help pay for their housing."

"That would be wonderful," Mom gushes. "She's the one person who loves that poor kid. Everyone in this world needs someone who loves them."

My chest tightens defensively against her words, which are like pounding fists knocking the wind out of me. I look down at my cart of gifts for Devon and know in my heart that even my best will never be enough.

Mom says, "When you see Devon, give him a hug for me. Tell him grammy loves him and that I'm worried about him."

"I have to go, Mom. The intake is in a few minutes, and I'm going to be late."

When I enter the conference room a few minutes later, I am late, but have a Dunkin' Donuts coffee in my hand. Devon has not arrived yet. Mr. Anil, the program director at Agape Houses, is a lanky man with a long face and stringy beard. Mr. Thomas is the manager of the specific Agape group home where Devon will be living. His six-foot, muscular frame is splayed out on a chair.

"Mrs. Williams, I want to talk with you about visits and clarify some of the information I received." Mr. Anil speaks slowly and steeples his long elegant fingers, which are stacked with silver rings. "I was told you're not open to having home visits, which is a problem since the goal is for Devon to transition back home. Having home visits is an important part of that. He's also legally entitled to two days of therapeutic leave a month."

Leaning back in my chair, I compose my thoughts into a palatable answer. "I want to have home visits, but I'm concerned about false allegations. If he made allegations against me or my husband, we could lose our other kids. I can't risk them going into foster care even for a couple weeks during an investigation."

He nods. "We'll make sure his new therapist addresses this right away. Our therapist is Ms. Jasmine." Curiously, he begins jotting notes on loose leaf paper in a three-ring binder. "We also need to talk about discharge planning. I understand the goal is for him to ultimately transition home?"

I have my answer ready for this too. "Yes, of course, we want him to move home. But I don't feel comfortable having him transition home directly from a group home."

"What do you see as the discharge plan?" Mr. Anil asks.

"He needs to be living in a foster home with younger siblings and not have had suicidal ideations or physical aggression for three months."

This plan effectively punts the ball at least a full year down the road, edging Devon ever closer to adulthood. But it is the only scenario where Devon would actually be able to demonstrate that his behavior is safe enough to move home. It's a big ask, but what they proport to be trying to achieve through this stepped approach. It's also just common sense and Mr. Anil can't argue with it.

We run through a few other standard intake questions. The answers are on the tip of my tongue. His dad is not involved in his treatment because he doesn't believe in mental illness. Devon has no physical health issues, although from time-to-time he claims to have asthma. Please don't encourage that. I'm flexible and can start family therapy any time. I'd like to go to any doctor or dentist appointments. Yes, I know parents don't usually attend appointments, and staff take care of that, but if the plan is for him to return home, don't you think I should be involved? No, he doesn't have an inhaler. No, he has never been prescribed one. Again, he does not have asthma.

Devon hasn't arrived by the time the meeting ends, and Mr. Anil encourages me not to wait. He feels it would be less disruptive for Devon to go straight into their orientation period without seeing me, a reminder of home. I leave the shopping bag of goodies with Mr. Thomas, who assures me that he'll pass them along to Devon.

While driving home, I call Becky. "I just left Agape Houses."

"What did you think?"

"They seemed nice."

She asks, "Did you see Devon?

"No. He was running late. Before going over there I talked to Mom. You won't believe what she said."

"I bet I will ..."

76

Devon refuses to follow even basic rules at Agape Houses. Doesn't matter what it is, if it's a rule, he's not going to cooperate. He's restrained at least a couple of times per week, sometimes a couple times a day. He refuses to shower, complaining of bugs in the bathroom—invisible bugs that no one else can see. He breaks into the medicine cabinet to sniff other kids' pills. Nearly all outings are canceled because of his outbursts. The frustrated workers are at their wit's end.

During one call home, Devon tells me that the workers won't let him have his turn playing video games. I complain on his behalf, hoping to ally with him. This is something I'm trying to do whenever I have the opportunity—like paying premiums on an insurance policy. I realize it's possible this dangerous teenager will be moving back home at some point and I want him to view me as his advocate and not his enemy. I no longer call out his behavior, at least in front of him. My only goal now is to keep everyone safe and that means if he comes home, he and I need to be on good terms at any cost.

This time, my plan backfires. When I complain, I find out that staff has been letting the kids—troubled kids with violent behaviors—play *Mortal Kombat*. Now Devon is furious with me because the contraband video games have been removed from the house.

Then, on December first, like clockwork, Devon's behavior transforms overnight. He's polite, compliant, and cooperative. The staff can't wrap their minds around it. He's not just being good—he's being "perfect." Mr. Anil begins discussing a discharge as soon as January, and Devon beams. I play the cheerleader mom as I'm expected to, but I know better. Devon has merely switched off his bad behavior in hopes of parlaying good behavior into Christmas presents.

On Christmas afternoon, Becky, Jason, and all of the kids, and I crowd into the group home. It's noticeably un-festive with no tree or decorations. It feels even more drab having left home, where our tree twinkles, scraps of wrapping paper litter the floor, and the smell of coffee and cinnamon fill the air.

Eagerly tearing into his gifts, Devon opens a football and

basketball from Auntie Becky. I give him a set of Percy Jackson books and an art kit. Grammy has sent a dress shirt with a matching tie.

Devon darts down the hallway. He returns with a tattered, green and red polka dot gift bag. "I have presents for you guys too." Looking at him standing in front of me, I'm struck by how big he is. A man-sized boy. The gifts aren't wrapped, but he's used orange sticky notes to label them. He has a worn Auto Guide booklet for Sam and Daddy. Devon asks me to take it to them, and I tell him I will.

"You'll have to share. You're twins, anyway," he shrugs, handing Becky a 100-piece holiday puzzle that's meant for me too. It has a garage sale 99-cent sticker on one corner. He gives Brandon a partially filled mini bottle of Axe cologne and Amias and Kayla a comic book to share. The last gift is a crumpled People magazine. On it, the orange sticky says, "To: Mom, Auntie Becky, Uncle Jason, Papa, and Grammy."

"You'll have to share," he apologizes again.

"That's okay. These presents are *so* nice," I say, meaning it.

"And look what I got." He pulls a plastic, dome shaped air freshener from the bag—the kind I use behind the toilet. "Staff gave us each five dollars and took us to Walmart. I got me a 42-ounce limited-edition gingerbread air freshener."

I hide my dismay behind a plastered-on smile. What 15-year-old uses his spending money on an air freshener?

The kids go to the kitchen table to play *Settlers of Catan*. They're teens and pre-teens now, no longer the gaggle of toddlers we had when we moved to Charlotte. Brandon is the only one who is still a little kid. Amias and Abby share a chair. Brandon, hardly able to contain his excitement at playing with the big kids, hops from one foot to the other. Devon, Kayla, and Jacob have the other chairs, and Uncle Jason stands at the end of the table. Die click-clack across the table, often rolling across the floor. Becky and I refresh sodas, chips, and cookies.

Mr. Thomas sits nearby at a computer playing solitaire and eating the cookies I brought as a gift for the staff. The other three residents have gone home for Christmas, and Devon is the only "client" spending the holidays at the group home.

I hit re-dial on Sarrah's number. No answer. She hasn't posted on Facebook since December 21st. I've left several voicemails and posted on her wall: "Call me. The kids want to say 'Merry Christmas.'"

It's unlike her not to respond, and I'm worried.

The excitement around the table heightens. They holler and pound the table. Jacob wins, and then it's time to go home. Leaning one hip against the worn countertop, I try Sarrah one last time, but the call goes straight to voicemail. Devon leaves a message: "Hi. Ummm, Merry Christmas, Sarrah. Hope you havin' a good day."

Over the next few days, I try Sarrah's number several more times. No answer. Something must be wrong. I scour the Internet, knowing to start with crime reports. Sure enough, a news story pops up:

> ```
> Three suspected members of a Texas-
> based group known to steal purses
> from vehicles, were arrested after a
> brief foot chase, police said
> Monday.
> ```

I scroll down. Sarrah's beautiful face is puffy and looks like she's aged a decade. She's been charged with three felonies, so I'm guessing she's facing serious prison time. My heart sinks. I'd hoped Devon might find a home with her when he turned 18. Unfortunately, that door likely slammed shut with her jail cell.

77

"Did Sarrah call me back?" Kayla asks, just before bedtime.

"I have some bad news." I hate to tell her this, but I don't want her thinking Sarrah disappeared willingly. "Looks like Sarrah got into trouble. She's in jail in Texas."

Kayla's chin quivers. "What did she do?"

"She had some drugs and committed grand larceny."

"What's that?"

I mentally kick myself. What a stupid thing to say: grand larceny. Of course, Kayla wouldn't know what that is. I start again. "She stole from a bank. She definitely would have called you back if she could. You know that, right?"

Kayla nods and turns away, but not before I see tears gloss across her eyes.

Late that night, my cell phone dings with a text. I reach blindly to grab it off the nightstand. The caller ID reads "911 Kayla." She programmed her number that way to remind me of the paramount importance of answering her calls at all times.

> Kayla: mom are you up
> Me: You're supposed to be asleep.
> Kayla: i need to talk to u
> Me: Can we talk tomorrow? You have school in the morning.
> Kayla: stop using punctuation in texts its weird
> Me: No, it's normal.
> Kayla: ur such a mom

There's a long pause, and I put the phone back down. Rolling over, I flip my pillow to the now-cooled side. I snuggle up to Brandon, who's better than a hot water bottle. My phone dings again.

> Kayla: its to weird to talk to u i need to text
> Me: Okay.

When I don't feel the vibration of a response, I squint at the screen. The text bubbles are dancing. She's taking a long time to type whatever it is.

Kayla: i don't know how to tell u this but im gay

I blink and read it again. I was expecting something about Sarrah. I'm surprised she's randomly texting me after midnight about this, but I've long suspected we'd have this conversation one day. My finger hovers uncertainly over the letters on my glowing phone screen. Afraid to let the seconds stretch into a message of their own, I respond.

Me: I will always love you. I'm fine with you being gay.
Kayla: k
Me: People have different feelings as they go through puberty. I think you should relax and take some time to grow up and figure things out.
Kayla: k
Me: Have you told anyone else?
Kayla: everyone at school knows
Me: I will always love you no matter what. Now go to sleep. We will talk tomorrow.
Kayla: i dont want to talk it will be weird
Me: Okay. Good night. xxxooo
Kayla: night

I lay in the dark, thoughts swirling through my mind. Moments later, the mattress bounces and Kayla burrows under the covers next to me. I scoot Brandon over to make room and lay sandwiched between the two of them. Levering up and resting on one elbow, I look at Kayla's face as she pretends to sleep. I kiss her cheek.

"Mom, stop that. Go to sleep," she says, in her best pretending-to-be-exasperated-but-really-loving-the-attention voice.

"But a freckle jumped off my face and onto yours," I whisper.

She sighs, but in the soft moonlight streaming through the window, I see her lips fighting back a smile.

78

Sleet slices through the air, pinging off the roof of my car, and heat pours from the vents to defrost the windshield. Hushing Amias and Brandon, I answer my cell phone.

It's Mr. Rob from Agape Houses. "Devon is AWOL," he says.

"What do you mean AWOL? You didn't stop him?"

Mr. Rob clears his throat. "No. Uh, we locked the door after he left."

"You locked him out?" My voice pitches with anger. "Has someone gone out looking for him?"

"Our policy is to wait an hour, then call the police to file a missing person report. Eventually kids come back on their own."

I hope Devon is wearing a sweatshirt. He's so impulsive, I imagine him leaving the group home wearing only shorts and a tee-shirt. Furious, I say, "Let me know as soon as he comes back."

By the time I reach the group home neighborhood, the street lights have switched on and are casting murky shadows. I can't help but wonder why he's doing this now. Is it about Sarrah's arrest? The therapist told me not to tell him, and I haven't. But Kayla might have told him. Or, if he looked her up online, the news story would have popped right up.

I watch to the left while Amias and Brandon watch to the right, but there's no sign of Devon. I circle back to the group home and see a police SUV parked alongside the road a few houses down.

"Stay here with Brandon. Lock the doors," I tell Amias and leave the car running with the emergency brake on. I head toward the police car. The officers are middle-aged men who look friendly enough. "Are you here about Devon?" I ask. "The kid who was reported missing?"

"Who are you?" the officer in the driver's seat asks.

"I'm his mom. He lives over there in a group home, but I have custody."

The other officer types into his laptop, scrolls, and reads. He turns back to me. "The report we're here about is for property damage.

There's no mention of a missing person."

"You've got to be kidding. They filed only the property damage?" I'm unable to hide the disgust in my voice. I show the officers several pictures of Devon on my phone. A seemingly normal, handsome, teenage boy. I give them his date of birth and my name and contact information. My teeth chatter. "I'm going to keep looking for him."

"Check the QT on the corner. Lotta teenagers hang out there. We'll put out a BOLO."

My car is warm as I slide in and switch off the obnoxious throbbing hip-hop music the boys are listening to. I circle the QT several times. When I don't see Devon, I send Amias in to check the men's bathroom. We check the Taco Bell and McDonald's bathrooms too. No luck.

Brandon falls asleep in the backseat, but Amias sits next to me in the front. He's wet and cold, but he's as determined as I am to keep looking. I circle the neighborhood again. We drive up and down the streets, my windshield wipers leaving a mucky mess with each swipe. Between that and the glaring headlights of the occasional oncoming car, I struggle to see even a short distance ahead.

"You should let him move back home," Amias says.

I wonder if he's right. It's been nagging at my conscience for years. Who's to say moving home wouldn't be the motivation that Devon needs to behave? It's what he's holding out for—waiting me out, refusing to comply with treatment.

On the chance that Devon has returned to the group home, I swing by. To my surprise, he answers the door with a grin plastered across his face as if we're guests arriving at a party. And here I was imagining him scared, cold, and sheltering in a filthy public bathroom. Turns out he was happily hitchhiking across the city and back.

Now that Devon knows he can up and walk away, he begins to do it with disconcerting regularity. Each time, I sit home nauseated with worry, but I don't go looking for him. Where would I look? With the flip of his thumb, he could be anywhere.

79

I address an envelope and stick a stamp in the corner then walk to Kayla's bedroom. "Why don't you write Sarrah a letter?" I suggest, holding out the envelope.

"I don't want to write to her." She lays on her belly on her bed, playing on her phone, with her legs folded at the knee and swaying in the air.

I'm surprised by her intense reaction. "Sarrah is a good person. We don't know the story, but I'm sure she just made a mistake."

"Why did she have to do it at three o'clock in the afternoon?" Kayla demands.

If she knows the time of the arrest, she must have looked up the news stories for herself. Thinking she's feeling embarrassed to have her mother in jail, I say, "She's doing the best she can."

"No, she's not," Kayla insists. "She could've at least done it in the middle of the night."

"I don't understand …"

"What if she hurt someone? Why would she rob a bank in the afternoon? I mean, kids are out of school."

"Are you thinking that she went into a bank with a gun?"

"Didn't she?" Kayla demands.

"It wasn't like that. She went through the drive through and tried to cash a check that didn't belong to her."

Kayla looks at me dubiously. She rolls over, sits up, and crosses her arms over her chest.

I continue, "Honestly. That's all she did. Write and ask her about it." My phone rings. I hand Kayla the envelope and answer.

Mr. Thomas tells me that Devon was bouncing a rubber ball against the wall. They told him to stop, but he wouldn't. Mr. Thomas had to restrain him. I wonder how throwing a bouncy ball against a wall justified a physical restraint, but I wait to hear the rest of the story. A little while later, he found Devon with a T-shirt wrapped around his neck and his face was turning red. After removing the shirt, they took him to Eastside.

"I'll come down," I say.

"Best you do, but no rush," Mr. Thomas drawls. "Looks like it's going to be a long wait."

"Has he seen anyone yet?"

"Yeah. They're not going to admit him. The doctor here, a Dr. Alexandria. She said she knows him. Says he don't need to be admitted. He's just acting out to get to the hospital."

I hang up and return my attention to Kayla. The envelope lays next to her on the bed, and she's focused back on her phone again. "Listen, Kayla, maybe this summer we can go visit Sarrah at the jail if she's still there. Think about it, okay?"

A couple of hours later, I back down the driveway, on my way to Eastside, and notice the mailbox flag is up and know Kayla must have decided to write to Sarrah after all.

I find Mr. Thomas in the waiting room slouched in a chair, his long legs extended and crossed at the ankles. I sit opposite him. "Do you think he was really trying to hurt himself this time?"

"I don't know. He was laughing one minute then twisting the shirt around his neck the next." Mr. Thomas stands and pulls a pack of cigarettes out of the back pocket of his joggers. "You know your son. He's gonna find a way to get what he wants."

Visiting hours are almost over, but the nurse takes me back for the last few minutes. Devon and I sit on two vinyl covered armchairs in the wide hallway. I watch a young mother who is sitting a few feet from us. She's holding a small boy in her lap. Devon was little like that the first time we came here too. Tears dribble down the woman's face and drop off of her chin. It's painful to watch.

"I wasn't doing nothin'," Devon says, belligerently. "It was just a ball."

Tearing my eyes away from the mother and her son, I focus back on Devon. "I know it's a silly rule, but they're the adults. They told you to stop. You have to start following the rules."

He grunts.

"There are going to be rules you have to follow your whole life. What are you going to do when your boss tells you to do something?" He doesn't respond and we sit in silence for a few moments. I say, "You know every trip to the hospital extends your treatment. Remember? It's like you're going in a circle." I make a circle motion in the air with my finger.

"I don't care."

"Well, I care. I want you to get better so you can come home." I find myself meaning it, but hopelessness settles over me like a heavy, wet blanket.

A nurse comes by and tells us visiting hours are over. The young mother hugs her son. "I'll be back soon to get you," she promises. I feel sick to my stomach watching them. She thinks her son will get better here. Thinks that they have the answers.

"Will you visit tomorrow?" Devon asks.

I stand to go. "If you're here, but I don't think they're going to admit you."

"If they take me back, I'm going to run away."

"Where would you go? It's cold out."

He has no answer as we walk toward the door. He obediently stops at the stripe that's painted on the floor a few feet from the exit. Patients aren't allowed beyond the line. He says, "I just wanna to go home. Give me one chance …"

His big brown eyes are watery, and love for him burrows into my heart. "Devon," I say softly. "If *they* can't keep you safe, how can *I* keep you safe at home? What would I do if you tried to hurt yourself?"

"But I won't. I promise." When I don't respond, he says, "Please I wanna go home. And to real school. The kids and staff always gettin' me in trouble at day treatment and Crossroads Academy. That's the problem."

"We can work toward you going to real school and coming home, but you have to cooperate with your treatment plan. It's up to you. It's like a game of Candy Land. You keep moving forward, and before you know it, you're at Candy Castle. Just follow the rules, and, before you know it, you'll be home."

I hug him tightly and say goodbye.

80

After Devon is released from Eastside, he continues to go AWOL and get himself into trouble. Agape Houses calls an emergency meeting because his behavior is becoming too dangerous for them to manage.

"Jasmine, you were there for this last incident," Mr. Anil says, stroking his beard. "Tell us what happened."

Mr. Thomas and James are also in the meeting and we're all sitting around the conference room table at the Agape Houses offices. Jasmine, Devon's therapist, leans forward and puts her elbows on the table. "I've never seen Devon like that before," she says. She describes how Devon tried to break a window with a chair, and how Mr. Thomas restrained him. Devon shouted he was going to get Mr. Thomas fired. He said Mr. Thomas was breaking his arms and choking him. Jasmine helped him calm down, but not before he bit Mr. Thomas's arm. "The blood was all over his mouth." She curls her lip at the memory.

Not long after, Devon went AWOL for several hours. He returned with the police. He was claiming to have been abused. CPS opened an investigation despite Jasmine's eye-witness statement and video footage. "Devon laughed and smiled and waved as Mr. Thomas was escorted off the property." Jasmine mimics Devon waving goodbye.

"Was it a psychotic break?" Mr. Thomas drawls.

"When he was throwing the fit?" Jasmine's bug eyes seem to pop out more. "Absolutely not. He was in complete control. He knew exactly what he was doing. There was nothing psychotic about what happened."

"Okay, well …" Mr. Anil taps his pencil on the paper. "As his clinician, what is your recommendation?"

Jasmine pushes her hair back off of her face. "He needs to be in a locked facility. He's not safe in the community. He has poor judgment and insight. He needs a higher level of care, probably for a long time."

"I can work on identifying a new placement," James says. "What therapeutic interventions would you recommend going forward?"

"There are *no* therapeutic interventions for this," Jasmine says. "The service where Devon would do well doesn't exist. He would need one-on-one 24/7, with no other kids. He would need to be able to do whatever he wants, whenever he wants, however he wants. No rules. No consequences. No expectations. That's the only environment where he's going to be successful."

There's a stunned silence in the room.

"I know it's not what you want to hear," Jasmine says, with a self-deprecating sigh. "For some kids, a locked facility really is the best and only option."

"She's not wrong," says James. "We need to prioritize keeping Devon safe and the community safe." As he begins to outline placement options he will begin looking into, I realize he's not looking to save Medicaid money by cutting corners as I'd feared. He's looking to get Devon into the right treatment. The problem is that treatment isn't available. "We can put in applications to all these places," he says, "but availability is tight for this level of care."

"It sounds like it will take some time to find a new placement," Mr. Anil says. "What do you suggest in the meantime?"

"Call the police," Jasmine says.

James shakes his head. "They won't do anything. He's under sixteen."

Jasmine arches an eyebrow at me. "Isn't his birthday in a few days?"

"Next week," I answer.

Mr. Anil tentatively asks, "What do you think about us calling law enforcement, Mrs. Williams?"

I've had several years to think about this question and I'm still uncertain of the right answer. I've often wondered if getting the law involved at ten or twelve or thirteen might have been the wakeup call that Devon needed. Or, perhaps, that would have made things worse. After a long moment of thought, I say, "It doesn't seem like there are any other options …"

Jasmine adds, "Until Devon is back in a locked facility, he needs to be under line-of-sight supervision. We all know he makes homicidal and suicidal threats. And, during our sessions, he's shared detailed plans to burn down the group home."

"You don't think he'd really act on those?" I ask, wistful for a bit of, even misguided, hope.

"Absolutely he would." Her response is unwavering. "That's what's dangerous about a kid like Devon. There's nothing he won't do to get what he wants."

81

I flip on the news. Over the sound of the running faucet, I catch snippets:

"AR-15."

"Students dead."

"School shooter."

"Parkland."

Images of grief-stricken parents flash across the screen. As I watch students run on a sidewalk in front of a concrete school building, fear traces its icy fingers down my spine.

"Mom, are we still going to see Devon?" Amias calls down from the top of the stairs. When I don't answer he calls again, "Mom …"

"Soon," I say, distractedly sinking to the couch.

The death toll is up to 17, and there's a suspect in custody. He's adopted.

The pundits rail about the need for mental health treatment, missed warning signs, and parents not getting appropriate help for their kids. There's a whooshing in my ears. I want to pound my fists on the television screen. I've heeded the signs. Devon's been in treatment for years. He's had literally thousands of hours of therapy. He's only gotten more violent. More dangerous.

The footage plays on a horrifying loop, and I can't look away for the longest time. Only reluctantly do I click off the TV. It's getting late. We need to go. The kids come down and pile into the car. Their chatter is like fuzzy background noise as I drive. The shooter's face flashes in my mind, and I shudder.

Then it hits me like a bullet. For years, Devon has used whatever's within reach as a weapon: books, trashcans, pencils. What could happen if a gun is ever within his reach? I wipe hot tears from my eyes, overwhelmed with grief. The scab on my heart tears wide open. I should have done more. Been a better mother. Found a solution. And now it's too late.

I pull into the group home, climb the stairs, and ring the doorbell. Inhale. Exhale. Five, four, three, two, one. The door swings open, and I hope that Devon doesn't notice that I'm forcing enthusiasm into my voice around the lump in my throat. "Happy Birthday."

"Hi, guys." A grin darts across Devon's face when he sees the presents Amias is carrying up the broken concrete walkway behind me. I'm holding him close in a hug, my heartbeat against his, full of apology and regret.

Devon pulls away. "Hey, Brandon, let me take those." He lifts the tray of vanilla cupcakes out of Brandon's hands.

Mr. Rob waves us into the front parlor. "They're here for my birthday," Devon tells him. In that moment, he's the same giddy birthday boy he was a decade ago, back when the future had been so bright. That's when I believed all Devon needed was the love of a forever family. Now there's a ball of paralyzing dread forming in the hollow part of my chest.

Kayla and Brandon sit on the threadbare couch. Amias leans awkwardly against a wall, rolling one of his shoulder-length dreads between two fingers.

"I'll be back here with the other boys." Mr. Rob's deep monotone voice draws my attention as he starts toward the back of the house.

"We need staff to supervise the visit," I remind him.

"I'm the only one here this afternoon."

I look into Devon's eager face, but I can't take the risk. "I'm really sorry, Devon, but we won't be able to stay without staff."

"But … but … it's my birthday." His voice cracks with emotion. His shoulders slump.

Turning to Mr. Rob, I ask, "Can you stay to supervise long enough to let him open his presents?"

He nods.

Pasting on a smile, I pat Devon's arm. "It'll be like when you were little, a speed birthday." His face brightens, and he tears the wrapping paper off of the first box. He pulls out a pair of white Adidas. He sits on a chair and shoves his bare feet into the sneakers, pacing to test them out.

He grabs the next present. It's from Amias and Kayla. He unwraps a small purple box and turns it over in his hands. "What is it?" he asks.

"It's *BeanBoozled*," Kayla says.

Amias adds, "It's awesome. It's really gross jelly bean flavors. You can play with the other kids that live here."

Devon reads off the box, "Rotten Eggs. Boogers. Dead Fish.

Strawberry Banana Smoothie?" He wrinkles his nose and Kayla and Amias laugh.

"Just be sure to have a trash can nearby to throw up in," I say, handing Devon another present.

Devon pumps a fist in the air when he sees that it's a remote-control helicopter. Brandon jostles against Devon's arm. "Let's try it," he says.

"Another time," I promise, stopping them from opening the packaging. Devon hands the helicopter to Brandon who admires it through the windowed box. I hold out a shiny red gift bag with white tissue paper. "This last one is special, because you're a Valentine's Day baby."

He pulls a heart shaped box of chocolate covered cherries out. He hugs it to his chest. "Thanks, Mom. I love it all."

"Daddy says happy birthday. He wanted to come, but he couldn't make it. He's working," I say. "Sam too. He's still on base in Georgia."

Mr. Rob clears his throat. "I gotta get back. We're not allowed to leave the clients unsupervised."

I gather the torn wrapping paper as Amias, Kayla, and Brandon wish Devon a happy birthday and head to the car. I stand on the stoop under the bright entry light and Devon seems swallowed up by the gloomy hallway. Crooked in one arm, he holds the helicopter box, and his hand clutches the chocolates and jelly beans. If I could erase all of my mistakes and erase all of his hurts, he'd be just another teenage boy having a milestone birthday.

Moving a step closer, I lower my voice to a whisper. "You're 16 now. If you act out, they're going to call the police. And you could be charged as an adult."

Devon nods, but skepticism fills his eyes.

Desperate to get through to him, I look him in the eye: "You've got to start making good choices. You're not a little kid anymore." I hug him once more. "I love you. Happy birthday."

Devon watches from the front stoop as I back the car out of the driveway. "Devon was almost crying," Amias says. "Don't you think we should let him move home? He's part of our family."

I flip the headlights on, and they light a path forward through the night. "He'll always be part of our family, but this is his home for now," I say, regretfully. Through the rearview mirror, I watch Devon wave goodbye. Tears gather in the corner of my eyes as he shrinks and disappears into the darkness.

Grief, I've learned, is really just love.
It's all the love you want to give but cannot.
All of that unspent love gathers in the corner of your eyes,
the lump in your throat, and in that hollow part of your chest.
Grief is just love with no place to go.

—Jamie Anderson, *As the lights wink out*

EPILOGUE

Our story didn't have to go this way. Devon came to us having been the victim of developmental trauma—chronic early childhood neglect and abuse—a pre-existing condition as real as diabetes or asthma. This is typically diagnosed as Reactive Attachment Disorder (RAD), which is rare in the general population, but it's far more common among kids who've spent time in the foster care system.

Developmental trauma impacts each child differently, and Devon is on the severe end of the spectrum. As a result, he had poor impulse control, impaired cause-and-effect thinking, and dysregulated moods. He also exhibited many of the extreme behaviors associated with RAD, including playing with feces, destructive rages, extreme manipulation and lying, and physical aggression.

As Devon grew bigger, stronger, and more violent, we faced an impossible dilemma. He desperately needed to be part of our family, but he was becoming too dangerous to live at home. Unfortunately, after he entered a treatment facility at the age of ten, he was never able to safely return home to live. He lost eight years of his childhood to institutions.

This didn't have to happen.

Like most adoptive parents, my husband and I jumped in heart-first. The foster and adoptive communities have come to recognize certain behaviors as "normal for foster kids" including hoarding, gorging, sleep disturbances, potty issues, tantrums, fear of being left alone, difficulty bonding, and more. Unfortunately, because these behaviors have been normalized, they didn't raise alarm bells during those early months with Devon and Kayla. My husband and I assumed, based on everything we were told from the child welfare professionals, they only needed stability and the love of a forever family.

Traditional parenting methods never worked with Devon, but I forged on, knowing no better way. He was defiant and rebellious, but those characterizations didn't tell the whole story. Devon had picked up an invisible rope, locking us into a tug-of-war, and was clinging on for dear life. This is common for kids with RAD who feel as though they must control people and situations around them because the world is unsafe. Not understanding this, I unwittingly played this game of tug-of-war with him. Looking back I wonder how our relationship might have developed differently if only I'd been equipped to recognize what was going on and able to implement therapeutic parenting methods.

For years, I was plagued with guilt, and I still am, for not loving Devon in the way that I wanted to. Our society views the judge's pen like a magic wand, and their signature on adoption finalization paperwork as some sort of enchantment. It's not. It takes time to build a relationship with your adopted child, and it can be extremely challenging if they have difficult behaviors. Further complicating things, Devon was actively thwarting our relationship through his behaviors, particularly his weaponization of his bodily functions, which he knew I was sensitive to.

This is common for kids with RAD because they don't know how to be in a healthy relationship and they feel safer pushing people away. If I had known, it would have changed how I interacted with Devon and how I internalized his actions. Instead, he felt rejected and unloved.

Devon's triangulation of adults was particularly difficult to handle. Kids with RAD are often superficially charming and adept at manipulating their fathers, teachers, and therapists. Family and friends usually side with the child in blaming the mother for his behaviors. The child with RAD sees the conflicts that he orchestrates as comforting evidence of his power. I did not realize that this was happening. If I had, I would have worked to educate my husband about the disorder and its symptoms instead of taking his dismissal of my concerns so personally.

Exactly when Devon's tantrums morphed into rages isn't clear to me. I was so focused on making it through each incident that I lost perspective. This resulted in a calamitous delay in getting treatment, and those seven years weren't merely wasted time and a delay in getting treatment. Every mistake and misstep that I made exacerbated Devon's condition and damaged our relationship. Meanwhile, my other children were being traumatized by the increasingly toxic situation.

Devon's behaviors impacted his ability to function in school, make friends, and have a peaceful home life. It also caused significant primary and secondary trauma for Amias, Kayla, and Brandon. I knew that things were getting worse and something was very, very wrong, but I had no idea where to start with getting help. Had I known, Devon could have received treatment sooner, and his siblings could have been protected earlier.

One notable clinician says that a tell-tale sign of a kid with RAD is a "pissed off mom"—a spot-on description of me in those early years.

Unfortunately, it didn't serve me or Devon well. Especially when working with inept professionals, "angry" doesn't work. I alienated the therapists, and Devon was able to triangulate between us. He was able to deflect attention away from himself and receive very little actual therapy. New Hope was not an appropriate placement, but we spent—wasted—two years there. They were never going to "get" it, and I should have moved on far sooner.

Throughout all the facilities and treatment programs that Devon went to, we rarely encountered individuals who were truly "trauma informed." This is devastating given that studies show that nearly half of all children in the United States have experienced at least one trauma, and one in six kids are diagnosed with a behavioral or psychological disorder.

In these programs, Devon did not receive specialized treatment for RAD. He was grouped in with kids who were suffering from depression, anxiety, and other disorders. Unfortunately, the treatments for these conditions are ineffective for RAD.

For kids like Devon to heal, we must acknowledge the need for research and new treatments. Imagine how our story might have been different if Devon received solid, trauma-based treatment with a focus on functioning in the family. He might have gotten his driving permit at 15, gone to prom, played high school football, gotten a summer job, and graduated from high school with his classmates—all milestones that he missed out on.

Devon has not had access to effective treatment and did not get early interventions. This forced us to make an impossible choice—for the safety of Devon and the other kids, we had to leave Devon in these facilities, even though he was not getting better. This is a choice that no parent should ever face. Yet, so many do. When children with RAD become too dangerous to live at home, for the safety of siblings, parents, and themselves, they are institutionalized or funneled into the juvenile justice system.

Unfortunately, even with early intervention and treatment, kids with RAD may suffer the effects for their lifetimes and pass the impacts to generations that come after them. There are no quick and easy solutions, but I'm convinced that two very basic, common-sense solutions would have changed the outcome for Devon and our family. First, we needed comprehensive training about developmental trauma and therapeutic parenting. We needed to know the warning signs and where to go for help. We needed this before our family was in crisis. By the time a family is in crisis, it's too late. Second, Devon needed access to specialized, effective treatments to heal the brain trauma caused by his early childhood abuse and neglect.

It seems unimaginable that adoptive parents don't already receive training, support, and resources for developmental trauma. It seems impossible that there aren't effective treatments for RAD. Yet, sadly, this is why thousands of kids are not able to thrive in their forever families.

In the aftermath of the 2018 Parkland school shooting, the most popular talking point, aside from calls for gun control, was the need for increased access to mental health services. I knew better. This isn't merely an access issue. The mental health system doesn't have answers. In fact, treatment centers are virtual incubators for violence, churning out angry, dangerous young people.

The link between developmental trauma and violence has been known for decades. Psychologists Terry Levy and Michael Orlando made this correlation in their article, "Kids who Kill," published by the *Forensic Examiner* in the aftermath of Columbine. Levy published an adaptation of the article in response to the Parkland school shooting where he noted the significant escalation in youth violence over the last two decades.

After the *Sun-Sentinel* published my op-ed, "A Mother's Take: I've tried the system and it doesn't work," an adoptive mother with a story like mine contacted me. She invited me to join her online private support group. In that group and several others, I found myself surrounded by a community of tens of thousands of parents with stories *nearly identical* to mine.

Why have we been forced underground into secret parenting groups? Because, when we do tell our stories to family, friends, law enforcement, educators, and mental health professionals, we are blamed and shamed into silence. As a result, our kids and families are not getting the help that we desperately need.

This problem is too big for parents to address alone. We need the community to work together to advocate for better support for adoptive parents and specialized treatments for our kids. This is why I've chosen to tell my story. Through the pages of this reads-like-fiction memoir, readers can walk in my shoes and begin to understand the complexity and nuances of these situations.

Our story has been tragic, but that doesn't have to be the future for the thousands of other children with developmental trauma. Their future has not yet been written.

AFTERWORD

Forrest Lien, LCSW, Lifespan Trauma Consulting. Forrest has consulted with *20/20*, *HBO*, and *The Today Show* and presented at the Mayo Clinic.

Unfortunately, Keri's story is not that of just one mother, a single troubled child or an isolated family. Families all over the world experience what this family did. Children like Devon and those struggling to raise them are not at fault. The Williams' story, and thousands like theirs, is the result of early childhood trauma left to its own devices.

Trauma during the critical first three years of life, including abuse and neglect, can disrupt a child's brain development. The impact is broad and varies in severity. Some develop developmental trauma disorder, also referred to as reactive attachment disorder. Victims struggle to form meaningful and authentic relationships, regulate their emotions and control their impulses. They have poor executive functioning skills, low self-esteem and may have issues with learning, eating and sleeping.

Some children, like Keri's son Devon, fall on the moderate to severe end of the spectrum for the disorder. These children may exhibit violent outbursts, actively thwart attachment with caregivers and sabotage their own healing. They may become too emotionally and mentally or physically dangerous to themselves and others to live safely at home. Siblings in the home often become collateral damage and suffer from secondary trauma alongside their parents. Simultaneously, the child only becomes more ill. Far too many children end up institutionalized or incarcerated from startlingly young ages.

The disorder is rare according to the Diagnostic and Statistical Manual of Mental Disorders. Indeed, for the general population, this is true. You may have never heard of the disorder before reading Keri's story. Yet, those raising and working with children impacted by early trauma—many times via the foster care system or through adoption—see it often. Even they rarely know what "it" is though.

Like Keri and Delano, many jump in heart-first without any knowledge or appropriate training. Adoptive and foster parents, educators and even clinicians rarely understand the complexity of developmental trauma.

Meanwhile, 100,000 children in the United States foster care system await adoption. Thousands more live in orphanages around the globe. Many of these children have histories of neglect, physical abuse, sexual abuse and emotional abuse. Developmental trauma is not rare in these populations. Yet, many children are placed in foster or adoptive homes far too quickly and without any critical information given about the child or their past. Most parents are left to figure out this incredibly complex disorder on their own, often to the detriment of their families.

Many people believe placing a child in a safe and loving home will make all the difference for those from hard places. It's often not that simple. Developmental trauma disorder, especially in the moderate to severe range, only intensifies without appropriate intervention. Love alone cannot undo the impact of early trauma. Trauma left untreated exchanges hands from generation to generation. Broken children grow into broken adults and the cycle is perpetuated.

There is still hope. With as much heartbreak as I've seen over 40 years in my career, I've also seen hundreds of children and families heal from developmental trauma and ultimately, thrive. Effective treatment is neither quick nor easy. A genuine attachment to a healthy caregiver is the key to positive outcomes for these children. Establishing this connection takes far more than love. A team of highly-specialized professionals surrounding the family is a strong start in leading a child toward the path of healing. Healthy parents are a vital part of the solution.

I invite you to join a growing movement to stop the cycle of childhood trauma. Together, we are stronger. The biggest obstacle faced by adoptive parents is inadequate education, resources and support. And like Keri, many are blamed and shamed for "inadequate parenting abilities." Even when parents find appropriate help—which is scarce—adoption agencies, insurance companies and human services departments typically deny the financial support necessary to utilize effective treatment.

A simple first step in your advocacy is to share Keri's story. Through a growing awareness about developmental trauma, continued research and greater access to effective treatment, we can heal more children—preventing trauma from hurting generations of our children, families and communities. There is hope. You can be that spark in your own community.

AFTERWORD

Chris Peters, LCMHC, Licensed Clinical Mental Health Counselor

There is so much to say, but I do not have the words to say it all.

I have worked in the mental health field as a licensed clinician for over 10 years in North Carolina. I have worked with hundreds of families and thousands of individuals. I wish this story was rare. Unfortunately, I have experienced it too many times through families who are seeking proper treatment, supportive providers, and appropriate care.

Stories like Keri's and Devon's are all too common in the mental health system. Frequently families enter the structure seeking help, often after years of attempting to address behavioral issues within the home and school setting. By the time the family receives significant interventions from providers, the child's behaviors have become too much to manage in the home.

What the families and children do not know, which many professionals fail to discuss, is that the help they need simply isn't there. That the solutions the families desire may not even exist. That the systems we have designed to help families and children are not always evidence-based and do not produce the outcomes desired, due to this omission. The mental health system, as it is designed, often makes children with these diagnoses much worse off.

It is not due to poor intentions. Indeed, the mental health system is devised to progress children through "levels of care" in North Carolina, starting with the least restrictive intervention if possible, and often with the end goal of reunification with the family. It is designed to not institutionalize children and to promote necessary mental health interventions in the least restrictive settings, ranging from the home setting to psychiatric residential treatment facilities (PRTFs). However, how the system is incentivized does not align with empirical treatment outcomes. Agencies are heavily monetarily incentivized to keep children in "higher" levels of care such as PRTFs and group homes because they pay the most from Medicaid. Even if this is the clinically appropriate level of care, these treatment facilities are often not specialized to treat children with specific diagnoses, like Reactive Attachment Disorder. It is not a prerequisite for treatment—only the "level of severity" or how harmful the child is to him/herself, the community, and the family is—and how this matches the "level of care."

This creates a doom loop cycle where, in cases like Keri's son Devon, it is in the interests of the family, the interests of the child, and it is the "clinically appropriate level of care," to keep the child out of the home. The child does not reintegrate back into the community or with their family because it is not safe for them to. However, they are also not receiving evidenced based treatment for the disorder—that is to say, if they are diagnosed correctly at all. They do not get better, and often get worse, due to improper treatment interventions and how the system is designed to address these behaviors.

We need proper diagnoses from experienced clinicians, evidenced based treatments, and supports for families of this disorder. Only by realigning the incentives of mental health care delivery and utilizing data along with families' concerns will stories like these become rare and not the norm. There is hope and it is why I continue to work as a mental health clinician.

By sharing their story, Keri and Devon are helping to bring awareness to issues we have not wanted to address. We can, and we will, do better.

FAQs

What gives you the right to tell Devon's story?
I don't have the right to tell Devon's story, and I am not. I am telling my story, the story of how I adopted a child with RAD and my struggle to navigate the child welfare and mental health systems. As part of sharing any experience, such as this, there is always the intersection of the stories of other people. As a society we routinely discuss the experiences of caregivers—caregivers to the chronically or terminally ill, to aging parents, to children with autism, to babies born prematurely, and to those with a myriad of other special needs. The experience of parents like myself, caregivers of children with RAD, needs to be told as well.

Did you receive Devon's permission to publish this book?
Devon has given me permission to share and publish what is contained in this book and he is benefiting financially from it. There are situations and events I have not included in this book at his request. Furthermore, I have chosen to exclude details that are unnecessarily gratuitous. Ultimately, though, this story is not about Devon. It is about how "the system" is failing our most vulnerable children and the families that care for them.

Why are you disclosing Kayla's sexual orientation?
Kayla specifically asked me to include the details that I have in this book. She has been open about her sexuality for several years and hopes that our story will encourage parents to be supportive of their LGBTQ+ children.

Is Sarrah okay with you telling this story?
Sarrah has consented to my sharing how she lost her children. She believes, as I do, that many birth mothers unfairly lose custody of their children when they should receive services and help. Sarrah is one of the most honest and courageous women I know, and I am honored to be able to speak up on her behalf about how she was victimized by the system.

Don't you realize you weren't a good mother to Devon?
Of course, I realize this. I deeply regret my inability to be the mother Devon needed. I hope my honesty and transparency in telling this story will make clear that mothers of kids with RAD are being asked to do the impossible and our best is literally not good enough. By blaming and shaming moms, child welfare and mental health professionals have been able to deflect away from their lack of effective treatments for RAD and other outcomes of early childhood trauma. As a result, our children and families are not getting the help we need.

Isn't RAD a "fake," defunct diagnosis?
Currently, Reactive Attachment Disorder is listed in the Diagnostic and Statistical Manual of Mental Disorders (DSM) as a "real" diagnosis alongside other mental health disorders we are familiar with like, bipolar, ADHD, and schizophrenia. The DSM is the standard classification of mental disorders used world-wide by mental health professionals and the health insurance industry. That said, there is much debate about the RAD diagnosis, in large part due to harmful attachment "therapies" associated with it in the past. Leading clinicians and researchers are promoting a shift towards Developmental Trauma Disorder (DTD) as a more comprehensive diagnosis for the impacts of early childhood trauma. Unfortunately, this was submitted for consideration as a new diagnosis in the most recent version of the DSM and was rejected. While I strongly support the move away from RAD to DTD as a more helpful diagnosis for our children, in this book I factually document the RAD diagnosis my son actually received from clinicians and psychiatrists.

What happened between the end of the book and when Devon turned 18?
Due to Devon's age and dangerous behaviors, it became increasingly difficult to find facilities willing to treat him. This was especially true when he began to get charged with misdemeanors and felonies. Ultimately, a facility filed a "Health and Safety Discharge" which enabled them to discharge him without securing a new placement. This meant he was being discharged to home. They contacted me with an ultimatum. They would withdraw the Health and Safety Discharge and keep him if I would pay them thousands of dollars out of pocket (under the table, and in addition to the Medicaid payments they receive). As this was my only option to keep Devon and his siblings safe, I made the payments to keep him in care until he turned 18.

What's your relationship with Devon like now?
When Devon became an adult, with real-world consequences and responsibilities, he began making better choices. Also, our relationship was no longer hostage to the dysfunctions of the "system"—I no longer had to fear Devon leveraging false allegations against me and the police would come to my aid if necessary. As a result, my relationship with Devon is on a path of healing. We have talked about what has happened and I've apologized for not being able to be the mother he needed. While nothing can ever make that right, I think Devon is coming to understand some of the "why."

Where is everyone now?
Devon is working to integrate into the community and to mitigate his outstanding criminal charges. He loves video games, Anime, and animals. Kayla is a young adult and is exploring potential career paths. She likes to skateboard, rap, and spend time with friends. Sam is working as a self-employed barber. Amias is serving in our military as an aircraft mechanic. Brandon is in high school and hopes to become a veterinarian. Delano passed away in 2019. Becky and Jason and I continue to go on vacations together with all the kids, now young adults and teenagers. We still celebrate holidays together at "Auntie Becky's house."

What does "based on a true story" mean?
Most importantly, it means that the substance of this story has not been fabricated. However, in order to write this as a reads-like-fiction narrative, I have taken non-material and other liberties. Dialogue has been reconstructed based on my recollections, the recollections of others, my journals, and other documentation. In addition, names and personally identifying details have been changed in most cases.

What documentation did you use while writing this book?
I leaned heavily on my own extensive journals and contemporaneous notes, as well as the recollections of others. I also relied on thousands of pages of formal and informal documentation I have collected over the years. When I began this project, I also requested records from the professionals and facilities our family interacted with to supplement my documentation.

Did therapists really say those things to you?
Many of the interactions with therapists that I've described in this book may be surprising or even hard to believe. However, these interactions did happen and I was able to very closely and accurately recreate the dialogue based on my contemporaneous notes and documentation. As other moms of kids with RAD will attest, this is the unhelpful advice and guidance therapists provide to our families. This is why developing effective specialized treatments for RAD must be a priority.

Why can't I find any of the facilities named in this book?
Most names of facilities and people, as well as identifying details, have been changed. This book is not intended to be an exposé of any specific organization or person. It is intended to be an exposé of the systemic failures and dysfunctions of the child welfare and mental health systems that are not adequately supporting children with RAD and their families.

Why did you write this to read like a novel?
The lives of moms of children with RAD are unimaginable for those who haven't experienced it. I wrote this story to read like a novel to enable readers to "experience for themselves" the struggles and nuances of a family in crisis and "see for themselves" the shocking dysfunctions of the systems that are failing our children and families.

My hope is that the community—therapists, doctors, mental health professionals, educators, and others—will gain a newly informed perspective to begin to rethink their assumptions about our families. My hope is that our family and friends will "get it" and begin to offer us empathy and support. My hope is that everyone who reads this book will become an advocate for the child welfare and mental health reforms our kids need.

Why did you use the stages of grief to structure this book?
C.S. Lewis wrote, "I sat with my anger long enough until she told me her real name was grief." Writing is a cathartic experience and ultimately it was how I "sat with my anger" and became introspective enough about these events to understand my own feelings. I realized that I was grieving the unfilled expectations I had for myself as a mother, and the unfulfilled expectations I had for adoption.

Do you still support adoption?
Absolutely. I believe adoptive parents should keep jumping in hearts-first, but also eyes-wide-open. This book was not written to discourage anyone from adopting. It was written to support adoption, by highlighting where the system needs to change to better support children and their families so adoptions can be more successful.

A note about active shooters
In the interest of telling this story accurately, I included the conversation I had with my kids about the "Batman shooting" true to what I said at the time. However, I've since learned from active shooter training to run if you can, hide and barricade if you cannot, and fight back as a last resort. Please educate yourself and your kids on how to stay safe.

Where can I learn more about your story?
You can find links to my published articles and interviews, as well as my blog posts, on my website www.RaisingDevon.com. I've also posted an album of pictures at www.RaisingDevon.com/album.

Where can I get help?
If you are caring for a child who has a history of early childhood trauma there are online support groups and several organizations that can provide you with information and help. You can find these resources, as well as my articles and blog posts at www.RaisingDevon.com. Or, find me on Facebook at www.facebook.com/RaisingDevon. My book, *Reactive Attachment Disorder: The Essential Guide for Parents*, is available on Amazon and Audible.

ACKNOWLEDGEMENTS

Although one of the most difficult and demoralizing parts of my journey was working with people in the mental health system, there were a few very bright lights. To A.L., C.P., N.P., N.U. and Z.S.: During my darkest, most hopeless moments, being believed by you is what kept me going and what saved my family. Thank you for your encouragement, invaluable advice, and help. Thank you for doing everything within in your power to help Devon and our family. I am forever grateful to you.

Writing such a personal story about this controversial topic has been incredibly challenging. To Becky, who is my editor: Thank you for the countless hours you have spent on this project from its inception through publication. This manuscript would not be what it is today if it weren't for you. To Nichole, who mentored me early on: Thank you for your wise advice on navigating the pitfalls before I even knew what the pitfalls were. Also, thank you to my beta readers who have offered invaluable feedback.

This memoir reveals intimate details about members of my family, details I have strived to handle with honesty and respect. To my children: Thank you for trusting me to tell these stories. Having you recollect your memories was a key part of ensuring the accuracy of this memoir. Thank you for being willing to "go back there" even when it was painful. You are everything to me. To my mom: Thank you for your unconditional support of this project. You are not only supporting me as your daughter, but countless other mothers and daughters who will gain common understanding through this book.

While this story recounts my personal experience, it is also the story of thousands of other moms. To Julia and Katie: You are an inspiration to me. Thank you for your love and support. To the community of moms of kids with RAD: Thank you for your overwhelming support as I educate others on RAD and the effect it has on our families. I wrote this book for each and every one of you.

Made in United States
North Haven, CT
26 August 2025